Company Secretarial Practice Manual

David Venus

GW00697085

Butterworths
London, Edinburgh
1990

United Kingdom	Butterworth & Co. (Publishers) Ltd, 88 Kingsway, LONDON WC2B 6AB and 4 Hill Street, EDINBURGH EH2 3JZ
Australia	Butterworths Pty Ltd, SYDNEY, MELBOURNE, BRISBANE, ADELAIDE, PERTH, CANBERRA and HOBART
Canada	Butterworths Canada Ltd, TORONTO and VANCOUVER
Ireland	Butterworth (Ireland) Ltd, DUBLIN
Malaysia	Malayan Law Journal Sdn Bhd, KUALA LUMPUR
New Zealand	Butterworths of New Zealand Ltd, WELLINGTON and AUCKLAND
Puerto Rico	Equity de Puerto Rico, Inc, HATO REY
Singapore	Malayan Law Journal Pte Ltd, SINGAPORE
USA	Butterworth Legal Publishers, AUSTIN, Texas; BOSTON, Massachusetts; CLEARWATER, Florida (D & S Publishers); ORFORD, New Hampshire (Equity Publishing); ST PAUL, Minnesota; and SEATTLE, Washington

A CIP Catalogue record for this book is available from the British Library.

ISBN 0 406 50502 0

Phototypeset by Cotswold Typesetting Ltd, Gloucester
Printed by Mackays of Chatham PLC, Chatham, Kent

Preface

This new book sets out and explains the company secretarial procedures required to be carried out by a company pursuant to the Companies Acts 1985 and 1989. Suitable precedents are provided to facilitate the performance of these procedures.

In recent years, company secretarial practice has become an increasingly complex and detailed field. The need for additional procedures obviously increases with new legislation and the Companies Act 1989 is no exception. The Act has introduced important new requirements for private companies, in particular 'elective resolutions' whereby a private company can 'opt out' of certain procedural requirements. Other important provisions include the abrogation of the '*ultra vires*' rule, the acceptability of written shareholder resolutions, new requirements as to the registration of charges and the appointment, resignation and removal of auditors. These matters are all dealt with fully by this book.

The procedures set out in the book are aimed primarily at private companies but reference is also made to the law and procedures relating to public companies, where these differ.

The book is wholly practical and has been written for the benefit of practitioners. There are now several secretarial and legal manuals detailing and explaining company secretarial procedures, nearly all following the format of large, loose-leaf, volumes. These works are ideal for those practitioners requiring detailed knowledge of both public and private companies. Most practitioners, however, deal almost exclusively with private companies and do not require the mass of material relating only to public companies. This book has been written as a handy, portable and easily referenced guide to company secretarial procedures designed for the general practitioner. The following may find the book particularly useful:

1) *Accountants/Auditors*—most accountants in general practice advise clients on company secretarial matters and this book sets out the procedures and precedents for dealing with all the company secretarial matters that a practitioner is likely to encounter on behalf of his private company clients.

2) *Solicitors*—whilst other volumes deal more extensively with listed public companies, solicitors advising private company clients on general company secretarial matters will find this book useful.

3) *Company Secretaries*—even those company secretaries who seek assistance from their accountants or solicitors should have a basic knowledge of company secretarial procedures, and have access to such textbooks as may enable them to properly advise their Board of Directors.

As a practitioner himself for some ten years, the author has sought to include all procedures and precedents that a secretary or practitioner is likely to need. Procedures are incorporated in the text, with suitable precedents set out as an appendix. No attempt has been made to give a detailed exposition of the law, as the work is intended as a practical guide to legal compliance. Relevant section numbers are given however so that reference may be made to the Acts where this is considered necessary or appropriate. Where further explanation is required, a telephone call to the Registrar of Companies can often produce the answer. The staff are generally very helpful and knowledgeable and a telephone call lasting a few minutes can often save much time spent in researching the Acts or consulting professional advisers or colleagues.

Whilst every effort has been made to ensure the accuracy of the contents of this book, neither the author nor the publisher can accept responsibility for a loss arising to anyone relying on the information contained herein.

The author would like to thank his colleague Douglas Armour for his contribution to certain chapters.

David Venus
January 1990

Note

This book includes all the Company Secretarial procedures introduced or amended by the Companies Act 1989. The provisions of the 1989 Act are to be brought into force by commencement orders during the course of 1990/91. The anticipated dates of introduction vary from section to section and, until all provisions of the 1989 Act become law, users of this manual are strongly advised to check which sections of the Act have been introduced.

David Venus
January 1990

Contents

Material and Precedents

Table of Statutes

References in this Table to *Statutes* are to Halsbury's Statutes of England (Fourth Edition) showing the volume and page at which the annotated text of the Act will be found.

1 Formation

TYPES OF COMPANY

The Companies Act 1985 (s 1) provides for three kinds of company:

(1) A company limited by shares. The liability of a member of this company is limited to the amount which he has paid or agreed to pay on his shares. Such companies may be private or public.
(2) A company limited by guarantee. A member contributes no funds to the company but guarantees to pay a certain sum (usually £1) in settlement of liabilities on winding-up.
(3) An unlimited company. Such companies, which may or may not have a share capital, have members whose liability is unlimited.

The vast majority of companies registered in the United Kingdom are limited by shares and this book is concerned with the practice applicable to such companies. However, notwithstanding the important differences associated with guarantee and unlimited companies, the procedures set out in this book are also, for the most part, substantially the same for such companies.

In choosing the suitable form of incorporation the following questions should be asked:

(1) *Is the company to trade for profit?* If so, the company should be limited by shares. This allows the company:
(a) To limit the liability of its members.
(b) To raise funds from its members as working capital.
(c) To facilitate the transfer of ownership by the sale of members' shares.
(d) To reward members by paying dividends from profits.
(e) To distribute capital and reserves amongst members, on liquidation or otherwise.
(2) *Will the company be non-profit making?* Such companies typically comprise trade and professional associations, social, sporting and other clubs, tenants' and residents' management associations and charities. In such cases, a guarantee company should be formed. It should be particularly remembered that the Charities Commission will not approve a company for registration as a charity unless it is limited by guarantee.
(a) The Registrar of Companies may agree to dispense with the word 'limited' from the name of a guarantee company if the requirements of s 30(3) can be met.
(b) A company which is a charity and whose name does not include the word 'charity' or 'charitable' must state the fact that the company is a charity on all business letters, cheques, invoices and other published documentation (CA 1989, s 111).

1

(c) A specimen set of Memorandum and Articles of Association for a guarantee company is laid out in Table C to the Companies (Tables A to F) Regulations 1985 and is reproduced in Precedent 1.1.

(3) *Is the liability of the members obliged to be unlimited for professional reasons?* Certain professional bodies permit their members to practise through companies but only if the liability of the members is unlimited. It is normal for such bodies to require certain restrictive clauses to be inserted in the Memorandum and Articles of Association, e.g. that only members of the particular professional body may be members.

(4) *Is it preferred not to disclose financial information to the public?* An unlimited company is not obliged to file copies of its annual accounts with the Registrar of Companies. However the disadvantage to members of unlimited liability and the possibility of filing modified accounts for small and medium sized limited companies, greatly reduce the attractiveness of this concession. In addition an unlimited company is required to file accounts if it is either a subsidiary or a parent undertaking of an undertaking which is limited (s 254; CA1989 s 17).

(a) An unlimited company is not obliged to file returns of allotment with the Registrar of Companies in respect of shares issued.

(b) The Memorandum and Articles of Association of an unlimited company must be in the form of Table E or as near thereto as circumstances permit (Precedent 1.2).

PRIVATE AND PUBLIC COMPANIES LIMITED BY SHARES

The respective advantages of private and public companies are contrasted below (page 3). The following fundamental differences should be noted:

(1) Only the shares and debentures of public companies may be offered to the public and listed on the Stock Exchange or traded on the Unlisted Securities Market or in the Third Market. This does not mean however that the shares of all public companies are traded and there is a growing tendency for public companies to be registered with no immediate intention of offering shares to the public. Such registrations are often for commercial and marketing reasons, permitting the company to describe itself as a 'p.l.c.'.

(2) A public company can only be registered after 22 December 1980 as a company limited by shares or by guarantee.

PRIVATE COMPANIES

This book is primarily concerned with private companies. Every private company must have a minimum of two members (s 24). This provision, which applies equally to public companies, can have important consequences. If the minimum number of members falls below two and the company carries on business in this state for more than six months, the sole member may, jointly and severally with the company, be liable for the debts of the company contracted during that period. It will therefore be seen that where one person is the beneficial owner of a company's entire issued share capital, it is essential that at least one share is held by a nominee. There is no restriction on the maximum number of shareholders in a private or public company.

The Companies Act 1985 makes the private company the residual form of company. That is to say that every company that is not a public company is a private company (s 1(3)). In this way, the Act only specifies one statutory requirement for a private company; it must not offer or allot or agree to allot to the public any shares in or debentures of the company.

The particular advantages and differences of a private company are as follows:

(1) The Memorandum and Articles of Association need not contain a clause indicating the nature of the company (s 1(3)(a));

(2) there is no minimum capital requirement (at present £50,000 for public companies) (s 117);

(3) in a public company each share allotted must be paid up as to not less than one quarter of its nominal value plus the whole of any premium payable (s 101(1)); there is no requirement in a private company that shares be paid up on allotment;

(4) the company may commence to trade and borrow immediately upon incorporation and need not obtain the trading certificate required by a public company under s 117;

(5) it may elect to dispense with the holding of annual general meetings (s 366A; CA 1989 s 115(2));

(6) it may elect to dispense with the laying of accounts and reports before the company in general meeting (s 252; CA 1989 s 16);

(7) it may have a sole director (s 282(3));

(8) the appointment of directors at a general meeting of the shareholders may be effected by a composite, rather than separate, resolution (s 292(1));

(9) the age limits for the appointment or re-appointment of directors do not apply unless a private company is a subsidiary of a public company (s 293);

(10) proxies at a general meeting of a company may not only attend and vote but may also speak at a meeting (s 372(1));

(11) only private companies can qualify as small or medium-sized companies which may enjoy exemption from filing full accounts with the Registrar of Companies (ss 246 to 249; CA 1989 s 13);

(12) whilst dormant, it may by special resolution make itself exempt from the obligation to appoint auditors (s 250; CA 1989 s 14);

(13) provisions relating to insider trading do not apply to private companies (Companies Securities (Insider Dealing) Act 1985 s 1);

(14) the directors of a private company may be authorised to allot shares pursuant to s 80 for an indefinite period (s 80A; CA 1989 s 115);

(15) the rights of pre-emption on the allotment of shares conferred upon members by s 89(1) may be excluded by the Memorandum and Articles of Association (s 91);

(16) many provisions relating to loans or quasi-loans to directors or transactions involving a company and a director apply only to a

public company or to private companies forming part of a public group (ss 311 to 347);

(17) it may elect to dispense with the obligation to elect auditors annually (s 386; CA 1989 s 119);

(18) a private company must deliver its accounts to the Registrar of Companies within 10 months of the end of the relevant accounting period; a public company must deliver its accounts within 7 months (s 244(1); CA 1989 s 11);

(19) the shares of a private company may be redeemed or purchased out of capital (ss 171 to 176);

(20) a private company, which is not a member of a group including a public company, may, subject to certain provisions, give financial assistance for the acquisition of its own shares (ss 155 to 158);

(21) a private company wishing to allot shares for a consideration other than cash need not obtain an expert's valuation report (s 103(1));

(22) only a private company limited by guarantee is capable of exemption from ending its name with 'Limited' (s 30(2));

(23) a private company which has lost half or more of its called up share capital is not obliged to convene an Extraordinary General Meeting to consider what measures should be taken to deal with the serious loss of capital (s 142);

(24) anything which may be done by a private company in a general meeting may be done by a written resolution of all the members entitled to attend and vote at such a meeting (s 381A; CA 1989 s 113); and

(25) the members of a private company may resolve by elective resolution to reduce the majority required for agreement at short notice to an extraordinary general meeting from 95% to not less than 90% (ss 369(4) and 378(3); CA 1989 s 115).

REGISTRATION OF COMPANIES

Company Registries

Registration must be effected at the Companies' Registry applicable to the situation of a company's registered office. The authority for England and Wales is:

The Registrar of Companies
Companies House
Crown Way
Maindy
Cardiff CF4 3UZ

Telephone: 0222–388588

The authority for Scotland is:

The Registrar of Companies
102 George Street
Edinburgh EH2 3DJ

Telephone: 031-225 5574/5

The authority for Northern Ireland is:

Companies Registration Office
ZIDB House
64 Chichester Street
Belfast BT1 4JX

Telephone: 0232-234488

Checklist—Questions to Consider when Deciding Upon Incorporation

(1) Should the company be public or private, limited or unlimited, limited by shares or by guarantee? The various considerations have been dealt with at the beginning of this chapter.
(2) Should the company be 'tailor-made' or 'shelf'? The choice here depends greatly upon whether the company is urgently required (see below).
(3) Is a particular name for the company required? Is the name available? (see below).
(4) Where is the registered office to be situated?
(5) What are to be the objects of the company?
(6) What authorised share capital will be required?
(7) Should the Articles of Association be in standard form or should special provisions be inserted?

'TAILOR-MADE' OR 'SHELF' COMPANIES

A 'tailor-made' company is one formed to the particular requirements of the promoter, with the required name, objects, share capital and articles. As incorporation normally takes some two to three weeks, it is necessary to acquire 'shelf' or 'ready-made' companies where the requirement for a company is more urgent. It will be appreciated that in such cases it will be necessary to change some or all of the name, objects, authorised share capital and articles and accordingly the final cost of establishing a 'shelf' company tends to be greater than that of setting up one which is 'tailor-made'.

SHELF COMPANIES

Most registration agents and many professional firms maintain stocks of 'shelf' companies. It would be normal to instruct the agents to change the name of the company to the required name. It should no longer be necessary for the main objects of a 'shelf' company to be changed to fit the required activity provided the Memorandum provides that the company is to carry on business as a general commercial company (s 3A; CA 1989 s 110). It may, however, be necessary to instruct the agents to amend the Articles of Association to include provisions in addition to or in substitution for the standard articles with which the company has been formed.

The agents will require delivery to them of Forms G288 detailing the new directors and secretary before they will release the Certificate of Incorporation and other documentation relating to the 'shelf' company. Upon receiving the 'company package', it will be necessary to hold a first board meeting of the new directors and to deal with other initial formalities (see Procedure 1A, paragraphs 8–15).

TAILOR-MADE COMPANIES

The detailed procedure for effecting registration is set out in Procedure 1A.

The following matters will require consideration and agreement before documents are lodged with the Registrar of Companies:

Name

(1) The name of the company must end with the word 'limited' in the case of a private company and 'public limited company' for a public company (or their respective Welsh equivalents for companies to be registered in Wales). The abbreviation 'ltd' may be used in place of 'limited' and 'p.l.c.' instead of 'public limited company' (s 27). If a company is registered with the abbreviation 'ltd' or 'p.l.c.', the abbreviated form of suffix must be used for all purposes.

(2) There are few restrictions on a name to be chosen. It can describe the type or nature of the activity to be undertaken, consist of or incorporate a surname or place name or geographical area or be otherwise distinctive as to trade name, service or profession.

(3) The Registrar or Companies will refuse to register a name if it is identical to one already registered, or if the Secretary of State for Trade and Industry considers the proposed name would be offensive or commit a criminal offence.

(4) In addition the Registrar of Companies maintains a list of 'sensitive' words to which his prior approval must be obtained. The full guidelines applied by the Registrar of Companies in determining the acceptability of a company name are set out in Precedent 1.3.

(5) Before deciding upon a name, it is essential that a check be made of the index of companies maintained by the Registrar to ensure that there is not a name registered which is identical or substantially similar to the desired name. A similar check might also be made with the Trade Marks Registry where this is felt appropriate. These checks are important as they will avoid any possible difficulties after registration either from the Registrar of Companies or from a company or firm claiming prior rights to the particular name or one very similar thereto. The difficulties could include:

(a) A company which has been registered by a name which appears to the Secretary of State to be 'too like' or 'the same as' a name already appearing on the Registrar's index may be directed by the Secretary of State within 12 months of registration to change its name (s 28(2)) The Secretary of State normally takes this action following receipt of a complaint by a company or firm with a similar name.

(b) If the Secretary of State considers that misleading information has been given for the purpose of securing a particular name or that undertakings or assurances given at the time of registration have not been fulfilled, he may within five years of the date of incorporation direct the company to change its name (s 28(3)). Such action might arise, for example, where a company undertakes to acquire two or more subsidiary companies in justification of the inclusion of the word 'Group' in its name, and such subsidiaries are not subsequently acquired.

(c) The Secretary of State may direct a company to change its name if he considers the name by which it is registered to give so misleading an indication of the nature of its activities as to be likely to cause harm to the public (s 32(1)).

(d) It could be open to any firm or company with prior rights to a name by which a company is registered, to bring an action against such a company for 'passing off'. Such actions may be the only available remedy where the 12 month period referred to in paragraph (a) has passed.

In view of the potential difficulties highlighted above, it may be advisable to 'keep a watch' on particular names where it is considered that the trading name employed is particularly valuable or sensitive. This can be done by conducting regular, periodic checks of the Registrar's index to monitor new registrations. Alternatively, firms of registration agents offer a computerised 'watching' service for a reasonable fee.

(6) On occasions, it may be decided to carry on business under a name which is different from the corporate name. This may happen where a 'shelf' company is acquired and it is not wished to register a change of name, or where the company intends to trade under more than one name. In such cases, the use of the business name will be governed by the Business Names Act 1985. Most importantly, the name of the company must appear on stationery and other documentation as well as the business name. This is normally done by way of a footnote.

Restrictions on the choice of a business name are few. Care should be taken however to ensure that the name does not conflict with a registered corporate name or a registered trade mark. In addition, a name implying a connection with central or local government or containing a word or words treated as sensitive by the Registrar of Companies (see Precedent 1.3), may only be used with the written approval of the Secretary of State.

The steps necessary to change the name of a company are set out in Procedure 1B.

Registered Office

Every company is obliged to have a registered office to which communications and notices may be addressed (s 287(1); CA 1989 s 136).

The Memorandum of Association must state the country in which the registered office is to be situated, i.e. England, Wales, Scotland or England and Wales. Where the registered office is to be situated in England or Wales, the company must be registered in Cardiff and where the registered office is to be in Scotland, registration must be effected in Edinburgh. If the Memorandum states that the company is to be registered in Wales, the

Welsh language may be used in the name and in the company documents. Such a company is obliged to maintain its registered office in Wales at all times.

The Act requires that certain documents are maintained at the registered office of a company. These documents are as follows:

(1) The register of directors and secretaries (ss 288 to 290).

(2) The register of directors' interests in shares or debentures (para 25 Part IV Schedule 13). If the company's register of members is not kept at the registered office, the register may be kept at the place at which the register of members is maintained. Notice must be given to the Registrar on Form G325 if the register is kept at a place other than the registered office. In no event can the register be kept at an address outside the country of incorporation.

(3) The register of members (s 353(1)). The register may be maintained at an address other than the registered office, in which case notice must be given to the Registrar on Form G353 of the address at which the register is kept. Again the register may be kept only at an address within the country of registration.

(4) The register of debenture holders (s 190(3)). The same provisions apply as to the location of this register as for the register of members. Notice should be given on Form G190 where the register is maintained at an address other than the registered office.

(5) The register of charges (s 411; CA 1989 s 101). Copies of the instruments creating any charge must also be maintained at the registered office.

(6) The register of substantial interests (public companies only) (s 211(1) and (8)). The register must be kept at the same place as the register of directors' interests.

(7) Copies of directors' contracts of service, or a written memoranda setting out their terms (s 318). Notice should be given on Form G318 if the copies or the written memoranda are maintained at an address other than the registered office.

(8) Minutes of general meetings (s 383).

(9) Accounting records (s 222). Alternatively, the records may be kept at such other place as the directors think fit. If accounting records are kept at a place outside Great Britain, accounts and returns relating to the business dealt with in the accounting records shall be sent to and kept in Great Britain and shall be available at all times for inspection by company officers.

Change in Registered Office

(1) A company may change its registered office from time to time by giving notice to the Registrar on Form G287 (s 287(3); CA 1989 s 136).

(2) A change takes effect upon notice being registered by the Registrar, except that within the 14 day period from the date of registration, a person may validly serve any document on the company at its previous registered office (s 287(4); CA 1989 s 136).

(3) The Directors should approve a resolution in the following terms:

'That the Registered Office of the Company be changed to
with immediate effect.'

It should be remembered that any change in registered office will require
reprinting of, or amendments to, company stationery and other documentation and the display of the company's name at the new registered office.

Objects

The Memorandum of every company must state the objects for which the
company is established (s 2(1)).

The Companies Act 1989 has introduced a number of innovations
regarding the 'ultra vires' rule:

(1) The objects of a company may be stated in any manner and it is
    sufficient for the objects to state that the company is to carry on
    business as a 'general commercial company' (s 3A; CA 1989 s 110).
    This allows a company to carry on any trade or business whatsoever
    and do all things 'incidental or conducive' to the business. The power
    to do all such things as are 'incidental or conducive' is however a
    matter of interpretation and it is recommended that certain specific
    powers continue to be included in the Memorandum e.g. the
    guarantee of a loan, charitable donations, certain pension arrange-
    ments etc.
(2) The validity of any act done by a company shall not be called into
    question merely because it is beyond the objects of the company
    stated in its memorandum of association (s 35(1); CA 1989 s 108). It
    remains the duty of the directors however to observe the provisions of
    the Memorandum and Articles and any action taken by the directors
    may only be ratified by the company by special resolution.
(3) Any person dealing with a company in good faith may assume that the
    power of the board of directors to bind the company, or to authorise
    others so to bind, is free of any limitation under the company's
    constitution (s 35A; CA 1989 s 108). It should be noted that a person
    shall not be regarded as acting in bad faith by reason only of his
    knowing that an act is beyond the powers of the directors under the
    company's constitution. The provisions of s 35A do not affect the
    rights of any member to bring proceedings to restrain the doing of any
    act which is beyond the power of the directors provided the act is not
    done in fulfilment of a legal obligation arising from a previous act of
    the company.
(4) A party to a transaction with a company is not bound to enquire as to
    whether it is permitted by the company's memorandum or as to any
    limitation on the powers of the board of directors to bind the company
    or authorise others to do so (s 35B; CA 1989 s 108).
(5) Where a transaction entered into by the company exceeds the power
    of the board of directors to bind the company and the transaction is
    between the company and a director or a director of its holding
    company or a person 'connected' with such director, the transaction is
    voidable at the instance of the company, unless ratified by the
    company in general meeting (s 322A; CA 1989 s 109).

The procedure for changing the objects of a company is set out at Procedure 1C.

Limited Liability

The memorandum of a company limited by shares or by guarantee must state that the liability of its members is limited (s 2(3)). If the memorandum were to be silent as to limitation of liability, the liability of the members would be unlimited.

Authorised Share Capital

The capital clause in the memorandum must state the amount of the share capital with which the company proposes to be registered and the division of the share capital into shares of a fixed amount (s 2(5)). The reference to shares of 'a fixed amount' makes it impossible to issue 'no par value' shares.

The authorised or nominal share capital of a company is the amount up to which shares may be issued and may be such size as the promoters wish. It is obviously wise to set the amount at a figure that takes account of immediate and foreseeable capital requirements. In the case of a public company, the authorised share capital cannot be less than the authorised minimum, i.e. at present £50,000 (s 11).

There is no provision in the Act which requires that the amount of the capital must be expressed in pounds sterling. Therefore it is possible for a private company to be registered with a share capital expressed in any currency divided into shares of a fixed amount in that currency. In the case of a public company however the authorised minimum, expressed to be £50,000, must be met and therefore where such company has only one class of share, that class must be expressed in pounds sterling and where there is more than one class, at least one of the classes must be in pounds sterling.

The Articles of Association

The Articles of Association of a company govern its internal affairs, and in the case of a company limited by shares may be registered with the Registrar of Companies (s 7). Such registration is optional for a company limited by shares as it may be decided to adopt Table A in its entirety, thus obviating the need for registration.

Table A is a model set of articles suitable for adoption by a public or private company limited by shares. Prior to the Companies Act 1985, Table A was set out in the Companies Act 1948 and any company incorporated under that Act (as amended) and adopting Table A in its entirety or in part, would continue to be governed by that Table A. Companies incorporated since 1 July 1985 are registered under the Companies Act 1985 and if no articles are adopted, such companies are assumed to have adopted Table A as contained in the Companies (Tables A to F) Regulations 1985. It is open for any company incorporated under the 1948 Act to resolve to adopt the Table A set out in the 1985 Regulations to the exclusion of the old Table A.

A company limited by shares may decide either to adopt Table A in full, to adopt Table A in part, or to exclude Table A completely and to adopt its own articles. The decision will be determined by the following factors:

(1) For a small private company, it is cheaper and more convenient to adopt Table A with amendments and additions. It is unusual to adopt Table A in its entirety as further powers and regulations are often required.

(2) It is the usual practice with larger private companies and public companies to exclude Table A entirely and to adopt individual articles. This has the advantage of ensuring that the regulations are 'tailor-made' and are fully set out for easy reference by shareholders and others.

Specimen articles prescribed by the Companies Act are as follows:

(1) Table A—a company limited by shares
(2) Table C—a company limited by guarantee and not having a share capital
(3) Table D—a company limited by guarantee and having a share capital
(4) Table E—an unlimited company having a share capital
(5) Table G—a partnership company, that is, a company limited by shares whose shares are intended to be held to a substantial extent by or on behalf of its employees (to be introduced by regulations pursuant to s 8A; CA 1989 s 128).

Various precedents are provided on pages 122 to 151 for Articles of Association. The precedents are as follows:

(1) Table A as contained in the Companies (Tables A to F) Regulations 1985 (Precedent 1.4).
(2) Short form of articles, incorporating Table A, suitable for a public company (Precedent 1.5).
(3) Articles suitable for a private company, incorporating Table A with amendments (Precedent 1.6).
(4) Articles suitable for a subsidiary company, incorporating Table A with amendments (Precedent 1.7).
(5) Individual regulations dealing with:
  (a) Full detailed pre-emption rights on the transfer of shares (Precedent 1.8).
  (b) Alternative form of pre-emption rights permitting transfers to 'privileged relations' (Precedent 1.9).

Articles setting out rights attaching to different classes of shares, together with suitable precedents, are discussed in Chapter 2.

The procedure for amending Articles of Association is set out in Procedure 1D.

PROCEDURE 1A

Registration of a Company—Procedure and Checklist

(1) *Incorporation, partnership or sole trader?* This fundamental question must be decided in conjunction with professional advisers. Factors

to be considered include cost, importance of limited liability, taxation and general commercial implications.

(2) *Type of company*—whether the company should be private or public, limited or unlimited, limited by shares or by guarantee.

(3) *Name*—the availability of the desired name should be checked with the Registrar of Companies and the Trade Marks Registry, if appropriate.

(4) *Memorandum of Association*—the objects of the company must be settled. The memorandum should be signed by two subscribers who must show their respective names and addresses and the number of shares they are to take. The signatures must be witnessed and the name and address of the witness must be inserted.

(5) *Articles of Association*—the articles of the company must be settled where Table A is not to be adopted without amendment. For a private company, the articles will usually be drafted in standard form but particular care should be taken to ensure that adequate provision is made for pre-emption rights on the allotment and transfer of shares where this is considered appropriate. Other matters to consider include special rights attaching to different classes of share (if any), the ability of the chairman to exercise a casting vote, the giving of notice of meetings to a member whose address is outside the United Kingdom (not required by Table A) and the retirement of directors by rotation. The articles should be signed in the same way and by the same persons as the memorandum except that the number of shares to be taken should not be stated.

(6) *Form G10*—this form must be completed giving particulars of those persons to be appointed as directors and secretary (or joint secretaries) together with their consents to act. The form must be counter-signed by the subscribers or their agent.

(7) *Form G12*—this is a statutory declaration of compliance with the requirements of the CA 1985 in respect of the registration of the company and of matters precedent and incidental to it. The declaration must be made either by a solicitor engaged in the formation of the company or by a person named as director or secretary in Form G10. Care should be taken to ensure that the statutory declaration does not predate the Form G10 or Form G12. The papers together with a cheque or banker's draft for the registration fee of £50 must be delivered to the Registrar of Companies.

(8) *Certificate of Incorporation*—provided the Registrar is satisfied with the documentation submitted, he will in due course issue a Certificate of Incorporation. The certificate is conclusive evidence that the requirements of the Act have been complied with in respect of registration (s 13(7)). A private company is capable of carrying on business immediately upon issue of the certificate, whereas a public company is not entitled to commence business or to exercise its borrowing powers until the Registrar has issued a certificate of compliance with the capital requirements for public companies. Application for the certificate must be made on Form G117, which consists of a statutory declaration to be made by a director or the secretary stating that the nominal value of the allotted share capital

of the company is not less than the authorised minimum, i.e. £50,000 and detailing the amount paid up on the allotted share capital. Such amount may not be less than one quarter of the nominal value of each share and the whole of any premium payable. It follows therefore that £12,500 is the minimum amount payable if the share capital requirements for a public company are to be met.

(9) *Company seal*—a company need not have a company seal but where a company seal is required, it should be adopted by the directors at the first board meeting (see s 36; CA 1989 s 130).

(10) *Statutory books*—the necessary minute books and registers must be obtained and established. For small 'owner-managed' companies, a combined register/minute book might be thought suitable, whereas for larger companies a separate register (preferably loose-leaf) and individual minute books for directors' and shareholders' meetings are recommended.

(11) *Board Meeting*—the directors should hold the first meeting of the board of directors of the company for the purpose of dealing with various matters consequent upon incorporation (see Precedent 1.10).

(12) *File forms with the Registrar of Companies*—the following forms should be submitted to the Registrar of Companies after the board meeting:

  (a) Form G288 detailing the appointment of any new directors or secretary. Where registration agents are employed and their staff appointed as first directors and secretary, it will be necessary to deliver the forms to the agents as they will wish to satisfy themselves that the forms are delivered to the Registrar. In addition the agents will not release the Certificate of Incorporation, copies of the Memorandum and Articles of Association and other documentation before delivery of the forms. It may therefore be necessary to deliver the forms before the first board meeting is held.

  (b) Form G287 detailing the new registered office if any.

  (c) Form G88(2) giving details of shares allotted and the names and addresses of those persons to whom the shares are issued. The two subscriber shares should not be included in the initial allotment; the names of the subscribers should be entered in the Register of Members upon incorporation and transfers then effected to the new shareholders.

  (d) Form G224 notifying the accounting reference date of the company. This form must be submitted to the Registrar within nine months of incorporation, failing which the company will be automatically awarded an accounting reference date ending on the last date of the month in which the anniversary of its incorporation falls.

  (e) Forms G325, G353 and G190, as appropriate. These forms notify the Registrar of the location of the register of directors' interests in shares or debentures, the register of members and the register of charges if they are kept at an address other than the registered office. If any or all of the registers are to be maintained at the registered office, no notification is necessary.

(13) *Arrange printing of stationery and display of company name*—the

name of the company must be given on all business letters, notices and other publications of the company, together with all bills of exchange, cheques, orders and invoices (s 349). All business letters and order forms must also state the company's place of registration, the number with which it is registered and the address of its registered office. This information is normally shown in the form of a footnote as follows:

Registered in England and Wales No.: 5000000, Registered Office: 3 City Road, London SW30.

It is not necessary for the names of directors to appear on business letters, but where it is decided to list them, the forenames or initials and the surnames of all the directors must be printed (s 305(1)).

Arrangements must also be made for the company name to be painted or affixed on the outside of every office or place in which its business is carried on, in a conspicuous position and in letters easily legible (s 348).

Where a company is trading under a business name (i.e. a name which does not consist of its corporate name without any addition) business letters, invoices, orders and other documents bearing the business name, must state in legible characters the full name of the company and an address in Great Britain at which service of any document relating in any way to the business will be effective. This address will normally be the registered office. The same information must also be displayed in a prominent position at any premises where the business is carried on and to which customers or suppliers have access (s 4 Business Names Act 1985). It should be remembered that the business letters and order forms of a company trading under a business name must also show the information required by the Companies Acts and described above.

(14) *VAT and PAYE*—arrange for registration for Value Added Tax and for PAYE, if appropriate.

PROCEDURE 1B

Change of Name

(1) *Check new name*—the proposed new name should be checked against the register maintained by the Registrar of Companies to ensure it is available. It may also be necessary to obtain approval if the name includes a 'sensitive' word.

(2) *Board Meeting*—the directors should hold a meeting of the board to recommend the change of name to the members and to convene an extraordinary general meeting of the members for the purpose of considering a special resolution changing the name. The form of resolution is as follows:

'THAT the name of the Company be changed to   .'

(3) *Extraordinary General Meeting*—the meeting should be held and the special resolution approved. Alternatively the members of a private

company may approve by written resolution. The chairman or secretary should sign a copy of the resolution in the form required by the Registrar of Companies.

(4) *Registrar of Companies*—the signed copy of the special resolution should be immediately delivered to the Registrar of Companies, together with a cheque for £40 in payment of the change of name fee. If the change of name is to be effective from a certain date, the Registrar must be clearly instructed as to the particular date required. The company must continue to use its existing name until the Registrar issues a Certificate of Incorporation upon change of name.

(5) *Change of Name Certificate*—immediately upon receipt of the change of name certificate, the following should be informed of the change:
   (a) staff;
   (b) customers and suppliers;
   (c) bankers;
   (d) auditors;
   (e) solicitors;
   (f) Inland Revenue
   (g) Customs and Excise; and
   (h) other interested persons.

(6) *Printing*—all company stationery and other printed material must be reprinted to show the new company name. The name must also be displayed at the registered office and at all offices where the company has a place of business.

(7) *Company Seal*—if the company intends to use a seal a new seal should be obtained in the new name.

(8) *Memorandum and Articles of Association*—a copy of the special resolution must be attached to all copies of the memorandum and articles held by the company and, in addition, copies should be sent to every person known to hold a copy of the memorandum and articles. For neatness and certainty, it is recommended that the memorandum and articles are reprinted to reflect the new name.

PROCEDURE 1C

Change of Objects

Section 4 permits a company to change its objects. Normally a company will alter its objects as a result of a change in its trading activities or to provide itself with some additional power.

The procedure for change is as follows:

(1) *Board Meeting*—the directors will resolve to recommend to the members that the objects of the company be amended and shall instruct the secretary to sign and issue a notice convening an extraordinary general meeting for the purpose of approving a special resolution (see Precedent 1.11). Care should be taken to send notice to the holders of any shares not normally entitled to vote but whose rights may be varied by the change or whose shares are enfranchised for the purposes of approving such a resolution. In such cases, it may

be necessary to hold separate class meetings. It may also be necessary to send notice to debenture holders, if the terms of the particular debenture issue require such notice to be given.

(2) *Extraordinary General Meeting*—the meeting should be held and the special resolution approved. Alternatively the members of a private company may approve by written resolution. The chairman or secretary should sign a copy of the resolution in the form required by the Registrar of Companies.

(3) *Registrar of Companies*—the signed copy of the special resolution should be delivered to the Registrar of Companies within 15 days of the meeting.

(4) *Application to Court*—it is open to any holders of not less than 15% in nominal value of the company's issued share capital, or the holders of not less than 15% of the company's debentures, or, if the company is not limited by shares, 15% of the company's members, to make application to the court to have the alteration in objects set aside (s 5(2)). Such application must be made within 21 days of the date of the meeting.

(5) *Memorandum of Association*—if no application for cancellation is made to court, the company must file a printed copy of the Memorandum of Association as amended within 15 days of the 21 day period. If application for cancellation is made, notice of this fact must be given to the Registrar of Companies, on Form G6, and once a court order has been made a copy of the order cancelling the alteration must be submitted to the Registrar within 15 days, or, if the application is unsuccessful, a copy of the memorandum as amended must be delivered.

(6) *Memorandum and Articles of Association*—these should be reprinted following the alteration to the objects and copies passed to those persons having need of an up to date copy.

PROCEDURE 1D

Alteration of Articles of Association

Section 9 provides that a company may alter its Articles of Association, subject to the Act and the provisions contained in its memorandum. A company may therefore amend any part of its articles or adopt entirely new Articles of Association. The necessary procedure is as follows:

(1) *Board Meeting*—the directors will resolve to recommend to the members that the articles of association be amended and shall instruct the secretary to sign and issue a notice on behalf of the board, convening an extraordinary general meeting for the purpose of approving a special resolution (see Precedent 1.12). If the alteration varies the rights attaching to a particular class of shares or if the terms of issue of a share provide for that particular class to be enfranchised upon a vote for the alteration of the articles, it may be necessary for a separate class meeting or meetings to be convened and held. In addition, it may be necessary to send notice to debenture-holders, if

the terms of the particular debenture issue require such notice to be given.

(2) *Extraordinary General Meeting*—the meeting should be held and the special resolution approved. Alternatively the members of a private company may approve by written resolution. The chairman or secretary should sign a copy of the resolution in the form required by the Registrar of Companies.

(3) *Registrar of Companies*—the signed copy of the special resolution should be delivered to the Registrar of Companies within 15 days of the meeting. If new articles have been adopted a copy, initialled by the chairman for identification, should be forwarded with the resolution.

(4) *Articles of Association*—a printed copy of the Articles of Association as amended must be delivered to the Registrar of Companies. In addition, it is recommended that the Memorandum and Articles of Association be reprinted and copies passed to those persons having need of an up-to-date copy.

2 Capital

SHARE CAPITAL

Authorised and Issued Share Capital

The authorised or nominal share capital of a company is the amount of share capital with which the company is registered. This may subsequently be increased by resolution of the shareholders. As well as being increased, the authorised share capital may also be consolidated and divided, converted into stock, sub-divided and cancelled.

The issued share capital of a company is that part of the authorised share capital which has been allotted and is in issue.

Classes of Shares

The shares of a company may be divided into various different classes, each having distinct rights and privileges. The usual classes are as follows:

Ordinary Shares

These are the 'risk-bearing' shares which, together with such other classes of shares carrying participating rights as to dividend and capital, constitute the equity share capital of the company. The shares carry voting rights, are entitled to received dividends of an unlimited amount and may participate in the surplus assets of the company upon winding up.

In some companies the ordinary share capital may be divided into 'A', 'B' or other classes of ordinary share. Such shares will bear different rights and characteristics but as ordinary shares, will together constitute the equity share capital. (See Precedent 2.1 for specimen articles setting out rights attaching to 'A' and 'B' shares.)

Non-Voting Shares

Such shares do not carry any right to attend or vote at a general meeting of the company, but normally rank equally with the ordinary share capital for dividend and return of capital. They are sometimes issued in private companies to enable employees to participate in the equity of the company without any loss of control for the owner/managers.

Founder Shares

Founder shares are issued to the promoters of a company to give them certain enhanced rights, usually dependent upon the success of the company. The issue of such shares has recently become more common, especially for public companies seeking to raise funds under the Business Expansion Scheme. In such cases, the promoters and the sponsors are

18

normally entitled to participate in a percentage of any profits achieved over a given figure (see Precedent 2.2).

Preferred Ordinary

Such shares are entitled, together with the other equity share capital, to participate in the surplus profits of the company. They will also carry preferential rights as to return of capital or participation in surplus assets upon winding-up, or will be entitled to an enhanced or additional dividend.

Preference Shares

As the name implies, these shares carry preferential rights as to dividend or capital or both. They do not normally form part of the equity share capital, although it is not uncommon for such shares to carry participating rights.

The usual characteristic of such shares is a right to receive a fixed dividend expressed as a percentage of a share's nominal value and the right on winding-up to return of the amount paid up upon each share in priority to any other class of share. The additional rights attaching to preference shares can however be many and varied. For example, such shares may be cumulative, redeemable, convertible, participating or voting.

(1) *Cumulative*. Unless expressly stated to be non-cumulative, preference shares are regarded as cumulative as to dividend. This means any arrears of dividend arising from an inability of the company to pay a dividend in a particular year or period, will be accumulated and become payable on the next due date for dividend payment. No dividend can be paid on ordinary shares before accumulated dividends on preference shares are satisfied. Where preference shares are expressed to be non-cumulative any dividend not paid on a due date is lost to the shareholder (see Precedents 2.3 and 2.4).

(2) *Redeemable*. Any private or public company may, if authorised by its articles, issue shares which are to be redeemed or are liable to be redeemed at the option of the company or the shareholder (s 159).

The Act permits any share to be capable of redemption but it is normally only preference shares that are expressed to be redeemable as a term of issue. The right of redemption will be set out in the articles, which will also provide for the timing of redemption and the procedure to be followed. The following requirements should also be noted:

(a) No redeemable shares may be issued if at that time there are no non redeemable shares in issue (s 159(2)).

(b) All shares to be redeemed must be fully paid (s 159(3)).

(c) The terms of redemption set out in the articles must provide for payment on redemption (s 159(3)).

(d) The date on or by which, or dates between which, the shares are to be or may be redeemed must be specified in the articles. If the articles provide for such date or dates to be fixed by the directors, such date or dates must be fixed before the shares are issued (s 159A(2); CA 1989 s 133).

(e) The articles must specify the amount payable on redemption or the manner in which payment is to be determined. In the latter case, such determination may not be at the discretion or opinion of some person (s 159A(4); CA 1989 s 133).

(f) A return must be made to the Registrar of Companies within one month of redemption specifying the shares which have been redeemed (s 122).

(g) Upon redemption the particular shares are cancelled and the issued share capital is reduced by that amount. The authorised share capital is not affected (s 160(4)).

(h) Shares may only be redeemed out of distributable profits or the proceeds of a fresh issue of shares made for the purposes of redemption and, in the case of a private company only, redemption may be made out of capital.

For specimen articles relating to redeemable shares (see Precedents 2.5 and 2.6). The procedures to be followed on the repurchase by a company of its own shares are discussed in Chapter 4.

(3) *Convertible*. Such shares carry the right to be converted into ordinary shares at a certain date or upon the happening of a certain event. This gives the holder the attraction of a set rate of return and preferential rights for a given period, followed by participation in the equity share capital. The right to convert is often exercisable upon the take-over of a company or immediately prior to flotation and in such circumstances, can be very valuable (see Precedent 2.6).

(4) *Participating*. These shares entitle the holder to participate in a return of dividend and/or capital beyond the fixed rate of dividend and return of capital normally associated with preference shares. To the extent that such shares are entitled to participate in the surplus profits of the company, the shares are regarded as equity share capital for taxation purposes.

(5) *Voting*. It is unusual for preference shares to carry voting rights. However, if dividends become overdue, the rights attaching to such shares may provide for the shares to be enfranchised. It is quite possible however for preference shares to be accorded voting rights at all times.

Application and Allotment

A private company is not restricted in its power to allot shares or debentures, and may allot shares immediately upon incorporation. A public company however must comply with the requirements of the Companies Act 1985 regarding the subscription of the authorised minimum (at present £50,000) and, if its shares are to be offered to the public, it must also comply with the legislation relating to the issue of a prospectus. This chapter is chiefly concerned with private companies, but the additional procedures to be followed by a public company are outlined.

Before shares may be issued, the directors must consider the following:

(1) Does the company have sufficient unissued shares in its authorised share capital to allow the allotment of further shares? If not, the authorised share capital must be increased.

(2) Have the directors been authorised to allot shares in terms of s 80 or

s 80A? This authority is either contained in the Articles of Association or conferred upon the directors by ordinary resolution of the shareholders.

(3) Are the shares to be offered to existing members or to new investors? If new investors are to be introduced, the directors must satisfy themselves that any rights of pre-emption set out in the Articles of Association or by s 89 are waived or exhausted.

(4) Is the allotment for cash or for consideration other than cash? Particular documentation and authorities may be required in the event of an allotment for non-cash consideration. For example if the allotment is in consideration of the purchase of property from a 'connected' person, the specific approval of the shareholders may be required to the transaction (s 320(1)) (see Chapter 8).

(5) Are the shares to be offered at par or at a premium?

(6) Are they to be issued partly or fully paid?

Increase in Authorised Share Capital

Section 121 permits a company to increase its authorised share capital by ordinary resolution. The articles of a company may provide that the authorised share capital shall only be increased by special resolution, and although it is unusual for the articles to so provide, they should nevertheless be checked.

It is normal in private companies to create a somewhat larger authorised share capital then is immediately required. This will avoid regularly reverting to the shareholders should further issues be required. It also obviates frequent amendment to the Memorandum of Association.

The procedure for increasing the authorised share capital is as follows:

(1) The articles must allow for an increase in authorised share capital and should be checked to ensure the company has the necessary authority (see Reg 32 Table A).

  The directors shall resolve at a board meeting to recommend to the shareholders that the authorised share capital be increased, and shall authorise the secretary to convene an extraordinary general meeting of the shareholders. Alternatively, the resolution to increase the authorised share capital may be proposed as special business at an annual general meeting or be approved by the members of a private company by written resolution. A resolution to increase the authorised share capital may read as follows:

  'THAT the authorised share capital be increased to £10,000 by the creation of an additional 9,000 Ordinary Shares of £1.00 each.'

(2) As it is necessary for the directors to be authorised to allot the new shares in the increased capital it is usual to include an ordinary resolution in the notice authorising the directors to allot shares in terms of s 80 or s 80A and also, if necessary, a special resolution waiving rights of pre-emption on the allotment of shares prescribed by s 89(1), or the Articles of Association (see below).

(3) Despatch the notice to the members upon 14 clear days notice if an ordinary resolution is to be approved (21 clear days notice if a special resolution is to be approved or the resolution or resolutions are

included as special business in the notice of an annual general meeting)). Alternatively, the EGM may be convened upon short notice (see Chapter 5).

(4) Hold the EGM or AGM and approve the resolution. Prepare minutes and a copy of the resolution for filing with the Registrar of Companies.

(5) File a copy of the resolution signed by the chairman, a director or the secretary with the Registrar of Companies within 15 days of the meeting together with Form G123.

(6) Whilst not a legal requirement, it is advisable to reprint the memorandum of association to record the increase in share capital, and for a copy to be filed with the Registrar. In any event, a copy of the resolution should be affixed to all existing copies of the memorandum of association and sent to all persons known to hold copies.

Section 121 also authorises a company to alter its capital in the following ways:

(1) to consolidate its shares;
(2) to subdivide its shares;
(3) to convert its shares into stock and vice versa; and
(4) to cancel unissued shares.

The procedures for altering the capital in these ways are similar to the procedure for increasing the authorised share capital. Accordingly, the alterations must be permitted by the Articles of Association and require approval by the company in general meeting, normally with the sanction of an ordinary resolution. The following points should be noted:

(1) *Consolidation of Shares.* This is the process of consolidating a class or specified number of shares of a certain denomination into shares of a greater denomination but retaining the same combined nominal value. For example, 100 ordinary shares of 10p each may be consolidated into 10 ordinary shares of £1.00 each. A resolution to consolidate shares may read as follows:

'THAT all the 10,000 Ordinary Shares of 5p each in the capital of the Company be consolidated into 500 Ordinary Shares of £1.00.'

As well as a copy of the resolution, notice of consolidation must be given to the Registrar on Form G122 within one month of the date of resolution.

(2) *Subdivision of Shares.* By this power the company may subdivide a class or specified number of shares of a certain denomination, into shares of a lesser denomination but having the same combined nominal value. For example, 10,000 ordinary shares of £1.00 each may be sub-divided into 40,000 ordinary shares of 25p each. A resolution to consolidate shares may read as follows:

'THAT all the 50,000 Ordinary Shares of 50p each in the capital of the Company be subdivided into 500,000 Ordinary Shares of 5p each.'

Again a Form G122 must be filed with the Registrar with a copy of the resolution. Where shares are not fully paid up, the proportion between the amount paid and the amount unpaid on each reduced share must be the same as it was before subdivision.

(3) *Conversion of shares into stock and vice-versa.* Stock may be divided into fractions rather than into equal parts. Stock was popular before the 1948 Companies Act as all shares were then obliged to be numbered. The 1948 Act empowered directors to dispense with distinguishing numbers if shares are fully paid (s 182(2)). Accordingly, it is now very rare for a company to have stock.

(4) *Cancellation of shares.* The cancellation of unissued shares in the authorised share capital must be distinguished from a reduction in issued share capital for which court approval is required. The procedure for cancellation is rarely used as it has little practical effect, but it may form part of a scheme of reconstruction or amalgamation whereby the issued share capital is also reduced. A resolution to cancel shares may read as follows:

> 'THAT the 99,000 Ordinary Shares of £1.00 each in the capital of the Company which have not been taken up or agreed to be taken up at the date of this resolution be cancelled so that the authorised share capital of the Company be reduced by £99,000 to £1,000.'

Notice of cancellation must be given to the Registrar on Form G122.

Sections 80 and 80A Companies Act 1985

Directors must be empowered to issue shares in terms of s 80(1). Authority to issue 'relevant securities' must be given either by the Articles of Association or by the company in general meeting.

'Relevant securities' are defined as all shares (other than subscriber shares or shares allotted under an employee's share scheme) and any right to subscribe for, or to convert any security into shares of the company (s 80(2)). Accordingly, directors do not require authority to issue debentures, but do require authority under s 80 to issue convertible debentures.

The authority which the shareholders may give or the articles confer is restrained by s 80(3) to (8):

(1) The authority may be general or limited to one particular issue.
(2) It must state the maximum amount of the relevant securities which may be allotted.
(3) The date upon which the authority shall expire must be stated.
(4) No authority may be given for a period exceeding five years.
(5) Any authority, given either in the articles or by the shareholders, may be revoked or varied at any time by resolution of the shareholders.

A private company is entitled to some relaxation from the provisions of s 80. It may elect, by elective resolution (see Chapter 5) to disapply the provisions of s 80(4) and (5) so that an authority given by the shareholders may be conferred for an indefinite period or for a period in excess of 5 years (s 80A; CA 1989 s 115). The authority must however state the maximum amount of relevant securities to be allotted. A suitable form of elective resolution is as follows:

> 'THAT the provisions of Section 80(A) of the Companies Act 1985 shall apply to the Company in place of the provisions of Section 80(4) and (5) of the said Act.'

A copy of the elective resolution must be forwarded to the Registrar (s 380; CA 1989, s 116(3))). Immediately following the election an ordinary resolution should be approved in the following terms:

'THAT the Directors be and are hereby generally and unconditionally authorised pursuant to Section 80A of the Companies Act 1985 to exercise all the powers of the company to allot relevant securities (within the meaning of Section 80 of the said Act) up to an aggregate nominal amount of £   at any time or times and upon such terms as they think fit and until otherwise revoked or varied by the Company in general meeting.'

An elective resolution under s 80A may be revoked or varied by an ordinary resolution.

Table A does not contain a power under s 80, but it is normal for the articles of a private company to include a general authority for the directors to allot shares at any time for a period of five years from the date of incorporation. A typical article might read as follows:

'The Directors are generally and unconditionally authorised for the purposes of Section 80 of the Companies Act 1985 to exercise any power of the Company to allot and grant rights to subscribe for or convert securities into shares of the Company up to the amount of the authorised share capital with which the Company is incorporated at any time or times during the period of five years from the date of incorporation and the Directors may, after that period, allot any shares or grant any such rights under this authority in pursuance of an offer or agreement so to do made by the Company within that period. The authority hereby given may at any time (subject to the said Section 80) be renewed, revoked or varied by Ordinary Resolution.'

Where authority is given by the shareholders, an ordinary resolution must be approved and filed with the Registrar within 15 days.

Pre-emption rights

(1) Section 89(1) provides that no new shares may be issued by a company unless existing shareholders are given an opportunity to subscribe for such shares pro-rata to existing holdings. Whereas a public company cannot exclude the provisions of s 89(1) (except by special resolution in the manner set out in s 95), a private company may exclude the requirements in their entirety by provisions contained in the articles, and either substitute amended rights of pre-emption or exclude rights of pre-emption completely.

(2) Section 89(1) applies only to 'equity securities'. Accordingly, the rights of pre-emption prescribed by s 89(1) do not apply to the following:

   (a) the issue of any shares carrying a fixed dividend. Non-participating preference shares may therefore be issued without reference to s 89(1).

   (b) the issue of shares under an employee's share scheme.

   (c) the issue of shares for a non-cash consideration.

(3) In practice, it is normal for the articles of a private company to exclude the provisions of s 89(1) and to provide for a non-statutory pre-emption right, over-riding the statutory provisions. Non-statutory provisions will normally be drafted in broader terms than s 89(1). For example, it would be unusual for such provisions to differentiate

between shares issued for cash or non-cash consideration. A typical pre-emption provision is set out in Article 3 of the specimen Articles of Association shown at Precedent 1.6.

(4) Where s 89(1) does apply, the provisions may be excluded by special resolution of the shareholders whether the company is public or private (s 95). The power of exclusion is, like s 80, limited to a period of five years, but is normally only applied to a particular issue or for a particular period (e.g. from one AGM to the next). The following is a simple form of resolution disapplying pre-emption rights, suitable for a private company.

> 'THAT pursuant to Section 95 of the Companies Act 1985 the provisions of Section 89(1) of the said Act shall not apply to the allotment of any shares which at the time of passing of this Resolution the Directors propose to allot provided that such allotment is made within one month of the passing of this Resolution and is limited to equity securities up to an aggregate nominal amount of £10,000.'

(5) Where the disapplication is for a specific allotment rather than a general allotment, a statement by the directors must be circulated with the Notice incorporating a resolution to disapply the provisions of s 89(1). (s 95(5).) This statement must set out the reasons for the directors recommending a disapplication, the amount to be paid for the shares to be allotted and the directors' justification of that amount. If in the case of a private company, it is proposed to pass the resolution by written resolution of the shareholders pursuant to s 381A (see Chapter 5), the statement must be sent to each shareholder at or before the time of supplying the resolution for signature.

(6) In the case of public companies and in particular listed companies, it is the practice to link a resolution for the disapplication of pre-emption rights to a resolution authorising the directors to allot shares in terms of s 80. In such cases, the disapplication would normally be for a period expiring upon the date of the next annual general meeting.

The following form of resolution may be used in such cases:

> 'THAT subject to the passing of Resolution no   hereof the Directors be empowered pursuant to Section 95 of the Companies Act 1985 until the Company's next Annual General Meeting to allot or agree to allot equity securities pursuant to the authority conferred by the said Resolution
> above as if Section 89(1) of the Companies Act 1985 did not apply to any such allotment provided that the Company may make any offer or agreement before the expiry of this authority which would or might require equity securities to be allotted after this authority had expired and the Directors may allot equity securities in pursuance of any such offer or agreement.
> For the purposes of the foregoing Resolution the expression "equity securities" and "allot" shall bear the meanings respectively given to the same in Section 94 of The Companies Act 1985.'

Shares Issued for Non-Cash Consideration

Shares may be issued for money or for money's worth, e.g. property, shares in another company, goodwill, etc. In a private company, the statutory provisions and resultant procedures are substantially similar whether consideration is for cash or other assets. In a public company, however, the issue of shares for consideration other than cash is strictly regulated.

These regulations are extensive but are briefly summarised below:

(1) A public company may not accept as payment for shares an undertaking given by any person that he or another should do work or perform services for the company or any other person (s 99).

(2) A public company may not allot a share unless it is paid up at least to a quarter of its nominal value and any premium is fully paid. This provision does not apply to shares allotted pursuant to an employee's share scheme (s 101).

(3) A public company may not allot shares in consideration of an undertaking to be performed more than five years after the date of allotment (s 102).

(4) An allotment for consideration other than cash may not be made by a public company unless the allotment has been independently valued and a report made to the company on the valuation within six months of the allotment and a copy of the report passed to the proposed allottee (s 103). This section does not, however, apply to allotments made in consideration, wholly or in part, of the transfer of all or some of the shares, or all or some of the shares of a particular class, in another company pursuant to a general offer made to all the shareholders or all the shareholders of the particular class ("a share exchange"). Accordingly most takeovers or mergers are excluded from the ambit of s 103.

(5) Except as provided in the Act, no public company may within two years of becoming entitled to trade (i.e. two years from the date of its s 117 certificate) enter into agreement with a subscriber to its memorandum for the transfer by him to the company of any non-cash assets for a consideration equal to one-tenth or more of the company's nominal share capital (s 104). The exceptions to this provision include the independent valuation of the consideration followed by the approval of the agreement by ordinary resolution of the shareholders.

(6) The form and content of the independent valuation (the so-called 'expert's report') are set out in ss 108 and 109.

The valuation must be made by someone qualified to be an auditor of the company, although if he considers it reasonable to do so, he may arrange for a valuation or part of it to be carried out by someone who appears to him to have the requisite knowledge or experience.

Issue of Shares at a Premium

Shares are issued at a premium if they are issued at a price greater than their nominal value.

For most purposes, share premium is treated as other share capital and may not be distributed to shareholders as dividend or otherwise. The Act does, however, make exceptions:

(1) the paying up of fully paid bonus shares to members;

(2) the writing off of the expenses of any shares or debentures of a company or any commission paid or discount allowed thereon;

(4) the providing of a premium payable by the company on redemption of debentures of the company (s 130(2)); and
(5) the providing of a premium upon the redemption of redeemable shares issued at a premium and redeemable at a premium (s 160(2)).

Partly-paid Shares

Subject to the provisions relating to public companies discussed above, there is no prohibition upon a company issuing a share, partly-paid as to its nominal value or even nil paid.

Shares are sometimes issued partly-paid in a private company where the owner/managers wish to demonstrate a sizeable capital commitment but do not have the wish or the ability to make immediate payment for shares in full. In such cases, it must be remembered that, at all times, a debt remains to the company in respect of the amount unpaid, and that this debt cannot be extinguished by, for example, sub-dividing the shares (see page 22). The amount unpaid will become liable for payment upon the winding up of the company or upon an earlier call made in accordance with the Articles of Association.

In the case of public companies, it is not uncommon for shares to be issued partly paid with the terms of issue provided for payment in full by fixed instalments rather than by means of calls resolved by the directors from time to time.

The CA 1985 does not make any provision as to the making of calls and the power of directors in this regard will be derived from the articles. Articles 12 to 19 of Table A provide, for example, that at least 14 clear days' notice must be given to members, specifying when and where payment is to be made, that joint holders will be jointly and severally liable for unpaid calls, and that interest may be charged on any unpaid calls.

Allotment for Cash—Procedure

(1) The directors must firstly satisfy themselves that they have the requisite authority to allot shares. They must ensure that either the articles or a resolution of the shareholders confers upon them the necessary authority to allot shares in terms of s 80 or s 80A. In addition, checks must be made to ensure that there is sufficient authorised share capital and that compliance is made with any rights of pre-emption (see above).
(2) Hold an extraordinary general meeting of the shareholders, if necessary.
(3) Applicants for shares should make formal application for the allotment of new shares (see Precedent 2.7).
(4) A board meeting should be held to approve the allotment of shares, the execution of a share certificate in favour of the allottee and the submission of Form G88(2) (Return of Allotments) to the Registrar (see Precedent 2.8).
(5) Execute share certificates and despatch to applicants.
(6) Make the necessary entries in the Registrar of Applications and Allotments (if any) and to the Registrar of Members.

(7) File Form G88(2) with the Registrar within one month of the date of the allotment.

Rights Issue

A rights issue is an issue for cash where all shareholders are invited to subscribe for additional shares, at a given price, in proportion to their existing holdings.

In the case of a private company, the procedure for allotment is as set out above. Regard should be paid to any pre-emption provisions set out in the Articles of Association to ensure that the issue complies therewith. Existing shareholders are often given the opportunity to transfer their rights to a third party by means of renounceable letters of allotment.

Board meeting minutes for a rights issue by a private company, together with a suitable form of application for shares and form of acceptance are set out at Precedents 2.9, 2.10 and 2.11.

Allotment for Consideration other than Cash—Procedure

(1) The directors should ensure they have the necessary shareholder approvals (see above).
(2) In the case of a public company, the directors must ensure compliance with the provisions relating to the allotment of shares for non-cash consideration and in particular the independent valuation of such consideration (see above).
(3) It is normal for a formal contract to be made for the transfer of a non-cash asset to a company in consideration of the allotment of shares. Such a contract will require the approval of the board and may require the approval of the shareholders (where, for example, the asset is being acquired from a connected person).
(4) Once approved, the written contract must be submitted to the Registrar together with Form G88(2). If the contract is not reduced into writing, details of the agreement must be set out, on Form G88(3), which will then be submitted with Form G88(2).

The most common form of allotment for consideration other than cash involves the purchase of shares of another company on the basis of an exchange of shares. Examples of resolutions, and letters of offer relating to an acquisition by exchange of shares involving private companies are set out in Precedents 2.12, 2.13, 2.14 and 2.15.

Bonus Issues

A bonus, scrip, or capitalisation issue involves the capitalisation of reserves and their allocation to shareholders as new fully-paid shares without any requirement for payment. The issue, which must be approved by the articles and by the company in general meeting, is made to existing shareholders in proportion to their present holdings. In public companies and on occasions in private companies, the issue is made by renounceable letters of allotment allowing the shareholder to sell or transfer his rights to the bonus shares.

It will be appreciated that a bonus issue raises no new capital and does not increase a shareholder's stake in the company. It does, however, allow a company to enhance its share capital and is often used merely for reasons of commerciality. In addition, by linking the issue with renounceable letters of allotment, shareholders are afforded the opportunity to profit from their entitlement.

Bonus Issue—Procedure

(1) Ensure that the directors have the necessary authority to allot shares (see above).
(2) Hold a board meeting to convene an extraordinary general meeting for the purpose of approving an ordinary resolution to capitalise reserves. It may also be necessary to increase the authorised share capital and to amend the Articles of Association. It should be remembered that there is no necessity to waive any rights of pre-emption (imposed either by s 89 or the articles) as a bonus issue is made pro rata to existing members.
(3) Convene the meeting upon 14 clear days notice for an EGM or 21 clear days notice for special business at an AGM. (The meeting may be convened upon shorter notice if the requisite members agree—see page 58.) Alternatively, the members of a private company may approve by written resolution.
(4) Hold the EGM and AGM and approve the resolution(s).
(5) Hold a further board meeting to resolve to allot the bonus issue.
(6) Issue allotment letters to shareholders or, if renunciation is to be permitted, renounceable letters of allotment.
(7) File a copy of the ordinary resolution with the Registrar of Companies within 15 days and Forms G88(2) (Return of Allotment) and G88(3). The Forms G88(2) and G88(3) may be submitted to the Registrar immediately upon allotment if renunciation is not to be permitted, but submission will obviously be delayed until the end of the renunciation period where renounceable letters of allotment are issued. In any event, Form G88(2) must be submitted within one month of the resolution to allot; accordingly, if the renunciation period is longer than one month, a Form G88(2) should be submitted at the end of the first 30 day period reflecting the acceptances and renunciations received by that date.
(8) Hold final board meeting, if necessary, to approve allotments.
(9) Issue share certificates, and write up Register of Members.

Precedents for the various board and shareholders' meetings required for a bonus issue are found at Precedents 2.16, 2.17, 2.18 and 2.19.

Reduction of Capital

A company may reduce its issued share capital by special resolution and subject to confirmation of the court (s 135). The Articles of Association must contain power for the company to reduce. The court has full discretion to refuse to sanction a reduction of capital and in this way is able to safeguard the interests of creditors.

A reduction of capital may be carried out in the following circumstances:

(1) *Over capitalisation*—to repay capital which is in excess of the needs of the company or to enable it to obtain fresh capital more cheaply from alternative sources. The reduction may be achieved either by extinguishing unpaid liability on partly paid shares, retrieving paid up capital or paying back paid up share capital with power to recall it, should it be necessary.

(2) *Loss of capital*—cancelling capital which has been lost or is unrepresented by available assets.

(3) *Order for purchase by the Court*—this would follow a member's petition relating to prejudicial conduct against him by the company.

Reduction of capital which involves the repayment of capital or the diminution of unpaid liability on shares requires the consent of creditors unless the court considers that it should dispense with such consent. As steps are normally taken by a company to ensure that all creditors' claims are satisfied, the court will normally dispense with seeking creditors' approval.

A special resolution to reduce capital may read as follows:

'THAT the capital of the Company be reduced from £100,000 divided into 100,000 Ordinary Shares of £1.00 each fully paid to £10,000 divided into 100,000 Ordinary Shares of 10p each fully paid and that such reduction be effected by returning to the holders of the said shares paid-up share capital of 10p per share and by reducing the nominal amount of each of the said shares from £1.00 to 10p.'

Serious Loss of Capital (Public Company only)

In the event of the net assets of a public company representing half or less of the amount of the company's called-up share capital, the directors are under a duty to convene an extraordinary general meeting of the shareholders for the purpose of considering whether any, and if so what, measures should be taken to deal with the situation (s 142).

The obligation to call the meeting arises when the fact that the net assets have fallen to half or less than half of its called-up share capital becomes known to any one director. The directors must act to convene the EGM within 28 days of the fact becoming known to the director and the EGM must be convened within 28 days of that date, i.e. within 56 days of the fact becoming known.

There is no necessity for any formal resolution to be put to the meeting.

Issue of Shares of a Discount

The issue of a share at a price less than its nominal value is prohibited (s 100). The issue of a share at a price less than its market value or equal to or greater than its nominal value is of course permissible.

Nominees

The beneficial owner of a share may not wish, for a variety of reasons, to be seen to hold shares in a company. In such cases, shares may be held on his behalf by a nominee.

The relationship between the beneficial owner and his nominee does not concern a company. A company is not permitted to recognise a trust and must regard the registered holder as the person entitled to deal with the shares held in his name (s 360) (but see Chapter 3 for position in Scotland).

Because a beneficial owner cannot enforce his rights against the company, he should protect his position by requiring the nominee to execute a Declaration of Trust in his favour and to complete a stock transfer form in blank. (A suitable form of declaration is reproduced at Precedent 2.20.) By holding a signed stock transfer form in blank, the beneficial owner may transfer the particular shares, at any time to any person, without further recourse to the nominee.

Nominee holdings are very common in small private companies and in wholly-owned subsidiaries. In such subsidiaries, and many other companies, there will be only one beneficial owner but to comply with company law, it is necessary for the company to have two registered shareholders. One share will therefore be registered in the name of a nominee. In private companies, the nominee will often be a spouse or close relation whereas in a subsidiary, the secretary or director will often hold the share, either solely or jointly with the holding company. In the latter case, the nominee should be the first named of the joint holders, as Articles normally provide that notices of meetings need only be given to the first named of two or more joint holders.

Variation of Rights

The rights attaching to shares are normally set out in the Articles of Association, but it is quite possible for the rights to be contained in the memorandum of association or some other document.

It may be wished to alter the rights attaching to shares from time to time and it will be necessary to study both the document setting out the rights and the Act to ascertain the correct manner in which to effect the variation. It is common for the rights attaching to a particular class of rights to declare that a variation shall be deemed to have occurred on the happening of some event not itself altering the class rights but nevertheless prejudicing the interests of the class as a whole, e.g. winding up, the sale of a substantial part of the company's undertaking, the issue of further shares, etc. On such occasions, it will be necessary to carefully consider the procedures to be followed, to ensure that the holders of the shares of the particular class give their approval to the variation or deemed variation.

The steps to be taken upon variation depend upon the terms of variation set out in the rights and the nature of the document in which the rights appear.

A. *Share Rights set out in the Memorandum*

It is unusual and inadvisable for special class rights to be set out in the memorandum. The normal rule that anything contained in the memorandum which could have been included in the articles may be altered by special resolution does not apply, as s 17 specifically excludes the variation of rights.

The procedure to be adopted upon variation depends upon what is or is not stated in the memorandum:

(1) *The memorandum provides for variation*—in such cases the rights may be altered by the stated procedure, except that if a separate class meeting is required or the consent of a specified proportion of the class is necessary, the holders of not less than 15% of the class may apply to the court to have the variation cancelled. However where the variation arises from the giving, variation, renewal or revocation of a s 80 authority or a reduction in share capital (s 135) the variation must be approved by an extraordinary resolution at a separate meeting of the holders of the particular class or the consent in writing of three quarters in value of the class. (An extraordinary resolution is one requiring the consent of not less than three quarters of the holders of the particular class present in person or by proxy at a separate class meeting called for the purpose of variation—see Chapter 5.)

(2) *The memorandum prohibits variation*—variation cannot be effected, except by a scheme of arrangement approved by the court (s 425).

(3) *The memorandum is silent as to variation*—the class rights may be varied only if all the members of the company consent.

B. *Share Rights set out in the Articles*

(1) *The articles provide for variation.* It is usual to find a clause in the articles permitting variation of rights with the approval of an extraordinary resolution at a separate class meeting or with the consent in writing of three-quarters of the issued shares of the particular class. (Table A contains no such provision, presumably because it is drafted for a company only having one class of share.)

The provisions of the Act relating to the length of notice for meetings (s 369), voting (s 370) and the circulation of resolutions (ss 376 and 377) shall apply to such meetings, together with the provisions of the particular articles so far as applicable (s 125(6)). Any provisions as to a quorum are over-ridden by s 125(6) which provides that the necessary quorum shall be two persons holding or representing by proxy at least one-third in nominal value of the issued shares of the class in question and, at an adjourned meeting, one person holding shares of the class in question or his proxy. Any holder present in person or by proxy may demand a poll. In addition, the holders of not less than 15% of the particular class may apply to the court to have the variation cancelled.

The same exceptions apply to a s 80 authority or a reduction of capital as set out in paragraph A(1) above.

(2) *The articles prohibit variation.* It is thought that the position is the same as where the memorandum prohibits variation (see paragraph A(2) above).

(3) *The articles are silent as to variation.* In such cases s 125(2) applies. This permits variation by an extraordinary resolution passed at a separate class meeting or the consent in writing of the holders of three quarters of the shares of the particular class. In addition, the holders of not less than 15% of the particular class may apply to the court to have the variation cancelled (s 127(2)).

(A notice convening a separate class meeting is set out at Precedent 2.21.)

DEBENTURES AND LOAN STOCK

Section 744 defines a debenture as including debenture stock, bonds and any other securities of the company, whether constituting a charge on the assets of the company or not. It is a document issued by a company as evidence of a loan and is usually secured by a charge.

Debentures may be in the following forms:

(1) Debenture—A debenture is always for a fixed or certain amount. It is not divisible in any way. Accordingly, a debenture for, say £10,000 may only be transferred in that one amount. A debenture is normally secured and issued in respect of a loan or a series of loans from one individual.

(2) Debenture stock—such stock is normally transferable in fractional amounts, in the same way as shares.

(3) Convertible debentures and convertible debenture stock—these confer upon the holder thereof an option to convert his loan into shares of the company upon the terms set out in the debenture or debenture stock deed.

(4) Registered debentures and bearer debentures—a debenture is normally issued to a registered holder, transferable to a further registered holder or holders. Bearer debentures are payable to bearer and rarely encountered in practice.

(5) Secured debentures—debentures may be secured either:
   (a) by way of a fixed or specific charge or mortgage on particular property of a company, e.g. a freehold property or an item of equipment or machinery;
   (b) by way of a floating charge over the whole of the assets and undertaking of the company; or
   (c) by way of both a fixed and floating charge.

   Where property of the company is subject to a specific or fixed charge, the company cannot dispose of the asset unencumbered without the consent of the holder or holders of the debenture. Where property is subject merely to a floating charge, e.g. as in the case of stock, cash, general equipment etc., the company is free to deal with the assets in the ordinary course of business. A floating charge will only crystalise and become a fixed charge on the happening of a certain event enabling the holder to exercise his security under the debenture deed.

   The registration of charges is considered at Chapter 11.

(6) Unsecured Loan Stock—being unsecured, such stock will normally carry a higher rate of interest than would attach to a secured debenture or debenture stock.

Issue of Debentures

There are no particular provisions at company law governing the issue of debentures. However in a public company the issue of debenture stock may be subject to legislation relating to prospectuses as well as Stock Exchange requirements.

The terms of issue of debenture stock are normally set out in a trust deed.

To issue convertible debentures the directors will require authority from the shareholders pursuant to s 80.

Unlike shares, debentures may be issued at a discount if the memorandum and Articles of Association permit.

Transfer of Debentures

A debenture to a registered holder may be transferred in accordance with the terms and conditions set out in the debenture deed. However s 183 does require a proper instrument of transfer to be prepared and delivered to the company. A transfer in the form prescribed by the Stock Transfer Act 1963 may be used for fully paid debentures. No stamp duty is payable on the transfer of a debenture, debenture stock or loan stock.

Redemption of Debentures

It is possible for debentures to be irredeemable or perpetual, but it is more usual to express a debenture to be redeemable by a certain date. Redemption may be effected by a new issue of shares or stock or, more normally, from profits. The terms of issue of the debenture will often provide for a sinking fund to be established whereby a predetermined sum is allocated to the fund each year for the purposes of redemption.

3 Shareholders

MEMBERS AND MEMBERSHIP

All companies must have at least two members. In companies limited by shares, each member must hold at least one share, i.e. a shareholder. For most purposes the expressions 'shareholder' and 'member' are synonymous.

The definition of a member is given in s 22:

'1. The subscribers of a Company's Memorandum are deemed to have agreed to become members of the Company, and on registration shall be entered as such in its register of members.

2. Every other person who agrees to become a member of a Company and whose name is entered in its register of members, is a member of the Company.'

Membership involves two important criteria:

(1) Agreement to become a member.
(2) Entry in the company's register of members.

Agreement to become a member can be given in a number of ways. An agreement to acquire shares is a form of contract and is governed by the law of contract. A formal written contract is not a necessity though a wise precaution so that agreement can be proved at a later date. The more common forms of agreement are:

(1) Subscribing to a company's memorandum.
(2) Applying to a company for shares.
(3) Acquiring shares by transfer.
(4) Acquiring shares by transmission on the death or bankruptcy of an existing member.
(5) By holding oneself out, or allowing oneself to be held out, as a member.

In all five cases it is also necessary to be entered in the company's register of members.

WHO CAN ACQUIRE SHARES?

(1) A minor or a person of unsound mind may become a member of a company. However any agreement by a minor to become a member is voidable during the period of minority (the age of 18 in England, Wales and Northern Ireland; see below for the position in Scotland). Accordingly it is not good practice to accept a minor as a member especially if the shares acquired are partly paid. If a minor or a person of unsound mind is registered as a member and this fact is discovered by the company at a later date, the company may repudiate the contract. In the case of an acquisition of shares by way of transfer, the transferor may be reinstated as the holder of the shares.

(2) Until repudiation a minor or person of unsound mind can enjoy full benefits of ownership.

(3) Any member transferring shares to a minor, even in ignorance, remains liable for any future calls on the shares whilst the minor is the registered holder. Any person who purchases shares and procures them to be registered in the name of a minor makes himself liable to indemnify the transferor against any call that may be made on such shares.

(4) A bankrupt may be a member of a company and has full rights of membership whilst registered as the holder of shares.

(5) In Scotland:

  (a) A person is a pupil until the age of 12 (girls) and 14 (boys) after which they become minors until the age of 18. Pupils have no capacity to contract although their guardian (tutor) may contract on their behalf. Minors who live independently and hold themselves out as having reached 18 have the capacity to contract. If a minor has a guardian (curator), contracts will usually be made with their approval.

  (b) A pupil or minor who validly acquires shares is able to reduce (or cancel) the contract not only whilst still a pupil or minor but also until the age of 22. (This extra age limit does not apply to business contracts.) The minor only has to show that the contract was unreasonable at the time.

  (c) Thus although minors and pupils can acquire shares, it may be disadvantageous to the company or transferor.

(6) Companies may also become members of other companies. There are a number of restrictions concerning the owning of shares by a company and these are dealt with more fully later in this chapter.

HOW TO BECOME A MEMBER

As mentioned above, there are five ways of becoming a member. These are considered more fully below:

Allotment

A person wishing to become a member can simply write to the board of directors of that company and apply for shares to be allotted to him. If the application is accepted by the board and provided any rights of pre-emption are followed or waived as appropriate, the shares will be allotted on receipt of the consideration monies. The new shareholder will then be entered in the register of members as holder of the shares, a share certificate issued and a form G88(2) submitted to the Register of Companies giving details of the allotment. Procedures upon allotment are considered in Chapter 2.

Transfer

(1) The shares or other interest of any member in a company are transferable in the manner provided by the company's articles.

(2) To effect a transfer of shares it is necessary for the transferor to

complete a stock transfer form in favour of the transferee, in the form prescribed by the Stock Transfer Act 1963 although the way is now clear for 'paperless' transfers top be introduced in due course (CA 1989, s 207). In most cases, a stock transfer form must be stamped with the appropriate duty by the Inland Revenue before the transfer can be registered in a company's statutory books. A form must be submitted for stamping within one month of execution or signature and ad valorem stamp duty is assessed at the rate of 50p per £100 or part thereof of the consideration paid.

(3) Stamp Duty is payable on any sale for cash or other consideration. Where the transaction is at arm's length and full value in cash is given for the shares, payment of stamp duty may be tendered at an Inland Revenue Stamp Duty Office either in person or by post. However, where full value is not given or where the consideration passing is not in cash but is for a consideration other than cash (such as shares in another company) the Inland Revenue will wish to assess stamp duty. In such cases the stock transfer form must be submitted to an Adjudication Office for this purpose.

The addresses of the various Stamp Offices are set out below:

Law Courts Buildings
Chichester Street
BELFAST
BT1 3JH

16 Picardy Place
EDINBURGH
EH1 3NF

Alexandra House
Parsonage
MANCHESTER
M60 9BT

Ground Floor
City House
140–146 Edmund Street
BIRMINGHAM
B3 2JG

42 Eastgate
LEEDS
LS2 7JL

Room 222
Aidan House
All Saints Office Centre
NEWCASTLE
NE1 2BG

First Floor
The Pithay
All Saints Street
BRISTOL
BS1 2NY

Tower Building
Water Street
LIVERPOOL
L3 1AE

Lower Ground Floor
Lambert House
Talbot Street
NOTTINGHAM
NG1 5NN

Companies House
Crown Way
CARDIFF
CF4 3UR

South West Wing
Bush House
Strand
LONDON
WC2B 4QN

South Block
  (Adjudication only)
Barrington Road
WORTHING
West Sussex BN12 4SF

(4) In some circumstances, a fixed duty of 50p is payable on the transfer, or it may be exempt from stamp duty altogether. The transactions to which these exemptions apply are set out on the reverse of a stock transfer form. They include a fixed duty of 50p for a transfer to or from a nominee or between nominees, and no stamp duty for gifts made inter vivos or in respect of shares bequeathed.

(5) A transferee of a valid transfer has an absolute right to be registered as the holder of those shares unless the company has the power, by the Articles of Association, to refuse registration and has exercised such power. Directors must exercise any right of refusal within a reasonable period, generally thought to be two months. Directors require a valid reason to refuse any transfer.

(6) A transfer is not complete until the name of the transferee is entered in the register of members as the holder of the particular shares. The transferee only has an equitable right to the shares and does not become the legal owner until his name is entered in the register.

(7) If registration of a transfer is delayed for any reason, the transferor remains liable for any calls made on those shares. To overcome this, the transferor is given the right to apply for registration of a transfer as if the application were made by the transferee (s 183(4)).

(8) Normally the transferee assumes liability for unpaid calls at the time of transfer. In the event of a winding up within a year of a transfer, the transferor may be liable for such amounts if the transferee is unable to meet the call.

(9) Many of the provisions relating to the rights of shareholders are contained in a company's Articles of Association. In the case of private companies, the articles often set out restrictions on the transfer of shares and care should be taken to carefully read the Company's articles to ascertain the precise provisions relating to transfers.

It is common for the articles to contain pre-emption provisions on transfer. The aim of such provisions is to preserve ownership within the existing membership. Accordingly, any shareholder wishing to dispose of his shares is initially obliged to offer such shares to existing shareholders for purchase in the same proportions as their current holdings. Only if the shares are not purchased by the members, may they be offered to a third party.

Pre-emption clauses can be very varied, depending upon the needs of the Company. For example, they may:

(a) Oblige all shareholders without exception to offer their shares for purchase by existing shareholders.

(b) Permit transfers to close relations but disallow any other transfer before rights of pre-emption are exhausted.

(c) Oblige any employee or director leaving office for any reason to offer shares for purchase by existing shareholders.

(d) Provide for rights of pre-emption on one class of share but not on another.

See Precedents 1.8 and 1.9 for suggested forms of pre-emption clauses.

Transmission on Death

(1) Upon the death of a member, any shares held by him vest in his estate which then becomes liable for any calls made on his shares. The executors or administrators of the estate are entitled to be registered as the holders of the shares unless the articles of the company state otherwise.

The executors do not become members of the company and must not be registered in the register of members as such. They may however, request their names to be entered in the register of members in which case a formal transfer will be required. If registered personally they should be treated as new members. If registered only in their capacity as executors, the register of members should be amended so as to note that the shares are held by executors and also to record their address. In this instance no stock transfer form is required and the company can rely on letters of probate, administration, or confirmation of executors, as sufficient evidence of their title.

(2) Executors may transfer shares although not registered as members. In such cases a stock transfer form must be signed by all the executors. They may also transfer shares to one of their number in which case they must also execute a share transfer form. Thereafter that executor will be treated as a new member.

(3) The articles of a company may provide that executors or administrators shall elect either to become registered as holders of the shares, or to transfer the shares. Where executors decide to transfer shares, the articles may stipulate that rights of pre-emption shall apply.

(4) Where a member has been resident abroad, a company may not recognise an overseas executor or administrator until an ancillary grant is obtained in England or Scotland as appropriate.

Transmission on Bankruptcy

(1) When a member becomes bankrupt his trustee in bankruptcy generally has the right under the articles to be registered in the company's register of members in respect of the bankrupt's shares. If the shares are onerous (as defined by s 315(2) of the Insolvency Act 1986) the trustee may at any time disclaim the shares in the prescribed form. It is left to the company to prove for any loss suffered as a result of the disclaimer.

(2) Any article allowing the directors to refuse to register the transfer of shares to any person indebted to the company does not apply to transmission of shares on death or bankruptcy.

(3) Provisions in a company's articles requiring the transfer of shares of a bankrupt at a pre-arranged value can be enforced by a company against a trustee in bankruptcy.

(4) Where a bankrupt remains as a member he retains rights of membership although beneficial ownership passes to his trustee in bankruptcy and his trustee is entitled to receive any dividends or other sums due in respect of the shares.

Subscription

This is now an unusual route to membership. The vast majority of companies are formed with only two subscribers, each subscribing for one share. It is however possible to have more subscribers or for them to subscribe for more shares.

Subscribers must sign the Memorandum and Articles of Association prior to incorporation and to have a large number of subscribers would be impractical. Additionally most companies are formed by registration agents who frequently provide their own subscribers so as to avoid delay and the necessity for documents to be passed back and forth.

Holding Out

It is possible to become registered as a member of a company by holding oneself out to be a member or allowing oneself to be so held out. A person is to be regarded as a member if his name appears on the register of members with his consent or if he cannot deny that he is registered with his consent. This could occur when a person is aware that he has been registered as a member but does not exercise his power to have his name removed. He may not have applied for shares and his name may have been entered without his consent but by agreeing to his name remaining on the register he is considered to be a member.

FORFEITURE OF SHARES

(1) The articles of a company normally contain provisions authorising forfeiture of shares for non payment of calls or other payments. These provisions cannot be used in the event of non payment of other debts to a company or this would be regarded as an unauthorised reduction in capital. As with all directors' powers, forfeiture may only be used for the benefit of the company.

(2) Once shares have been forfeited, the holder ceases to be a member and is no longer liable for any future calls on those shares. The articles usually provide that the holder shall remain liable for any amounts called or due and unpaid at the time of forfeiture.

(3) Care must be taken when shares are to be forfeited as the slightest irregularity can result in the forfeiture being restrained by the courts. Thus it is essential that both the forfeiture procedures are carried out accurately and that the call or payment which remained unpaid has been correctly made. Any error in giving notice (either length of notice, service of notice or its content) will result in the forfeiture being cancelled.

(4) Where the shareholder is a bankrupt or has died, notice of forfeiture should be sent to the trustee in bankruptcy or the executors as appropriate.

    The articles usually give power to directors to sell any shares that have been forfeited. They may be sold at a price less than the amount paid up prior to forfeiture, but the transferee will become liable for amounts unpaid and due at the time of purchase. Thus the transferee may hold shares on which money is due and thus be debarred from voting. Any amounts paid by the previous member should be credited to the new holder of the shares.

(5) A shareholder whose shares have been forfeited invalidly can sue the company for damages.

(6) Sometimes articles permit directors to accept the surrender of shares. This power will only be recognised if it is used purely to avoid the formality of forfeiture. Accordingly, the shares must already be liable for forfeiture. Surrender cannot be used as a means of escaping from an uncalled liability.

(7) It is normal practice to inform a shareholder that his shares have been forfeited and to request the return of his share certificate. As a certificate may not be returned, the articles normally provide that a statutory declaration by a Director that shares have been forfeited, shall be conclusive evidence of that fact.

THE REGISTER OF MEMBERS

(1) Every company is required by s 352(1) to keep a register of members. The register must contain:

  (a) The name and address of each member and, for a company with a share capital, the number of shares held, the distinguishing numbers of the shares if relevant, the class of shares held and the amount paid up on the shares. Where all the issued shares of any class are fully paid it is not necessary for the shares to have distinguishing numbers.

  (b) The date on which each member was registered.

  (c) The date each member ceases to be a member.

(2) The register should normally be kept at the company's registered office and when this is not the case notice must be given to the Registrar of Companies on Form G353. This exception does not allow a register to be held outside England and Wales for a company registered at Cardiff, outside Scotland for a company registered in Edinburgh or outside Northern Ireland for a company registered in Belfast.

  The company must register any changes in the particulars required to be entered in the register as soon as it is made aware of them. Thus any changes of address or, in the name of the holder of shares, must be entered. In the case of joint holdings, it is normal for a company's articles to stipulate that notices need only be sent to the first named joint holder.

(3) All entries and amendments to the register can only be made after they have been approved by the board. The secretary does not have the power to alter the register without the approval of the board.

(4) Although partnerships in England do not have a separate legal identity, any holdings are entered in the register of members in the name of the firm. Scottish partnerships do have a legal identity.

(5) *Trusts*

(a) Companies registered in England and Wales are prevented by s 360 from entering details of trusts on their register of members or to receive notice of them. Thus it is the registered holder whom is regarded as the beneficial owner and will always be held liable for any calls. Additionally the true beneficial owner of shares held by nominees cannot interfere with a transfer of those shares to protect his interest except through the courts.

(b) Section 360 does not apply to Scottish Companies. They may amend their register of members in accordance with a deed of assumption on a change of trustees and may take notice of trusts and nominee holdings, although this does not affect the position of the registered holder. Although shares are held in trust this does not concern the company which must still deal with the registered holder of those shares.

(c) To prevent abuse of s 360 there are four safeguards which apply to English and Scottish companies alike:

  (i) The register of directors' interests must show details of any shares held in trust for directors. If the company is quoted then the stock exchange must also be informed.

  (ii) Public companies are required to maintain a register of substantial interests for any person holding at least 3% in nominal value of the voting share capital of a company (s 198; CA 1989 s 134(2)). These interests must include details of any trusts or nominee holdings.

  (iii) Public companies have the power to require shareholders to disclose the nature of their interest and to reveal whether the shares are held for a third party and if so, the identity of that party (s 212).

  (iv) The Department of Trade and Industry has the power to appoint inspectors to investigate the true ownership of shares.

(d) Companies are sometimes asked to split a share account into separate designated accounts in the same name. Care must be taken when doing so in order that no notice of a trust, whether express or implied, is shown on the register. The company is not able to split a holding in this manner unless authorised by its articles. If shares are moved from one designated account to another of the same holder no transfer document is required as there has been no change in ownership.

(6) Companies having more than 50 members are obliged to keep an index of members unless the register itself is in index form or in alphabetical order. Any alterations to the register must be also made to the index within 14 days. The index must be kept with the register.

(7) The register of members is only prima facie evidence of those matters required to be registered and is not conclusive.

(8) *Inspection of the Register*

(a) The register of members of every company must be available for inspection for at least two hours each day. The register may be inspected without charge by members and by any other person on payment of a fee not to exceed five pence. Copies may not be taken immediately, though a copy can be requested and must be sent within 16 days. Where copies are required a fee of 10 pence per 100 words can be made.

(b) Companies are allowed to close the register for not more than 30 days each year and this fact must be advertised in a newspaper in the area of the company's registered office. Public companies may close their register prior to the payment of dividends or the issuing of notices. However, even when the register is closed, notice of change in name or address, letters of probate and charge letters must still be registered. As a result many companies will specify that dividends will be paid or notice given to those members registered on a certain date. Thus the board may declare a dividend on 1 January to be paid on 30 January to the members registered on 20 January.

(9) *Rectification of Register*

(a) Where a person's name is entered in the register of members in error, it is possible for such a person to have the register corrected. This power of rectification is given by s 359. Rectification can only be made by order of court. s 359 provides two instances when rectification might be appropriate:

    (i) Where a person's name has been entered on the register or omitted from the register in error.

    (ii) Where there is default or unreasonable delay in recording that a person has ceased to be a member.

(b) In Scotland operation of this section is often by summary procedure rather than ordinary jurisdiction of the courts and is invoked by petition of the company, shareholder or aggrieved person.

(10) *Overseas Registers*

(a) Where a company undertakes business in a foreign country and has shareholders in that country it may operate a register of those members, referred to as a branch register. The Registrar of Companies must be notified of the place where such a register is kept. (Form G362).

(b) Any entries kept on the branch register must not also be entered on the main register though a copy of the branch register must be kept with the main register. This copy must be updated as soon as possible following any alterations. The branch register and duplicate copies are deemed to be part of the main register and so all the provisions relating to the operation of the main register apply to the branch register. If rectification is required, application to a local court would be made.

(c) In some cases a company may wish to keep a copy of its main register abroad and this copy is referred to as a duplicate register. The duplicate has no standing in law and so changes in the entries must be made simultaneously, so that the duplicate at all times is a true copy of the company's register.

(11) *Share Certificates*

(a) A share certificate issued to a member is prima facie evidence of the title of that member to those shares and a company cannot deny that title or any of the details on the certificate, such as the number of shares or the amount paid up.

(b) Whenever shares are issued or shares transferred the company must deliver a share certificate to the new member within two months of the allotment or transfer of shares. This will also apply to a member who has only transferred part of his holding and has delivered his old certificate for cancellation.

(c) There are no statutory requirements concerning the form of a share certificate. A certificate will usually cover all the shares of one class of each individual member. However, where a member subsequently acquires more shares it is common practice to issue him with a certificate for the additional shares rather than for his total holding. The certificate should state the shareholder's name and address, the number of shares the certificate represents and the amount paid up on those shares.

(d) The articles of a company will usually require that the certificate is signed by two officers of the company under the company's seal.

(e) Where a share certificate is damaged, worn out or defaced it is usual to replace it free of charge although certain expenses are sometimes levied. When a certificate has been lost the directors should obtain an indemnity from the shareholder before raising a duplicate share certificate. A suitable form of indemnity is found at Precedent 3.1.

(12) *Companies as Shareholders*

(a) A company authorised to do so by its memorandum can hold shares in another company.

(b) However, a company may not hold shares in its holding company except in the following circumstances:-

   (i) the subsidiary holds shares as a personal representative or trustee.

  (ii) the subsidiary is concerned only as a market maker.

 (iii) the company became a holder of shares in a company before 1 July 1948, or after that date but before the commencement of s 129 of the Companies Act 1989, in circumstances in which the previous law applied. In either case, the subsidiary has no right to vote at any general or class meeting in respect of the shares (s 23; CA 1989 s 129).

(c) A company is a subsidiary of another company:-

   (i) if the other holds a majority of the voting rights in it, or

  (ii) if the other is a member of it and has the right to appoint or remove a majority of its board of directors, or

 (iii) if the other is a member of it and controls alone, pursuant to an agreement with other shareholders or members, a majority of the voting rights in it.

In addition, a subsidiary of a subsidiary is also a subsidiary (s 736; CA 1989 s 144).

This definition of a holding company and a subsidiary is used for most purposes of the Acts but should not be confused with the definitions of 'parent undertaking' and 'subsidiary undertaking' introduced by the Companies Act 1989 for accounting purposes only (s 258; CA 1989 s 21).

4 Purchase by a Company of its own Shares and Financial Assistance

PURCHASE OF OWN SHARES

Any private or public company may, if authorised to do so by its Articles, purchase its own shares. (s 162). Regulation 3 of the Table A gives a company the appropriate authority. For a company adopting the old Table A set out in the Companies Act 1948, it is necessary to amend or replace Regulation 3 of that Table to provide the necessary authority.

The following points should be noted:

(1) The articles need not provide for the terms and manner of purchase. This contrasts with shares which are expressed to be redeemable upon issue, in which case the articles must set out such terms and manner (s 159A; CA 1989 s 133).

(2) No shares may be purchased if this would result in only redeemable shares being in issue (s 162(3)).

(3) The shares to be purchased must be fully paid (s 159(3)).

(4) Payment must be made on purchase and may not be deferred (s 159(3)).

(5) A public or private company may purchase its shares out of distributable profits or out of the proceeds of a new issue of shares made for the purpose. In addition, a private company may, in certain circumstances, purchase shares out of capital (s 160(1); s 171(1)).

(6) Any premium payable upon purchase must be paid out of distributable profits, unless the shares were originally issued at a premium in which case any premium payable on purchase may be paid from the proceeds of a fresh issue of shares made for the purpose. Any premium to be paid from a fresh issue may not exceed the lesser of the premium received on the issue of the shares being purchased and the amount standing to the credit of the Company's share premium account (s 160(1) and (2)).

(7) Shares shall be treated as cancelled on purchase and the issued share capital reduced by the nominal value of the shares. The authorised share capital is not reduced by purchase (s 160(4)).

The procedure to be followed depends upon whether the purchase is a market or off-market purchase. A 'market' purchase is one made by a public company on a recognised stock exchange. Other purchases by public or private companies are 'off market'. These must be made pursuant to a contract of purchase approved by a special resolution of the company (s 164(2)).

Procedure for Private Company Purchasing Shares out of Distributable Profits

(1) Check the Articles of Association to ensure that the company has the necessary authority to purchase its own shares. If the Articles do not

provide the necessary authority, it will be necessary to convene an extraordinary general meeting for the purpose of amending the articles. (See Precedent 4.1.)

(2) Ensure that the company has sufficient distributable profits to redeem shares. If such profits are not available, it may be possible to finance the purchase by the issue of fresh shares or by payment out of capital.

(3) Where appropriate, ensure that necessary tax clearances have been obtained.

(4) Check that after the repurchase the Company will have at least two shares remaining in issue which are not redeemable and that the Company will have a minimum of two members. Check that the shares to be repurchased are fully paid.

(5) A purchase of own shares may only be made pursuant to a contract (s 164) (see Precedent 4.2). The terms of the proposed contract must be authorised by a special resolution of the company before the contract is entered into.

(6) A company may also enter into a 'contingent purchase contract' (s 165). This is a contract whereby the company *may* become entitled or obliged to purchase shares; such contract also requires approval of the shareholders prior to execution.

(7) Convene an extraordinary general meeting of the shareholders for the purpose of approving a special resolution authorising the purchase (see Precedent 4.3). Where the company has more than one class of share, it may also be necessary to convene a separate class meeting or meetings.

(8) A copy of the proposed contract of purchase or a written memorandum of its terms, must be available for inspection by the members of the company at the meeting and also at the registered office for 15 days prior to the date of the meeting. Any memorandum of the terms of the contract must include the names of the members to which the contract relates. Where it is proposed to approve the contract by written resolution of the shareholders, the contract or a written memorandum of its terms must be supplied to each member at the same time or before presenting the resolution for signature (Para 5 Part II Sch 15A; CA 1989 s 114).

(9) The votes of any member whose shares are proposed to be purchased shall not be counted. Likewise the signature of such member to a written resolution shall be disregarded (Sch 15A).

(10) A copy of the special resolution should be filed with the Registrar of Companies within 15 days.

(11) Within 28 days of the date of purchase, a return must be made to the Registrar of Companies on Form G169 setting out details of the purchase.

(12) Stamp duty, chargeable at the rate of 50p per £100 (or part thereof) of the purchase price, is payable. This payment should be made to the Registrar of Companies at the same time as submitting Form G169.

(13) The relevant Share Certificate or Certificates should be delivered to the company for cancellation and the appropriate entries made in the Register of Members. As mentioned above, the issued share capital

should be reduced by the nominal value of the shares purchased; the authorised share capital is not reduced by purchase.

(14) The amount by which the company's issued share capital has been reduced on purchase must be transferred to 'capital redemption reserve' (s 170).

(15) The contract of purchase or a memorandum of its terms must be kept available at the registered office for inspection by members for 10 years after completion of purchase.

Procedure for Private Company Purchasing Shares from the Proceeds of a Fresh Issue

(1) The same procedures apply as set out above. A capital redemption reserve will be unnecessary unless the proceeds of the fresh issue is less than the nominal value of the shares purchased, in which case the difference must be transferred to capital redemption reserve (s 170(2)).

(2) Checks must be made to ensure that the company has sufficient authorised share capital, that it is authorised to allot shares in terms of s 80 or s 80A and that all or any rights of pre-emption are waived, if necessary. (Any resolutions that are required may be incorporated in the notice convening an extraordinary general meeting for the purposes of approving the proposed contract or included in the written resolution).

(3) File Form G88 (2) with the Registrar within one month of the allotment of the new shares.

Procedure for Purchase of Shares out of Capital—Private Companies only

(1) A private company may, if authorised by its articles, make a payment in respect of the redemption or purchase of its own shares out of capital. The payment to be made out of capital is defined as the 'permissible capital payment' (s 171(3)). The 'permissible capital payment' is the amount paid for the purchase after deducting all distributable profits and the amount of any funds raised from a fresh issue of shares made for the purpose of purchase. Accordingly no payment may be made out of capital until all distributable profits have been exhausted and/or the proceeds of a fresh issue applied. 'Capital' is defined as any payment made other than from 'distributable profits' and would therefore include any payment made from a loan made by a director or a bank or other source.

(2) Check that the articles permit the purchase of shares from capital, that at least two shares will remain in issue which are not redeemable, that the company will have a minimum of two members after purchase, and that the shares to be purchased are fully paid.

(3) Check that any required tax clearances are obtained.

(4) To ascertain the 'permissible capital payment' and the 'distributable profits', reference must be made to 'relevant accounts' made up to a date not later than three months prior to the date of a statutory declaration to be made by the directors. The 'relevant accounts' are

defined as such accounts as are necessary to enable a reasonable judgement to be made as to the amount of the permissible capital payment and distributable profits (s 172(3)). In practice these accounts will normally be the audited accounts of the company in which case the purchase of shares out of capital will have to be made within three months of the company's year end.

(5) The directors are required to make a statutory declaration on Form G173 specifying the amount of the permissible capital payment for the shares in question and stating that, having made full enquiry into the affairs and prospects of the company they have formed the opinion that:-

(a) as regards its initial situation immediately following the date on which the payment out of capital is proposed to be made, that there will be no grounds on which the company could then be found to be unable to pay its debts; and

(b) as regards its prospects for the year immediately following that date, that, having regard to their intentions with respect to the management of the company's business during that year and to the amount and character of the financial resources which will in their view be available to the Company during that year, the company will be able to continue to carry on business as a going concern (and will accordingly be able to pay its debts as they fall due) throughout that year (s 173(3)).

There must be attached to the statutory declaration an auditors' report to the directors of the company stating that

(i) they have enquired into the company's state of affairs; and

(ii) the amounts specified in the declaration as the permissible capital payment for the shares in question is in their view properly determined in accordance with Sections 171 and 172; and

(iii) they are not aware of anything to indicate that the opinion expressed by the directors in the declaration is unreasonable in all the circumstances.

(6) Convene an extraordinary general meeting to pass a special resolution approving payment out of capital (see Precedent 4.4). The resolution must be approved on the same day as the making of the statutory declaration or within one week of such declaration being made. The declaration and auditors' report must be available for inspection at the extraordinary general meeting or the resolution will be invalid. (Where a written resolution is employed, the document must be supplied to each member at the same time as or before the resolution (Para 6(3) Part II Sch 15A; CA 1989 s 114). Where the company has more than one class of share, it may be necessary to hold a separate class meeting or meetings.

(7) The votes of any members whose shares are proposed to be purchased shall not be counted. Likewise, the signature of such member to a written resolution shall be disregarded.

(8) Within one week of the date of the resolution for payment out of capital, the company must publish a notice in the Gazette:-

(a) stating that the Company has approved the payment out of capital for the purpose of acquiring its own shares by redemption or purchase or both;

(b) specifying the amount of the permissible capital payment for the shares in question and the date of the special resolution;

(c) stating that the statutory declaration of the directors and the auditors' report are available for inspection at the company's registered office; and

(d) stating that any creditor of the Company may at any time within the five weeks immediately following the date of the special resolution apply to the court for an order prohibiting the payment.
(See Precedent 4.5 for a specimen notice).

A copy of the notice must also be published in a national newspaper or, alternatively, written notice must be given to each of the company's creditors (s 175(2)).

(9) The statutory declaration and auditors' report must be kept available for inspection by members or creditors at the registered office from the date upon which notice appears in the London Gazette or Edinburgh Gazette, (as appropriate) until five weeks after the date of the passing of the resolution for payment out of capital.

(10) A copy of the special resolution, the statutory declaration and the auditors' report must be filed with the Registrar of the Companies not later than the date of publication of the notice in the London or Edinburgh Gazette.

(11) Any member who did not approve the special resolution or any creditor may, within five weeks of the date of the special resolution, apply to the court to cancel the purchase. Where an application is made, the Company shall immediately give notice to the Registrar of Companies on Form G176 and within 15 days of an order of court being given, deliver an office copy order to the Registrar (s 176).

(12) Payment out of capital must be made not earlier than five weeks and no later than seven weeks after the date of the special resolution.

(13) Make return to the Registrar on Form G169 within 28 days of the date of purchase. Pay stamp duty on the amount of consideration at the rate of 50p per £100 (or part thereof).

(14) If new shares are issued as a part of the exercise, make return to the Registrar on Form G88(2).

(15) Recall share certificate or certificates, cancel issued share capital and make appropriate entries in the Register of Members.

(16) To the extent that distributable profits are used in the purchase, make appropriate transfer to capital redemption reserve. In this regard the following points should be noted:

(a) If the permissible capital payment is less than the nominal amount of the shares purchased, the amount of the difference must be transferred to the capital redemption reserve.

(b) If the permissible capital payment is greater than the nominal amount of the shares purchased, the amount of the difference may be used to reduce the amount of the fully paid up share capital, the capital redemption reserve, share premium account or revaluation reserve.

(c) Where a fresh issue of shares is made in connection with the purchase, the amount to be transferred to the capital redemption reserve, in (a) above, will be the difference between the purchase price and the amount of payment from capital and the proceeds of the fresh issue. Where the permissible capital payment and the proceeds of the fresh issue, taken together, are greater than the nominal amount of the shares to be purchased, the difference may be used to reduce any of the amounts specified in (b) above.

Financial Assistance for Acquisition of Own Shares

(1) Except as set out in the Acts and with the safeguards provided therein for creditors and shareholders, it is not lawful for a company, directly or indirectly, to give financial assistance for the acquisition of its own shares or any shares in its holding company before or at the same time as the acquisition takes place (s 151). It is also unlawful for financial assistance to be given after acquisition, by reducing or discharging any liability incurred by any person in connection with the acquisition of shares.

Financial assistance is defined as:

(a) financial assistance given by way of gift;

(b) financial assistance given by way of guarantee, security or indemnity (other than an indemnity in respect of the indemnifier's own neglect or default) or by way of release or waiver;

(c) financial assistance given by way of a loan or any other agreement under which any of the obligations of the person giving the assisitance are to be fulfilled at a time when in accordance with the agreement any obligation of another party to the agreement remains unfulfilled, or by way of the novation of, or the assignment of rights arising under, a loan or such other agreement; or

(d) any other financial assistance given by a company the net assets of which are thereby reduced to a material extent or which has no net assets (s 152(1)).

(2) Section 153(1) permits a company to give financial assistance for the purpose of an acquisition of shares in it or its holding company if:-

(a) the company's principal purpose is not to give financial assisitance for the purpose of any such acquisition or the giving of assistance is but an incidental part of some larger purpose of the company; and

(b) the assistance is given in good faith in the interests of the company.

These exceptions are also available where the financial assistance is given to reduce or discharge any liability incurred by a person for the purpose of an acquisition.

Legal advice would clearly need to be taken if a Company were to rely upon these exceptions.

(3) Section 153(3) sets out various transactions not subject to the general prohibition. These include the distribution of a company's assets by way of dividend lawfully made, any distribution made in the course of winding up, the allotment of bonus shares or the redemption or purchase by a company of its own shares. In addition s 153(4) does not prohibit financial assistance where:-

(a) the lending of money is part of the ordinary business of the company and the loan itself is made within the ordinary course of that business;

(b) it is given in good faith in the interests of the Company for the purposes of an employee's share scheme (s 153(4) and (6); CA 1989 s 132); or

(c) the loan is made to those employed in good faith by the company (other than directors) with a view to their purchasing shares in that company or its holding company for their beneficial ownership.

(4) The three exceptions provided by s 153(4) are only available to a public company to the extent that its net assets are not reduced thereby or, if so reduced, the assistance is provided out of distributable profits.

(5) The principal relaxation of s 151 is provided only to private companies. Accordingly, a private company may give financial assistance for the acquisition of its own shares or the shares of its holding company if either:

(a) its net assets are not thereby reduced; or

(b) to the extent that they are reduced, if the assistance is provided out of distributable profits (s 155(1) and (2)).

'Net assets' are defined by s 154(2), whilst 'distributable profits' are to be determined in accordance with Part VIII of the Companies Act 1985.

The procedure for a private company providing financial assistance pursuant to s 155 follows.

Procedure for Financial Assistance upon the Acquisition of Own Shares

(1) Check the Memorandum and Articles of Association to ensure that the company is properly authorised to provide financial assistance. In particular companies incorporated prior to 3 December 1981 and adopting Regulation 10 of Table A to the Companies Act 1948, will need to remove reference to Regulation 10.

(2) In determining whether net assets are reduced, consideration must be given to the form of financial assistance to be provided. For example, financial assistance by way of gift would clearly reduce net assets, whilst assistance in the form of a secured loan would not. Where net assets are reduced, sufficient distributable profits must be available for financial assistance to be given. In this regard, directors must consult management accounts made up to a date immediately prior to the proposed date for financial assistance; reference to the last audited accounts would not normally be sufficient.

(3) A statutory declaration on Form G155(6)(a) must be made by the directors of the company proposing to give financial assistance. Where the shares to be acquired are shares in its holding company, the directors of the holding company and of any other company which is both the company's holding company and a subsidiary of that other holding company, must make a similar statutory declaration. The declaration must contain particulars of the assistance proposed to be given, the person to whom the assistance is to be given and particulars of the business of the company. In addition the declaration must state:-

"that the directors have formed the opinion, as regards the company's initial situation immediately following the date on which the assistance is proposed to be given that there would be no ground on which it could then be found to be unable to pay its debts; and either—

(a) if it is intended to commence the winding up of the company within twelve months of that date, that the company will be able to pay its debts in full within twelve months of the commencement of the winding up, or

(b) in any other case, that the company will be able to pay its debts as they fall due during the year immediately following that date" (s 156(2)).

It is necessary for all the directors of the company (and of the holding company or companies as appropriate) to make the declaration.

(4) There must be annexed to the statutory declaration a report by the auditors of the company addressed to the directors stating that:-

(a) they have enquired into the state of affairs of the company, and

(b) they are not aware of anything to indicate that the opinion expressed by the directors in the declaration is unreasonable in all the circumstances. (s 156(4)).

(See Precedent 4.6 for a suitable form of auditors' report.)

(5) An extraordinary general meeting of the shareholders of the company must be convened to approve a special resolution of the company authorising the giving of financial assistance. Such special resolution is not required where the company proposing to give the financial assistance is a wholly-owned subsidiary. Where a company proposes to give financial assistance for the acquisition of shares in its holding company, special resolutions are required of the company, the ultimate holding company and any intermediate holding company, (wholly-owned subsidiaries excepted).

The special resolution must be approved on the same day as or within one week of the making of the statutory declaration. The statutory declaration and the auditors' report must be available for inspection at the extraordinary general meeting (s 157). Where a written resolution is employed, the documents must be supplied to each member at the same time or before the resolution (Para 4 Part II Sch 15A; CA 1989 s 114).

(A suitable form of special resolution is set out at Precedent 4.7.)

(6) A copy of the special resolution, the statutory declaration and the auditors' report must be filed with the Registrar of Companies within 15 days of the date of the resolution.

(7) Unless all the members of the company (or of all the companies where more than one company was obliged to give approval) voted unanimously in favour of the resolution or resolutions, the financial assistance may not be given until after the expiry of four weeks from the date of the resolution or the last resolution where more than one was necessary (s 158(2)). This waiting period is to allow any members who did not vote in respect of the resolution, and holding at least 10% in aggregate in nominal value of the company's issued share capital or any class thereof, to apply to court for cancellation of the resolution. If no application is made for cancellation, the financial assistance may be made at any time after the expiry of the four week period but no later than eight weeks from the date of the statutory declaration, or the earliest of the declarations where there is more than one.

5 Meetings

MEETINGS OF DIRECTORS

Board Meetings

The articles of association will normally set out the procedure for convening and holding board meetings. Regulation 88 of Table A states that the directors may regulate their proceedings as they think fit. In addition 'a director may, and the secretary at the request of a director shall, call a meeting of the directors'.

There are no statutory provisions relating to the length of notice to be given for a board meeting and 'reasonable' notice should be given to all directors. In larger companies, board meetings are often held at regular, predetermined intervals of which due notice is given, but in smaller companies and, from time to time in larger companies, meetings are called as and when necessary. The notice reasonable for a particular meeting will depend, amongst other things, on the urgency and importance of the business to be discussed and the availability of the directors.

Notice of a board meeting may be given verbally, although it would be usual for written notice to be given. Notice of a board meeting need not specify the business to be transacted. A specimen notice is set out at Precedent 5.1.

Quorum of Directors

The necessary quorum for a meeting of the directors is normally fixed by the articles. Regulation 89 of Table A provides that the quorum may be fixed by the directors and, unless so fixed at any other number, shall be two. This provision will need to be varied where a private company has a sole director. Where a quorum is not present at a meeting of the directors, the proceedings will be invalid. However, Regulation 90 of Table A provides that if the number of directors in office falls below the number necessary for a quorum, those directors may act, but only for the purpose of filling vacancies or of calling a general meeting.

A quorum must be disinterested. Regulations 94 and 95 of Table A, for example, provide that, except for certain specified transactions, a director interested in business to be conducted at a meeting may not be counted in the quorum for the particular business to be transacted nor may he vote upon such a matter. Where a quorum cannot be raised for a particular item of business, it may be necessary for the matter to be placed before the company in general meeting.

It is common in small private companies for the articles to relax the provisions of Regulations 94 and 95 of Table A so that any director who declares an interest in a contract or arrangement made, or proposed to be

53

made, with the company may, having declared such interest, be counted in the quorum of the meeting and be entitled to vote in respect thereof.

Resolutions of Directors

Resolutions are normally decided by a majority of votes of those present. Proxies are not normally permitted at directors' meetings but may be allowed if the articles so provide.

Regulation 88 of Table A provides that the chairman shall have a casting vote but if the articles are silent as to a casting vote, a chairman has no right to such a vote at common law.

It is now common for the articles of a private company (but not Table A) to permit meetings to be held by telephone, or similar means. A suitable article to permit such meetings will be found at Precedent 5.2.

Resolutions in writing of directors are commonly used in private companies. Regulation 93 of Table A provides that a resolution in writing signed by all the directors shall be as valid and effective as if it had been passed at a meeting of directors. A resolution in writing may consist of one document or several documents, in like form, signed by each of the directors (see Precedent 5.3).

Examples of general board resolutions are set out at Precedent 5.21.

Committee of Directors

The powers of the directors may not be delegated to a committee unless the articles so provide. Regulation 72 of Table A specifically provides that the directors may delegate any of their powers to a committee consisting of one or more directors. The articles will normally prescribe regulations governing the proceedings of such committees and, as far as they are relevant, the provisions regulating the proceedings of directors shall apply.

MEETINGS OF MEMBERS

Meetings of members are regulated both by the Articles of Association and by the Acts. There are three kinds of meetings of members of a company:-

(1) annual general meetings,
(2) extraordinary general meetings, and
(3) separate meetings of classes of shareholders.

Annual General Meetings

An annual general meeting must be held once in every year and not more than 15 months after the date of the last such meeting (s 366). The first annual general meeting however, must be held within 18 months of incorporation.

The directors of a company will normally convene an annual general meeting (see Regulation 37 of Table A) but if the directors default in convening such meeting within the statutory period, the Department of Trade and Industry may call or direct the calling of a general meeting upon the application of any member (s 367). The usual business of an AGM comprises the consideration of the annual report and accounts, the declaration of a dividend (if any), the election of directors and the appointment or reappointment of auditors and the fixing of their remuneration. A specimen notice of an annual general meeting, together with appropriate minutes of an AGM are set out at Precedents 5.4, 5.5 and 5.6. A suitable script for use by a chairman of an AGM is set out a Precedent 5.7.

The following points of practice should be noted with regard to the business of an annual general meeting:-

(1) Any business that may be transacted at an extraordinary general meeting of the company may also be included as special business at an annual general meeting.
(2) Except where the members of a private company have approved an elective resolution, the directors are obliged to lay audited accounts before the company in general meeting within 10 months of the end of an accounting period for a private company, and within seven months for a public company (s 244; CA 1989 s 11). It is therefore necessary to consider these time limits when setting the date of an annual general meeting.
(3) It is practice in some companies for the notice convening the AGM to be read at the meeting but, more often than not, the notice is taken as read with the consent of the meeting. The auditors' report, however, must be read at the meeting.
(4) There is no obligation on the company to adopt or approve the annual accounts. The requirement is merely that the accounts be laid before the company (s 241(1); CA 1989 s 11).
(5) Motions for the appointment or reappointment of directors must be proposed separately at an AGM of a public company; a composite resolution is not sufficient.

Election to Dispense with an AGM

A private company may elect, by elective resolution, to dispense with the holding of annual general meetings (s 366A; CA 1989 s 115(2)). An elective resolution is one approved by all the members entitled to attend and vote at a general meeting (s 397A; CA 1989 s 116 and see page 62).

An election has effect for the year in which it is made and subsequent years. An election cannot be used however, to correct a default that has already taken place in failing to hold an AGM.

Where an election is in force and no AGM has been held for a particular year, any member may give notice to a company not later than three months before the end of the year, requiring the holding of an annual general meeting in that year.

Where an election ceases to have effect (as a result, for example, of the company in general meeting approving an ordinary resolution to that effect), the company is not obliged to hold an AGM if less than three months of the year remains when the election ceases to have effect.

Suitable forms of elective resolution are set out at Precedent 5.8. These precedents show how elective resolutions may be approved by written resolution or at a general meeting of the company.

Coupled with an election to dispense with the holding of AGMs, may be elections to dispense with the laying of accounts and reports before a General Meeting and to dispense with the obligation to appoint auditors annually. These are considered in Chapters 9 and 10 respectively.

Extraordinary General Meetings

All general meetings other than the annual general meeting are termed extraordinary general meetings. It normally falls to the directors to convene an extraordinary general meeting but s 368 provides that on a members' requisition the directors of a company shall forthwith proceed to convene an extraordinary general meeting.

Members holding not less than one tenth of the paid up share capital of the company carrying the right to vote (or in the case of a company without a share capital, members representing not less than one tenth of the total voting rights of all members) may requisition the directors to convene an extraordinary general meeting of the company (s 368). The requisition must state the objects of the meeting, be signed by the requisitionists and be deposited at the registered office. The directors are obliged to convene a meeting within 21 days from the date of the deposit of the requisition and if they do not, the requisitionists (or any of them representing more than one half of the total rights of all of them), may themselves convene a meeting for a date not more than three months thereafter. To avoid delay by the directors, they are not deemed to have duly convened a meeting if the meeting is to be held for a date more than 28 days after the date of the notice convening the meeting (s 368(8); CA 1989 Para 9 Sch 19).

A specimen notice convening an extraordinary general meeting and draft minutes of an extraordinary general meeting are set out at Precedents 5.9 and 5.10. A form of requisition by members for an extraordinary general meeting is set out at Precedent 5.11.

Class Meetings

Separate class meetings are necessary when provided by the Acts or by the articles of association and are normally held when it is proposed to vary or otherwise amend the rights attaching to a particular class of share. Where a class meeting is required, it is normally necessary to hold a general meeting of all the shareholders as well as a separate class meeting or meetings. The procedure for convening and holding class meetings is the same as for general meetings, as far as circumstances allow.

All resolutions to be proposed at a class meeting are extraordinary resolutions. These are resolutions requiring approval of three quarters of the holders of the particular class attending, and entitled to attend and vote, in person or, where proxies are allowed, by proxy at a separate class meeting (see s 378(1) and hereafter).

A specimen notice of a class meeting is set out at Precedent 5.12.

Written Resolutions of Private Companies

It has been generally accepted that where all members demonstrate their consent to a particular matter which a general meeting of the shareholders has authority to approve, the consent will be as binding as a resolution of the shareholders at a general meeting properly convened and held.

This principle is now accepted into statute law by the Companies Act 1989 which provides that anything which in the case of a private company may be done by resolution of the company in general meeting, or by resolution of a meeting of any class of members of the company, may be done without a meeting, and without any previous notice being required, by resolution in writing signed by or on behalf of all the members of the company who at the date of the resolution would be entitled to attend and vote at such meeting. (s 381A; CA 1989 s 113).

The signatures may appear either on the same document or on several documents in like form. The resolution is dated when the resolution is signed by or on behalf of the last member to sign.

All resolutions agreed to in writing shall have effect as if passed by the company in general meeting or by meeting of the relevant class of members of the company, as the case may be. Any resolution whether ordinary, special, extraordinary or elective may be approved by resolution in writing.

A copy of any written resolution proposed to be agreed in accordance with s 381A must be sent to the company's auditors (s 381B; CA 1989 s 113). If the resolution concerns the auditors as auditors, they may within seven days from the date on which they receive a copy give notice to the company stating their opinion that the resolution should be considered by the company in general meeting or, as the case may be, by meeting of the relevant class of members of the company.

A written resolution shall not have effect unless the period of seven days elapses without any notice being given by the auditors to the Company or the auditors notify the company that in their opinion the resolution does not concern them as auditors, or does concern them but need not be considered by the company in general meeting or, as the case may be, in separate class meeting.

All written resolutions must be entered in a book, in the same way as minutes of proceedings of a general meeting of a company. Any such record, if purporting to be signed by a director of the company or by the secretary, would be evidence of the proceedings in agreeing to the resolution (s 382(A); CA 1989 s 113).

There are two exceptions to the acceptability of written resolutions:-

(1) the removal of a director under s 303 before the expiration of his period of office; and
(2) the removal of an auditor under s 391 before the expiration of his period of office.

In both cases the resolutions must be proposed at a general meeting duly convened and held.

The acceptance of written resolutions has necessitated the introduction of various procedural changes relating to the circulation of documents to shareholders. Thus, the following documents which are required to be circulated to shareholders with the notice of a general meeting or available for inspection by members at a general meeting, must, where a written resolution is to be employed, be circulated to each relevant member at or before the time the resolution is supplied to him for signature:-

(1) the written statement to be given by directors pursuant to a special resolution, waiving rights of pre-emption on the allotment of shares (s 95(5)).
(2) The statutory declaration and auditors' report relating to an approval for financial assistance by a company for the purchase of its shares (s 157(4)).
(3) The copy of the purchase contract, or written memorandum of its terms relating to the off-market purchase or contingent purchase by a company of its own shares (s 164(6)).
(4) The statutory declaration and auditors report relating to the purchase by a company of its own shares from capital (s 174(4)).
(5) A written memorandum setting out the terms of a proposed director's service contract for a term of more than five years (s 319(5)).
(6) Disclosure of matters relating to the approval of a director's expenditure to enable him to properly perform his duties (s 337(3)).

In the same way as the votes of a member whose shares are to be purchased by a company are to be disregarded in respect of the particular resolution, it is provided that a member so interested shall not be regarded as a member for the purposes of a written resolution.

NOTICE OF GENERAL MEETINGS

The length of notice of general meetings is as follows:

(1) Not less than 21 days for an annual general meeting (s 369(1)).
(2) When a special resolution is to be proposed at a meeting, not less than 21 days notice must be given, whether or not the meeting is an annual general meeting or other general meeting of the company (s 378(2)).
(3) Not less than 14 days notice for an extraordinary general meeting (s 369(1)). In the case of an unlimited company, not less than seven days notice shall be given of a general meeting.
  The articles of a company may not provide for shorter notice periods. However meetings may be called at shorter notice upon the agreement of members as follows:
  (a) In the case of an annual general meeting, by all members entitled to attend and vote,
  (b) In the case of any other general meeting, by a majority in number of the members having a right to attend and vote at the meeting and holding not less than 95% in nominal value of the shares giving a right to attend and vote at the meeting. (s 369(3) s 378(3)). In the same way, a resolution may be passed as a special resolution at a meeting of which less than 21 days' notice has been given (s 378(3)),
  (c) The 95% in nominal value required for agreement to short notice set out in (b) above, may, in the case of a private company, be reduced to not less than 90% by elective resolution of the members (CA 1989 s 115(3)),

(d) The provisions set out in (b) and (c) apply equally to separate class meetings.

Specimen agreements to short notice are set out at Precedents 5.13, 5.14 and 5.15.

Calculation of Notice

The articles will almost invariably provide that 'clear days' notice is required, ie excluding both the day of service of the notice and the day of the meeting. The position may be further complicated by a provision in the articles stating that notice will be deemed to be given at the expiration of a certain period. For example Regulation 115 of Table A provides that a notice shall, unless the contrary is proved, be deemed to be given at the expiration of 48 hours after the envelope containing it was posted. It is common for other articles to provide that service shall be deemed to be given at the expiration of 24 hours.

Great care must therefore be taken to ensure that the correct period of notice is given and in this regard, it is essential that reference be made to the articles. For example, a Company adopting Table A should give notice as follows:-

Date of Notice:	1 October
Deemed date of service:	3 October
21 days run from:	4 October
Expiry of 21 days:	24 October
Earliest date for meeting:	25 October

Entitlement to Notice

Notice of a meeting must be given to all those persons entitled to receive notice. This includes the following:

(1) every member, except those members whose shares do not carry the right to vote, e.g. non voting shares or preference shares;
(2) the auditors of the company;
(3) the directors of the company; and
(4) all persons entitled to a share in consequence of the death or bankruptcy of the member.

The articles of a company often provide that notice need not be given to those shareholders resident abroad and who have not provided an address within the United Kingdom for service of the notice (Regulation 112 Table A). It is also common for the articles to provide that in the case of joint holders of a share, notice need only be given to the joint holder whose name appears first in the register of members in respect of the joint holding (Regulation 111 Table A).

An omission to give due notice to any person entitled to receive it invalidates the meeting. However, the articles normally provide that an accidental omission to give notice, or the non receipt of notice by a person, should not invalidate the proceedings (Regulation 39 Table A).

Contents of Notice

A notice convening a general meeting must show the following:-

(1) the date, place and hour of the meeting and the general nature of the business to be transacted;

(2) if the meeting is the annual general meeting, the notice must state that it is so;

(3) the resolutions to be proposed at the meeting;

(4) a statement that a member entitled to attend and vote may appoint a proxy;

(5) the name of the director or secretary authorised to sign the notice and their office of director or secretary;

(6) a public company must also have regard to stock exchange requirements. Therefore a listed company must also include in the notice of an AGM a statement as to the availability for inspection of certain directors' service contracts at the meeting.

It is common for the last item of business on a notice for an AGM to state 'To transact any other ordinary business'. As any business to be transacted at an AGM must be set out in full in the notice, such a statement has no force or effect and as a matter of practice should be omitted.

QUORUM

The quorum for a general meeting will be set out in the articles of association. Regulation 40 of Table A provides that a quorum shall constitute two persons present in person or by proxy. The articles will also need to be consulted to ascertain the procedure should a quorum not be present, or maintained, at a meeting.

CHAIRMAN

The articles will normally provide that the chairman of the board of directors of the Company shall preside as chairman of the general meeting. If the chairman is not present, the directors may elect one of their number to act as chairman of the meeting or, if no director is willing to be chairman or if no director is present, the members themselves may choose one of their number to be chairman. (Regulation 42 and 43 of Table A).

RESOLUTIONS

The Acts and, on occasions the articles, provide for the type of resolution required for decisions of a company. The most common types of resolutions are:-

(1) ordinary resolutions,

(2) special resolutions,

(3) extraordinary resolutions,

(4) ordinary resolutions requiring special notice,

(5) elective resolutions, and

(6) resolutions requiring a specific majority under the articles.

Ordinary Resolutions

An ordinary resolution is approved by a simple majority of those members entitled to attend and vote, and present and voting at a general meeting in person or by proxy. It should be noted that a simple majority is required only of those shareholders present at a meeting, voting, and entitled to vote and not all the shareholders entitled to vote, whether at the meeting or not. Thus, if there are twenty shareholders of which only ten attend the meeting, an ordinary resolution is carried if six vote in favour and four vote against. In the same way seven of the ten shareholders present abstain, whilst two vote in favour of the resolution and one against, the resolution is carried.

Where the Acts or the articles are silent as to the resolution required, an ordinary resolution will be sufficient. Ordinary resolutions are required for the following decisions, amongst others:-

(1) the increase, consolidation and subdivision of authorised share capital (s 121);

(2) authority to allot securities (s 80);

(3) the declaration of a bonus issue;

(4) routine business at an annual general meeting;

(5) approval of a transaction with a 'connected person' (s 320); and

(6) the revoking of an elective resolution (s 379A; CA 1989 s 116).

Special Resolutions

A special resolution is one which has been passed by a majority of not less than three-quarters of such members as, being entitled so to do, vote in person or (where proxies are allowed) by proxy at a general meeting of which notice specifying the intention to propose the resolution as a special resolution has been duly given. Not less than 21 days clear notice must be given of the intention to propose a resolution as a special resolution (s 378(2)).

The following are examples of decisions requiring approval by special resolution:

(1) Alteration of the objects clause (s 4).

(2) Alteration of the articles (s 9).

(3) Change of name (s 28).

(4) Ratification of an act beyond the powers of the directors (s 35; CA 1989 s 108).

(5) Reduction of share capital (s 135).

(6) Disapplication of pre-emption rights prescribed by s 89(1) (s 95(1)).

(7) Re-registration of companies from private to public (s 43(1)).

(8) Approval of financial assistance by a private company for the purchase of its own shares (s 155).

(9) Purchase by a company of its own shares (s 164).

(10) A resolution for placing the company in members' voluntary liquidation (Insolvency Act 1986 s 84).

Extraordinary Resolutions

An extraordinary resolution is one which has been passed by a majority of not less than three-quarters of such members as, being entitled so to do vote in person or (where proxies are allowed) by proxy at a general meeting of which notice specifying the intention to propose the resolution as an extraordinary resolution has been duly given (s 378(1)).

The length of notice to be given depends upon the meeting at which the resolution is to be proposed. If an extraordinary resolution is to be proposed at an annual general meeting, it is necessary to give 21 clear days notice, whilst if the resolution is to be considered at an extraordinary general meeting of a limited company, 14 days' clear notice is required.

An extraordinary resolution is required to approve the following matters:

(1) Variation of class rights at a separate class meeting (s 125(2)).
(2) A resolution to place the company into creditors' voluntary liquidation.

Ordinary Resolutions Requiring Special Notice

Certain resolutions require 'special notice' to be given to the company. These resolutions are as follows:

(1) The removal of a director (s 303(2)).
(2) The appointment in a public company of a director over 70 years of age (s 293(5)).
(3) The appointment as auditor of a person other than the retiring auditor (s 391A; CA 1989 s 122).
(4) The removal of an auditor before the expiration of his term of office (s 391A; CA 1989 s 122).

How Special Notice Must be Given

Notice of the intention to move the particular resolution must be given to the company at least 28 days before the meeting at which the resolution is to be proposed (s 379). The company must give notice of the resolution at the same time and in the same manner as it gives notice of the meeting or, if that is not practicable, it should give notice either by advertisement in a newspaper having an appropriate circulation or in any other manner allowed by the articles, at least 21 days before the meeting. Where special notice has been given of the intention to remove a director or an auditor, a copy of the notice must be given to the particular director or auditor (and the auditor proposed to be appointed, if appropriate) and both are given the right to make representations in writing for circulation to the members (ss 304 and 391A; CA 1989 s 122).

For examples of special notice, see Precedents 5.16 and 5.17.

Elective Resolutions

The Companies Act 1989 has introduced what is known as 'the elective regime'. This permits a private company to 'opt out' of certain statutory obligations, thereby easing the burden of legislative requirements. To secure these benefits, the members of a private company must approve 'elective resolutions' by unanimous decision (s 379A; CA 1989 s 116).

Elective resolutions can be approved to achieve the following concessions:

(1) The grant of authority to directors to allot shares in terms of s 80 for an indefinite period or for a fixed term greater than five years (s 80A; CA 1989 s 115).
(2) Dispensing with the laying of accounts and reports before the company in general meeting (s 252(1); CA 1989 s 16).
(3) Dispensing with the holding of annual general meetings (s 366A; CA 1989 s 115).
(4) Reducing the majority required to authorise the holding of general meetings or class meetings upon short notice (ss 369(4) or 378(3); CA 1989 s 115).
(5) Dispensing with the requirement to reappoint auditors each year (s 386; CA 1989 s 119).

The following points should be noted concerning an elective resolution:

(1) It must be approved by unanimous resolution at a general meeting of the company (or by written resolution).
(2) At least 21 clear days' notice in writing must be given of the general meeting.
(3) The notice must state that an elective resolution is to be proposed and state the terms of the resolution.
(4) The resolution must be approved by all the members, in person or by proxy, entitled to attend and vote at the meeting. This should be contrasted with other resolutions which require only a stated majority of those eligible members *present* in person or by proxy.
(5) It may be revoked by an ordinary resolution at any time.
(6) It shall cease to have effect if the company is re-registered as a public company.
(7) A copy must be filed with the Registrar of Companies within 15 days of the date of approval of an elective resolution.
(8) A copy of the resolution revoking an elective resolution must be filed with the Registrar of Companies within 15 days of the date of approval.

Examples of elective resolutions are set out at Precedent 5.8.

Resolutions Requiring Special Majorities

On occasions, the articles of a company may require a special or extraordinary resolution to be approved where, in terms of the Acts, an ordinary resolution is merely required. This is sometimes encountered with an increase in a company's authorised share capital. In addition, when a company's share capital is divided into different classes, the articles may provide that certain events or changes in the company's structure must be approved by special resolution of all the shareholders, e.g. the sale of a substantial part of a company's undertaking, the formation of a subsidiary or the declaration of a bonus issue.

Filing of Resolutions with the Registrar

Section 380 sets out those resolutions that must be filed with the Registrar. These include:-

(1) special resolutions;
(2) extraordinary resolutions;
(3) elective resolutions and any ordinary resolutions revoking such resolutions;
(4) an ordinary resolution giving, varying, revoking or renewing an authority to directors under s 80;
(5) an ordinary resolution to increase authorised share capital (s 123); and
(6) an ordinary resolution giving authority to a public company for a market purchase of its own shares (s 166(7)).

VOTING AT MEETINGS

Questions are normally decided, in the first instance, by show of hands. This does not take account of the number of shares held by each member present.

It is open to any one member to demand a poll. The articles will normally provide the number of votes attaching to each share. This will generally be one vote for each share held, but, on occasions, the articles may confer upon the holders of a particular class of share the right to an enhanced number of votes for each share of that class held.

PROXIES

Section 372 provides that a member entitled to attend a general meeting or a class meeting is entitled to appoint a proxy (who need not be a member) to attend and vote instead of him. In the case of a private company, a proxy appointed to attend and vote instead of a member has the same right as the member to speak at the meeting. In a public company, unless the articles otherwise provide, a proxy has the right to attend the meeting or any adjournment thereof but has no right to speak at the meeting except to demand or join in demanding a poll. A proxy may only vote on a poll, whether the company be public or private.

The articles normally set out the form of proxy to be used at a general meeting of a company. These will either be in ordinary form or be a 'two way' proxy. An ordinary form of proxy is normally used in a private company, whereas two way proxies are required for any company whose shares are listed on the stock exchange. The articles will normally provide for the manner of signature or execution of the proxy. Thus it should be executed by or on behalf of the appointor or, in the case of a corporation, be under its seal or under the hand of an officer duly authorised.

Specimen forms of ordinary and two way proxies are set out at precedents 5.18 and 5.19.

VOTING BY CORPORATIONS

The company may appoint a proxy or, alternatively, appoint a representative pursuant to s 375. Under that section a company may authorise any person it thinks fit to act as its representative at any meeting of a company of which it is a member and a person so authorised is entitled to exercise the same powers on behalf of the company which he represents, as that company could exercise if it were itself an individual shareholder. Under a s 375 appointment, the representative has the right to vote on a show of hands and to speak at meetings of both public and private companies.

A specimen letter of appointment of representative for delivery to a company pursuant to s 375 is set out at Precedent 5.20.

6 Re-registration of Companies

CONVERSION OF PRIVATE COMPANY TO PUBLIC COMPANY

This is the most common form of re-registration. A company wishing to trade its shares must be registered as public and often the decision to convert to 'p.l.c.' status is prompted by the desire to seek a quote on the stock exchange or to raise funds under the Business Expansion Scheme. Increasingly, however, private companies are being re-registered as public companies for merely commercial and marketing reasons. Many directors and shareholders consider that p.l.c. status can enhance the standing of their company in the public mind and many re-registrations are now being effected without any immediate plans for a public offer. Any company considering conversion must be mindful of the differences between public and private companies, details of which are set out in Chapter 1.

A private company cannot be re-registered as a public company unless it satisfies the statutory requirements of a public company. These are as follows:

(1) The memorandum of the company must state that the company shall be a public company (s 1(3)).
(2) The name of the company must end in the words 'public limited company' or if the company has its registered office in Wales it may, if it chooses, use the Welsh equivalent (s 25(1)). It is permissible to use the abbreviation 'p.l.c.'.
(3) The issued share capital must be not less than the 'authorised minimum' (ss 11 and 118). This amount is at present £50,000.
(4) Each of the shares in issue must be paid up as to one quarter of its nominal value plus the whole of any premium payable on it (ss 101 and 112).

Procedure for re-registration

(1) Hold a board meeting to convene an extraordinary general meeting of the shareholders for the purpose of approving a special resolution re-registering the company as a public company and approving the necessary changes to the memorandum and articles of association. Whilst it is not a statutory requirement to amend the articles of association, it would be normal to amend the existing articles or to adopt new articles suitable for a public company. For example, the articles of a private company may permit a minimum of one director and exclude the rights of pre-emption on the allotment of shares prescribed by s 89(1); a public company must have a minimum of two directors and is not permitted to exclude the provisions of s 89(1). (See Precedent 1.5 for a short form of articles for a public company

and Precedents 6.1 and 6.2 for specimen board meeting minutes and a notice setting out the special resolution required for re-registration.)

(2) Application for re-registration must be made to the registrar of companies on Form G43(3). This must be accompanied by the following documents:

(a) A printed copy of the memorandum and articles of association as amended.

(b) An audited balance sheet prepared to a date not more than seven months prior to the company's application for re-registration (this is because a public company must file its accounts with the Registrar not more than seven months after the year end). It would be normal for the balance sheet to be taken from the last audited accounts but it is quite permissible for the auditors to draw up a separate balance sheet to a date other than the Company's normal accounting year-end. The auditors' report to the balance sheet should be unqualified or without 'material qualification' (s 46).

(3) A written statement from the auditors that in their opinion the company's balance sheet shows that the amount of the company's net assets are not less than the aggregate of its called up share capital and its undistributable reserves (s 43(3)(b)). Where a report is qualified, the written statement must make it clear that the qualification is not 'material' for the purposes of s 46. (See Precedent 6.3.)

(4) If between the balance sheet date and the passing of the special resolution shares have been allotted for a consideration other than cash, a copy of a valuation report, as required for a public company, must be forwarded to the registrar of companies (s 44). A bonus issue of shares is not regarded as an allotment for consideration other than cash for this purpose.

(5) A statutory declaration on Form G43(3)(e), made by a director or the secretary of the Company stating as follows:-

(a) The required special resolution has been duly passed.

(b) The provisions of ss 44 and 45 have been satisfied (requirements as to issued share capital).

(c) That between the balance sheet date and the application for re-registration, there has been no change in the company's financial position that has resulted in the amount of its net assets becoming less than the aggregate of its called up share capital and undistributable reserves.

(6) The Registrar will issue a certificate of incorporation stating that the company is a public company. Upon the issue of this certificate, the company becomes a public company and may commence or continue to trade without the requirement for a certificate under s 117.

(7) It will be necessary to reprint stationery, and the Memorandum and Articles of Association, and to arrange for the new name of the company to appear at the registered office and at all business premises. If the company has a company seal, this will also have to be changed.

It should be noted that a fee is payable to the Registrar upon re-registration (at the time of writing £50). If a change of name is also involved (by the addition, amendment or deletion of a word other than 'limited') it will also be necessary to pay the necessary fee for change of name (at the time of writing £40).

CONVERSION OF PUBLIC COMPANY TO PRIVATE COMPANY

A public company may re-register as a private company, although this is rarely encountered in practice. There may be occasions when a public company is *obliged* to re-register as a private company following a fall in the issued share capital below the authorised minimum. This could occur through a reduction in issued share capital below £50,000, by, for example, a forfeiture of shares, or the acquisition by a company of its own shares.

Procedure for Re-registration from Public to Private

(1) An extraordinary general meeting of the shareholders must be convened to approve a special resolution amending the memorandum of association, and deleting the clause that the Company is to be a public company. In addition the resolution may make necessary incidental amendments to the Memorandum and Articles. The name of the company will also be changed by the deletion of the words 'public limited company' (or appropriate abbreviation) and the substitution therefore of the word 'limited' (ss 53 and 55).

(2) Application for re-registration must be made to the registrar of companies on Form G53. A printed copy of the memorandum and articles of association as amended by the resolution must accompany the form.

(3) A copy of the special resolution must be filed with the registrar within 15 days of the passing of the resolution.

(4) A minority of shareholders may apply to the court for cancellation of the resolution (s 54). This minority may consist of the holders of not less in the aggregate than 5% of the company's issued share capital, (or if the company is not limited by shares, by not less than 5% of its members), or not less than 50 members. The objection must be lodged within 28 days from the date of passing of the resolution. Upon hearing the application, the court may either cancel or confirm the resolution.

(5) If no application is made within the 28 day period or if an application is made and is dismissed by the court, the registrar will re-register the company as a private company and issue a certificate of incorporation appropriate to a private company.

(6) Stationery and the Memorandum and Articles must be reprinted and the new name of the company must appear at the registered office and at all business addresses. If the company employs a company seal, this will need to be changed.

CONVERSION OF LIMITED COMPANY TO AN UNLIMITED COMPANY

A company registered as a limited company may apply for re-registration as an unlimited company (s 49). A public company cannot be so re-registered nor may a company which has previously been re-registered as a unlimited company. An application for re-registration must be approved by *all* the members.

Re-registration from limited to unlimited is not uncommon and is chiefly effected to relieve a company from the necessity of filing audited accounts with the Registrar of Companies. It must be remembered however, that an unlimited company which is the subsidiary of a limited company or is a parent company of a limited company is *not* relieved from the obligation to deliver accounts (s 254; CA 1989 s 17).

Procedure for Re-registration from Limited to Unlimited

(1) An application for re-registration on Form G49(1) must be made to the Registrar, signed by a director or the secretary. The application must set out the necessary amendments to the Memorandum and Articles appropriate to a unlimited company and a printed copy of the altered Memorandum and of the altered Articles should be attached.

(2) The application should be accompanied by a form of assent, on Form G49(8) (a), signed by or on behalf of every member. A statutory declaration must also be made by all the directors on Form G49(8) (b) confirming that the persons signing the form of assent constitute the whole membership of the company and that they have taken all reasonable steps to satisfy themselves that a person subscribing to the form on behalf of a member, has been lawfully empowered to sign on that person's behalf. In such cases, the directors must have sight of any powers of attorney, probate, letters of administration, etc.

(3) A fee is payable upon re-registration (at the time of writing £5).

(4) The Registrar will issue a new certificate of incorporation stating that the company is unlimited.

(5) Stationery and the Memorandum and Articles must be reprinted and the new name of the company must appear at the registered office and at all business addresses. If the company employs a seal, this will need to be changed.

CONVERSION OF UNLIMITED COMPANY TO LIMITED

An unlimited company may re-register as limited (ss 51 and 52).

Procedure for Re-registration from Unlimited to Limited

(1) An extraordinary general meeting of the shareholders of the company must be convened to approve a special resolution, stating that the company is to be limited by shares or by guarantee, specifying the amount of the share capital, if any, and making such necessary amendments to the Memorandum and Articles as appropriate to a limited company.

(2) A copy of the special resolution must be filed with the Registrar of Companies within 15 days.

(3) Application for re-registration must be made on Form G51, signed by a director or the secretary, and accompanied by printed copies of the

memorandum and articles as amended. A re-registration fee is payable (at the time of writing £50).

(4) The Registrar will issue a certificate of incorporation as a limited company.

(5) Stationery and the Memorandum and Articles must be reprinted and the new name of the company must appear at the registered office and at all business addresses. If a seal is employed by the company, this will need to be changed.

(6) Protection is given to creditors should a company be wound up within three years of the date of re-registration as limited. In such cases, a person who was a member of the company at the time of re-registration will be liable to contribute to the assets of the company in respect of any debts or liabilities contracted before that time.

7 Dividends

Every company has an implied power to distribute profits to its members in the form of dividends. The articles of a company will normally contain an express power and also set out the manner and proportion in which dividends are to be paid. For example Regulation 102 of Table A provides that 'subject to the provisions of the Acts, the Company may by ordinary resolution declare dividends in accordance with the respective rights of the members, but no dividend shall exceed the amount recommended by the directors'. Regulation 103 confers upon the directors a similar power in respect of interim dividends.

It is a general rule of company law that dividends may only be paid if sufficient profits are available and for this purpose profits are strictly defined. Profits available for distribution may well differ from those profits revealed in the company's accounts. Reference must be made to ss 263 to 281 of the Act to determine what profits are available for payment as dividend.

PROFITS AVAILABLE FOR DISTRIBUTION

No company is permitted to make any distribution except from assets available for the purpose (s 263(1)). A 'distribution' includes not only dividends but any other payment made to shareholders whether in cash or in kind. The following are, however, excepted from any restrictions placed upon distributions—

(1) The issue of fully or partly paid bonus shares.
(2) The redemption or purchase by a company of its own shares.
(3) A reduction in share capital.
(4) The distribution of assets to members on winding up (s 263(2)).

On all other occasions, payments of dividend or other distribution may only be made from accumulated realised profits less accumulated realised losses (s 263(3)). The distinction therefore is between realised and unrealised profits and no discrimination is made between capital profits and profits arising from income.

The terms 'accumulated' and 'realised' require consideration. It is not sufficient that a company makes a realised profit in one year and regard must be made to the cumulative realised profits of a company. A dividend may only be declared where a company's cumulative realised profits exceed the cumulative realised losses.

'Realised' profits are not defined by the Act, except that paragraph 91 of Schedule 4 states that realised profits shall be those determined in accordance with principles generally accepted for accounting purposes. Accordingly, the final arbiter of what constitutes realised profits will be a company's auditors who shall have regard to Statements of Standard

Accounting Practice. Where doubts arise, careful consideration should be given to the legislation and clearance sought from the company's auditors. For general guidance, however, the following points may be noted:-

(1) Where the directors of a company are unable to determine whether a particular profit made before 22 December 1980 is realised or unrealised, they may treat the profit or loss, as the case may be, as realised (s 263(5)).

(2) Profits arising on the revaluation of an asset or assets are regarded as unrealised. However, the amount of depreciation charged against a revalued fixed asset may be treated as realised profit to the extent that it exceeds the depreciation which would have been charged if the asset or assets had not been revalued (s 275(2)).

(3) A provision for depreciation or a diminution in value of assets or a provision for any liability or loss shall be treated as a realised loss (s 275(1)).

(4) Development costs, shown as an asset in a company's accounts, are to be treated as a realised loss (s 269).

(5) Additional provisions apply to public companies as regards distribution of profits. Accordingly, a public company is prevented from making any distribution unless at the time, its net assets are not less than the aggregate of its called up share capital and undistributable reserves and the distribution itself would not result in a reduction of the net assets below that level (s 264).

RELEVANT ACCOUNTS

A company must have regard to the 'relevant accounts' to determine whether a distribution may be made. The 'relevant accounts' will normally be the last annual accounts laid before the company in general meeting but, if those accounts would not allow a distribution to be made, reference may be made to subsequent interim accounts or, to initial accounts where the distribution is proposed during the course of the company's first accounting period (s 270).

Whether reliance is placed upon annual, interim or initial accounts, it is necessary that they must be properly prepared in accordance with the provisions of the Acts. The following additional requirements apply to the particular accounts:-

(1) *Last annual accounts.* The auditors must have given an unqualified report to the accounts or, if the report is qualified, they must have stated in writing (either at the time or subsequently) whether the qualification is relevant for the purposes of whether the distribution may lawfully be made. A copy of such written statement must have been laid before the company in general meeting. (See Precedent 7.1 for a specimen auditors' statement.)

(2) *Interim Accounts.* These accounts must be such as are necessary to enable a proper judgement to be made as to the amount of the figures necessary to determine whether a distribution can be made (s 270(4)). A public company must also deliver a copy of the interim accounts to the Registrar.

(3) *Initial Accounts*. Again, these accounts are such as are necessary to enable a proper judgement to be made as to the amounts of the figures necessary to determine whether distribution can be made (s 270(4)). There are additional requirements for public companies, including a report by the auditors thereon and the delivery of the accounts to the Registrar (s 273).

DECLARATION OF DIVIDENDS

The Articles of Association of a company normally contain provisions for the declaration of dividend and, almost invariably, it is for the company in general meeting to decide upon the payment of the final dividend. However, directors will normally have the power to declare and pay interim dividends; i.e. dividends between one annual general meeting and another. They will also have authority to pay fixed dividends on preference or other shares as they fall due for payment under the terms of issue. This is the position with companies adopting the provisions of Regulations 102 and 103 of Table A. Regulation 102 acknowledges that powers of management reside with directors, by providing that no dividend (i.e. final dividend) shall exceed the amount recommended by the directors. (See Precedents 7.2 and 7.3 for resolutions relating to the declaration of dividends.)

On occasions certain shareholders may wish to waive some or all of their entitlement to dividend. A suitable form of precedent is set out at 7.5.

UNPAID AND UNCLAIMED DIVIDENDS

In England an unpaid dividend is regarded as a simple contract debt and the time limit for recovery is six years (Limitation Act 1980 s 5). In Scotland unclaimed dividends remain outstanding for five years (Prescription and Limitation (Scotland) Act 1973 s 6).

Regulation 108 of Table A, however, provides that any dividend remaining unclaimed for 12 years from the date on which payment becomes due shall, if the directors so resolve, be forfeited and cease to remain owing by the company.

DIVIDEND WARRANTS

Payment of dividend is normally made by dividend warrant consisting of two parts:-

(1) an advice setting out details of the dividend for attention by the shareholder and production to the Inland Revenue in support of any claim for recovery of tax credit, and
(2) a cheque for presentation to the company's bank.

An example of a dividend warrant suitable for a private company is set out at Precedent 7.4.

8 Directors

A director is defined by the Acts as any person occupying the position of director, by whatever name called (s 741(1)). This definition is necessarily loose to ensure that any person acting in the capacity of a director, whilst not bearing that title, does not escape from the responsibilities and obligations imposed by company law. Therefore, any person in accordance with whose directions or instructions the directors are accustomed to act will be deemed to be a 'shadow director' (s 741(2)). Professional advisers, upon whose advice directors may act, will not normally be regarded as shadow directors (s 741(2)).

NUMBER OF DIRECTORS

A public company must have a minimum of two directors. A private company must have at least one director (s 282). Furthermore, every company must have a secretary but a sole director cannot also act as secretary (s 283). It is not possible for a company to have as secretary, a corporation, the sole director of which is the sole director of the company, nor to have as sole director of the company, a corporation, the sole director of which is secretary to the company (s 283).

The Act does not contain any limit on the maximum number of directors, although a company's articles may specify a maximum number. Whilst Table A does not specify a maximum it does provide for a minimum of two directors and it will be necessary to amend Table A if it is proposed that a sole director should act.

Where the number of directors falls below the minimum number required by the Act or by the Articles, the remaining directors have no power to act except as may be prescribed by the articles. Regulation 90 of Table A permits the remaining directors in such circumstances to act only for the purpose of filling vacancies or of calling a general meeting.

There is no requirement in the Acts for a director to have a share qualification and it is uncommon for Articles to require a director to hold such a qualification. The articles usually provide, however, that even though a director may not be a member he shall be entitled to receive notice of and to attend and speak at general meetings of the company. Such a director will not have a right to vote unless he is chairman and the articles provide him with a casting vote.

APPOINTMENT

The first directors are those persons named in the statement (Form G10) delivered to the Registrar of Companies prior to incorporation. The statement must be signed by or on behalf of the subscribers to the

74

Memorandum of Association and must contain a consent to act signed by each of the directors.

The appointment of any subsequent directors will be governed by the Articles of Association. It is usual for the Articles to provide as follows:-

(1) The board of directors is normally empowered to fill casual vacancies or to appoint additional directors up to any maximum set by the Articles. Where the Articles give the directors exclusive power to appoint additional or new directors, the company in general meeting will have no power of appointment as this would usurp the powers delegated to the directors.

(2) Any person appointed by the directors as an additional director will normally hold office only until the next annual general meeting when an ordinary resolution must be proposed for his re-appointment (Regulation 79 Table A).

(3) The company is normally empowered by the Articles to appoint, by ordinary resolution, a person to fill a vacancy or as an additional director.

Procedures for appointing a director

(1) Check the Articles of Association for the mode of appointment. Ensure that the additional appointment will not cause the number of directors to exceed any maximum prescribed by the Articles.

(2) Obtain approval of the appointment at a board meeting or at a general meeting, as appropriate (see Precedent 8.1). It should be noted that a composite resolution to appoint two or more directors, proposed at a general meeting of a public company is void (s 292). Accordingly, all resolutions at a general meeting to appoint or re-appoint directors to a public company must be voted upon individually.

(3) Supply a Form G288 to the new director for completion. In particular, the appointee must sign a form of consent to act.

(4) Submit Form G288 to the Registrar within 14 days of the date of appointment.

(5) Enter details of the appointee in the Register of Directors of the company. The particulars to be inserted are his name, any former name, usual residential address, nationality, business occupation (if any), particulars of past and present directorships and his date of birth (s 289; CA 1989 Para 2 Sched 19).

(6) Remind the director of any share qualification required by the Articles. Where a qualification is required, the Articles will often provide a maximum period within which the qualification must be acquired, such period not to exceed two months (s 291).

(7) Invite the director to make disclosure of any interest in shares and debentures of the company and also to give general notice of any interest in contracts. He should also be reminded of his obligation to keep the company informed, from time to time, of any changes in interests in shares, debentures or contracts and he should be provided with pro-formas on which to make such disclosure.

(8) Notify the company's bankers of the appointment and, if the appointee is to be a bank signatory, amend the bank mandate.

(9) Remind the director of his responsibility to notify the company of any

change in address or personal details, and any changes in other UK directorships.

AGE LIMIT

There is no limit to the age of a director in a private company, unless it is a subsidiary of a public company. In the case of such subsidiaries and any public company, a person of 70 years of age or over may not be appointed as a director except by ordinary resolution of the shareholders of which special notice has been given (see Chapter 4). Any person in office attaining that age must vacate office at the conclusion of the annual general meeting immediately following his 70th birthday (s 293). These provisions may be excluded by the articles.

ALTERNATE DIRECTORS

The Act provides no power for the appointment of alternate directors and reference must be made to the Articles to ascertain whether alternate directors are permitted. The appropriate provision must be carefully considered as they can differ considerably from company to company. For example, Table A provides that an alternate may be either an existing director or some other person approved by the board of directors as suitable (Regulations 65–69). Other articles may provide that all appointments of alternate directors be approved by the board or may give the appointee the power to appoint any person as alternate director without the need for any board approval.

An alternate director is subject to all the statutory obligations and responsibilities of other directors. Accordingly, he must complete and sign a Form G288 and his details must be entered in the Register of Directors. He will also be subject to the rules relating to disclosure of interests in shares and transactions of the company. A form of appointment and revocation of appointment of an alternate director is set out at Precedent 8.2.

EXECUTIVE AND NON-EXECUTIVE DIRECTORS

These terms are commonly used to describe a full-time, working director (executive director) and a person who devotes only part of his time to the business and affairs of the company (non-executive director). Neither term is recognised by the Companies Acts and if a non-executive director qualifies as a director in terms of s 741, he is subject to the same statutory obligations and liabilities as any other director. If, however, a non-executive director fulfils his duties diligently and exercises the measure of skill and the duty of care which a part-time director might reasonably be expected to demonstrate, a court may apply different standards of responsibility from those reasonably expected of a full-time director.

It is common practice in some larger companies for senior managers to be provided with courtesy titles, such as associate director or divisional director. Such appointments are not intended to be board appointments but merely to confer a status upon the appointee. Provided the appointee does not hold himself out as a full board director and does not act as a director within the meaning of s 741, he will not be subject to the statutory responsibilities and liabilities attaching to full board directors.

MANAGING DIRECTOR

The position of managing director is not recognised by the Companies Acts and his power is derived from any provisions in the Articles of Association. For example, Regulation 72 of Table A permits the directors to delegate to any managing director 'such of their powers as they consider desirable to be exercised by him'.

Regulation 84 sets out the manner of appointment and termination of appointment of a managing director. The Regulation provides that a managing director and any other director holding an executive office shall not be subject to retirement by rotation. This does not, in any way, inhibit the company's power to remove a director pursuant to s 303. A managing director so removed may, however, have a claim for damages under the terms of his service contract.

CONTRACTS OF EMPLOYMENT

A director holding an executive office with a company may have a contract of employment. Section 319 provides that no contract of employment for a term exceeding five years may be granted to a director unless such contract is approved by an ordinary resolution passed at a general meeting of the company. Where a person is a director of a holding company and has a contract of employment for a term exceeding five years with a subsidiary company, it is necessary for the shareholders of both the holding company and the subsidiary (if not a wholly-owned subsidiary) to approve the contract.

A contract for a period exceeding five years is defined by s 319 as one 'that cannot be terminated by the company by notice or can be so terminated only in specified circumstances'. A written memorandum setting out the terms of the proposed contract must be available for inspection by members of the company at the registered office for a period not less than 15 days ending with the date of the meeting and, at the meeting itself. Where a written resolution of the members is to be sought, a copy of the memorandum must be supplied to each member before or at the same time as the written resolution (Para 7 Part II Sch 15A; CA 1989 s 114).

REMUNERATION

A director is only entitled to remuneration if the articles so provide. Fees payable to a director in that capacity should not be confused with any remuneration received by him under a contract of employment in an executive or management capacity.

Regulation 82 of Table A provides that directors shall be entitled to such remuneration as the company may by ordinary resolution decide. Regulation 83 permits payment of travelling, hotel and other expenses properly incurred by directors in connection with their attendance at meetings or otherwise in connection with the discharge of their duties. All remuneration or fees paid to directors must be paid after deduction of income tax. Any payments that are made gross will be treated by the Inland Revenue as net payments and the company will be liable to account to the Revenue for tax payable thereon.

COMPENSATION FOR LOSS OF OFFICE

No compensation for loss of office may be made to a director, nor may any payment be made in consideration for or in connection with his retirement from office, without particulars of the proposed payment, including the amount, being disclosed to members and the proposal being approved by ordinary resolution of the company. (ss 312 and 313). The amount of compensation paid must also be disclosed in the company's annual accounts (s 232 and Sch 6; CA 1989 s 6).

A Form of Resolution approving payment of compensation for loss of office is set out at Precedent 8.3.

RETIREMENT

There is no requirement in the Acts for directors to retire by rotation or otherwise. It is, however, common (see Regulations 73–80 in Table A) for the articles of the company to provide for:

(1) the retirement at the first annual general meeting of all directors then in office,
(2) the retirement at an annual general meeting of all directors appointed by the board since the date of the last annual general meeting, and
(3) the retirement at every annual general meeting (other than the first) of one third of the directors who are subject to retirement by rotation.

It is essential that the articles are consulted as it is common for private companies to exclude retirement by rotation. It is a Stock Exchange requirement that the articles of all listed public companies include provision for the retirement of directors appointed by the board during the year, but there is no similar requirement for retirement by rotation. It is unusual, however, for the articles of a public listed company to exclude retirement by rotation.

If the provisions of Table A are adopted the following points should be noted:

(1) The directors to retire, comprising one third of those in office, shall be those directors who have been longest in office since their last appointment or re-appointment.
(2) Where directors were appointed or reappointed on the same day, those to retire shall be determined by lot unless they otherwise agree amongst themselves.
(3) Where the number to retire is not three or a multiple of three, the number nearest to one third shall retire from office.
(4) If a company has a sole director who is subject to retirement by rotation, he shall retire.

(5) A director appointed by the board during the year and retiring at the annual general meeting, shall not be taken into account in determining the directors who are to retire by rotation.

(6) A managing director and a director holding any other executive office will not be subject to retirement by rotation.

(7) The company may fill the vacancy created by a director retiring by electing some other person in his place. If such vacancy is not filled, the retiring director will be deemed to have been re-elected (provided he has offered himself for re-election), unless the meeting expressly resolves not to fill the vacancy or a resolution for his re-election is put to the meeting and lost.

VACATION OF OFFICE

The office of director is personal to the appointee and is therefore vacated upon death. Termination of a director's appointment may also occur in the following circumstances:-

(1) resignation;

(2) removal from office (see below);

(3) disqualification by court order, e.g. for offences under the Companies Acts;

(4) upon bankruptcy (unless permitted by the Court to continue);

(5) failure to obtain any share qualification required by the articles within two months of appointment (s 291).

(6) at the AGM next following his 70th birthday (for those companies to which such age restriction applies).

In addition the Articles of Association will normally provide certain additional circumstances in which the office of director will be vacated. Regulation 81 of Table A, for example, provides that a director shall cease to act if:

(1) he is suffering from mental disorder and is admitted to hospital pursuant to the Mental Health Act 1983 or a Court Order is made on the grounds of his mental disorder.

(2) he is absent without permission of the directors from meetings of directors for more than six consecutive months and the directors resolve that he shall vacate office.

(3) he has a Receiving Order made against him or if he compounds with his creditors generally.

On every occasion of vacation of office, notice of that fact must be submitted to the Registrar of Companies on Form G288 and the fact must be recorded in the Register of Directors.

A draft letter of resignation and a resolution of the board accepting such resignation are set out at precedents 8.4 and 8.5.

REMOVAL OF DIRECTOR

A director may be removed before the expiration of his period of office by ordinary resolution of the company (s 303). Special notice is required of the

intention to propose a resolution to remove a director or to appoint somebody in place of a director so removed at the meeting at which he is removed. The following points should be noted:

(1) The intention to propose a resolution to remove a director must be given by a member to the company at least 28 days before the meeting at which the resolution is to proposed (s 379).
(2) Notice of the resolution must be given by the company to its members at the same time and in the same manner as it gives notice of the meeting. If this is not practicable, notice shall be given either by advertisement in a newspaper having an appropriate circulation or in any other manner allowed by the company's Articles, at least 21 days before the meeting.
(3) The company must send a copy of the special notice received to the director concerned. Such director has the right to speak on the resolution at the meeting at which it is proposed and also has the right to make written representations to the company. At the request of the director, and if time allows, the company must send a copy of the written representations to every member to whom notice has been given.
(4) If the representations are received too late to circulate to members prior to the meeting, the director concerned may require that they be read out at the meeting.
(5) A resolution proposing to remove a director must be put before the members in general meeting. It may not be dealt with by a written resolution (Para 1 Part I, Sched 15A; CA 1989 s 114).

An example of a special notice to be sent to the company and a form of notice to be sent thereafter to members are set out in Precedents 8.6 and 8.7.

POWERS OF DIRECTORS

The Articles of Association normally provide that the business of the company shall be managed by the directors. Directors' powers are limited in two ways:

(1) Being agents of the company, the directors cannot exercise any power which the company does not have itself. As regards outsiders, however, any person dealing with the company in good faith may assume that the power of the board of directors to bind the company or to authorise others so to bind it, is free of any limitation under the company's constitution (s 35A; CA 1989 s 108 and see Chapter 1).
(2) The abolition of the ultra vires doctrine by the Companies Act 1989 only extends to third parties and survives as between the company and its directors. Therefore a member may bring proceedings to restrain the doing of an act which is beyond the company's capacity, although a member can do nothing about an agreement already entered into (s 35(2); CA 1989 s 108). Directors remain bound by their duty to observe any limitations on their powers flowing from the Memorandum (s 35(3); CA 1989 s 108). Any act of the directors beyond the powers set out in the objects may be ratified by special resolution of the members but such resolution will not affect any liability incurred

by the directors which may only be relieved by a separate special resolution.

Special rules apply to transactions with a 'connected company' and these are discussed in the following section.

TRANSACTIONS WITH DIRECTORS (ENFORCEMENT OF FAIR DEALING)

There are numerous provisions in the Acts enforcing a director's duty to act, at all times, in the best interests of the company as a whole, and not to take advantage of his privileged position vis-à-vis the company. Accordingly, Part X of the Companies Act 1985 imposes various obligations of disclosure to members and others as well as in some cases, approval of the shareholders, to transactions or interests of directors. The various provisions are as follows:-

Interest in Contracts

It is the duty of a director of a company who is in any way, whether directly or indirectly, interested in a contract or proposed contract of the company, to declare the nature of his interest at a meeting of the directors (s 317). This duty also extends to a shadow director who is obliged to declare his interest, not at a meeting of the directors, but by a notice in writing to the directors. The following points concerning disclosure of interest should be noted:

(1) A director must declare his interest at the first possible opportunity. Thus an interest should be declared at the meeting at which the question of entering into a proposed contract is first raised (or if the director is not present at that meeting at the next meeting, whether or not he is present). If a director becomes interested in an existing contract, the declaration should be made at the first meeting of the directors to be held after the interest arose (s 317(2)).

(2) A director who is a member of a specified company or firm may give a general notice to the directors that he is so interested and such notice will act as sufficient notification in respect of any contract or proposed contract to be made with such company or firm. Where an interest arises as a result of a director being a director of another company, it is not sufficient for a general notice to be given and specific disclosure of an interest must be given on each occasion upon which it arises (s 317(3)). An example of a general written notice is set out at Precedent 8.8.

(3) Interests in contracts which are disclosable include loans by a company to a director or to a person connected with such director. 'Connected persons' chiefly comprise the spouse, minor children, business partners and companies in which the director or persons connected with him have an interest in at least one-fifth in nominal value of the equity share capital (s 346).

(4) The provisions of s 317 are normally tempered by the Articles of Association. Accordingly, Regulations 85 and 86 of Table A state that providing a director declares his interest, he may be a party to

transactions with the company and may provide a general notice in respect of all such interests as they arise.

(5) The Articles of Association may provide that a director interested in a contract may not vote upon any question put to a meeting of the directors concerning such transaction. Regulation 94 of Table A so provides but also sets out various transactions upon which a director may vote even though he may be interested. Regulation 95 provides that a director not entitled to vote as a result of his interest may not also be counted in the quorum of the meeting. However, by Regulation 96, the company may by ordinary resolution, relax or suspend any provisions of the Articles relating to voting on interested matters.

(6) Directors' interests in contracts must be disclosed in the notes to audited accounts (s 232; CA 1989 s 6).

Directors' Service Contracts

Copies of all directors' service contracts must be available for inspection at a company's registered office, or at the place where its register of members is kept or at its principal place of business. Notice of the location must be given to the Registrar of Companies where the copies are kept at a place other than the registered office (s 318).

Substantial Property Transactions

The approval of an ordinary resolution in general meeting is required where a director of the company acquires a 'non-cash asset' from a company or disposes of such an asset to a company (s 320(1)). The following points should be noted:-

(1) If the director or connected person is a director of its holding company or a person connected with such a director, a resolution in general meeting of the holding company will also be required.

(2) Approval of the shareholders is only required if the value is more than £1,000 and exceeds the lesser of £50,000 or 10% of the company's net assets.

(3) Approval of the shareholders is not required where the transaction is between companies within a wholly-owned group.

(4) A transaction which does not receive the approval required by s 320 will generally be voidable.

(5) Where a company enters into a transaction which includes a director or a director of its holding company or a person or company connected with such a director, and the board of directors exceed any limitation on their powers under the company's constitution in relation to the transaction, it will be voidable at the instance of the company (s 322A; CA 1989 s 109). Whether or not, the transaction is avoided, the director or connected person who is a party to the transaction and any director who authorised it, will be liable to account to the company for any gain made directly or indirectly from the transaction and shall indemnify the company for any loss or damage arising. The transaction will cease to be voidable if ratified by the company in general meeting.

(6) The provisions of s 320(1) do not now apply to any transaction on a recognised investment exchange carried out by an independent broker on behalf of a director or a person connected with him. 'Independent' in this context means the broker 'selects' the person with whom the transaction is to be effected (s 321(4); CA 1989 Para 8 Sched 19).

An example of an ordinary resolution approving a substantial property transaction is set out at Precedent 8.9.

Interest in Shares and Debentures

Sections 324 and 325 require a director to notify a company of his interests in shares and debentures of the company or a related company and for a register to be maintained by the company for the purpose of recording the information so notified.

Directors are obliged not only to disclose their own interest but also the interests of their spouses and infant children, including step-children (s 328).

'A related company' for the purposes of diclosure, consists of a subsidiary or holding company or a subsidiary of the company's holding company.

All notifications under s 324 must be in writing and must state the subsistence of the interest and the number or amount of shares or debentures of each class involved. The events requiring notification are as follows:-

(1) any interest in shares or debentures existing at the time of a director's appointment, and thereafter;
(2) the fact of becoming or ceasing to be interested in shares or debentures, or the making of a contract to sell any shares or debentures;
(3) the assignment of a right to subscribe to shares or debentures; and
(4) the grant by a related company of a right to subscribe to shares or debentures of that company, or the exercise or assignment of such a right.

Notification must be given within five days of the date of the event. In calculating the period for notification, Saturdays, Sundays and Bank Holidays are excluded.

In general, any interest whatsoever in shares or debentures must be notified, as well as the additional interests set out in Sch 13. In particular, the Schedule provides that the interest of a body corporate in a company is deemed to be the interest of a director if that body corporate or its directors are accustomed to act in accordance with his instructions or he controls one third or more of the voting power at any general meeting of that body corporate.

Schedule 13 also sets out various interests which do not require notification. These include the holding of shares as a bare nominee. In addition, certain exemptions have been prescribed by statutory instrument. These include:-

(1) Interests as a trustee of, or a beneficiary under certain approved pension schemes.

(2) **Interests in shares or debentures of a company which is a foreign** holding company of a wholly-owned subsidiary incorporated in Great Britain.

(3) Interests of a director of a wholly-owned subsidiary company who is also a director of the holding company and a register of such interests is maintained by the holding company.

The company must maintain a register for the purpose of recording directors' interests. Entry must be made in the register within three days of the date upon which it is received, excluding Saturdays, Sundays and Bank Holidays.

Where a director is granted a right to subscribe for shares or debentures of the company or exercises such a right, the company must make the appropriate entry in the register without any notification.

The register must be kept at the company's registered office or where the Register of Members is kept if at a location other than the registered office. Notice of the location must be given to the Registrar of Companies on Form G324 if the register is not kept at the registered office. The register must be available for inspection by members and other persons and must be produced at the commencement of every annual general meeting of the company and be available for inspection during the meeting by any person attending.

To assist directors with their obligations under s 324 it is usual and advisable to pass each director a supply of suitable forms on which notification may be made to the company. Examples of disclosure letters are set out at Precedents 8.10, 8.11 and 8.12.

Loans to Directors

Generally, a company is not permitted to make a loan to a director of the company or of its holding company or to enter into any guarantee or to provide any security in connection with a loan made by any person to such a director (s 330(2)).

Further restrictions apply to public companies with regard to 'quasi-loans'; these are very complex and reference should be made to ss 330–344 of the Act and, if considered appropriate, legal advice should be taken. It should be remembered that the restrictions relating to quasi-loans also relate to private companies which are part of a group containing a public company.

The general prohibition on loans by a private company to a director is relaxed to allow the following loans to be made:-

(1) A loan by a company to its holding company or the giving of security in relation to a loan by another to the holding company (s 336).

(2) Loans or the giving of guarantees made by a company whose ordinary business includes the making of loans or the giving of guarantees (see s 338). Such loans may not exceed £100,000 in amount (s 338(4); CA 1989 s 138).

(3) Subject to approval by the company in general meeting, a director may be provided with funds to meet expenditure incurred or to be incurred by him for the purposes of the company or for the purpose of enabling him properly to perform his duties (s 337). In such cases the expenditure must not exceed £10,000. As an alternative to prior

approval, the loan may be made on condition that if approval is not given at the next annual general meeting it will be repaid within six months of that meeting. Certain details concerning the loan must be disclosed to the shareholders when approval is sought, or, if approval is to be obtained by written resolution, details must be circulated to the relevant members, before or at the same time as the resolution is supplied (Para 8 Part II Sch 15A; CA 1989 s 114).

(4) Any company may make a loan to a director or to a director of its holding company if it does not exceed the sum of £5,000 (s 334; CA 1989 s 138).

It must be remembered that the provisions relating to loans to directors relate also to 'connected persons' of a director. These include his spouse, minor children, partners or any company in which he is interested in at least one fifth of the equity share capital or in which he can control the exercise of more than one fifth of the votes.

Insider Dealing

Insider dealing does of course extend to persons other than directors, but it is likely to be directors who are most readily in possession of price sensitive information. The provisions relating to insider dealing apply only to public companies and are set out in the Company Securities (Insider Dealing) Act 1985.

It should be noted that s 323 prohibits the director of any company from dealing in share options of that company.

INDEMNITY INSURANCE FOR OFFICERS AND AUDITORS OF THE COMPANY

There has been debate in recent years as to whether it is lawful for a company to effect insurance on behalf of directors and other officers to indemnify them against any liability incurred as a result of proceedings taken against them in the course of their duties. This was in the light of s 310 of the 1985 Act which rendered void any provision for exempting an officer or auditor from liability incurred in respect of any negligence, default, breach of duty, or breach of trust in relation to the company.

The Companies Act 1989 removes such doubt and makes it lawful for a company to insure against or to indemnify director or other officer against any liability incurred by him:-

(1) in defending any proceedings (whether civil or criminal) in which judgement is given in his favour or he is acquitted, or

(2) in connection with any application under s 144(3) or (4) (acquisition of shares by innocent nominee) or s 727 (general power to grant relief in case of honest and reasonable conduct) in which relief is granted to him by the Court (s 310(3); CA 1989 s 137).

The fact that such insurance has been effected must be disclosed in the Directors' Report of a company's audited accounts for any period during which the insurance is purchased or maintained (Para 5A, Part I, Sch 7; CA 1989, s 137).

9 Accounts and Records

COMPANY ACCOUNTS

The Companies Act 1989 introduces new ss 221–262 to replace the corresponding sections of the Companies Act 1985. The change of law was inspired by the EEC 7th directive on group accounts but the opportunity has been taken to also amend the form, content, filing and publication of individual company accounts. In particular, the law relating to accounting reference periods, the approval, signing, laying and delivery of accounts, and the exemptions available for small and medium sized companies have been considerably amended.

ACCOUNTING RECORDS

Every company is obliged to keep accounting records which are sufficient to show and explain the company's transactions (s 221(1); CA 1989 s 2). These records must disclose with reasonable accuracy, at any time, the financial position of the company and enable the directors to prepare a balance sheet and profit and loss account in accordance with the Act. In particular, the records must contain:

(1) day-to-day entries of all sums of monies received and expended by the company;

(2) a record of the assets and liabilities; and

(3) if a company deals in goods, statements of stock held by the company at the end of each financial year, statements of stocktakings and, except for companies engaged in the ordinary retail trade, statement of all goods sold and purchased giving sufficient details to identify all buyers and sellers.

The accounting records must be kept at the registered office or at such other place as the directors think fit (s 222; CA 1989 s 2). These records must be open at all times to inspection by the company's officers. The records must be maintained, in the case of the private company, for three years, and in the case of the public company for six years. Both for administrative reasons and to meet the requirements of the Inland Revenue and the VAT authorities, it would be normal for management to retain accounting records for longer periods.

If accounting records are kept outside Great Britain, accounts and returns sufficient to disclose with reasonable accuracy the financial position of the business at intervals of not more than six months and, such as to enable the directors to prepare a balance sheet and profit loss account, must be sent to and kept at a place in Great Britain.

ACCOUNTING REFERENCE PERIODS

A company's financial year begins with the first day of its accounting period and ends with the last day of that period or a date not more than seven days before or after the end of the period (s 223; CA 1989 s 3). It will be seen therefore that a company may adjust its accounting period, at any time, by not more than seven days without restriction or the need for any secretarial formalities.

A company's accounts must be prepared for an accounting reference period, to be determined as follows:

(1) A company's first accounting reference period must be for a period of more than six months but not more than 18 months, beginning with the date of its incorporation (s 224(4); CA 1989 s 3).

(2) A company has nine months from the date of incorporation to choose an accounting reference date. This will be the date upon which the accounting reference period will end in any calendar year. (s 224(2); CA 1989 s 3). Notice of this date must be given to the Registrar of Companies on Form G224 within the nine month period.

If the company fails to give notice to the registrar within the nine month period, it will be automatically awarded an accounting reference date ending on the last day of the month on which the anniversary of its incorporation falls (s 224(3); CA 1989 s 3). This applies to all companies incorporated after the commencement of Part 1 of the Companies Act 1989. Companies incorporated before that date and failing to notify the Registrar of Companies of an accounting reference period, have been awarded 31 March in each year as their year end.

The provisions ensure that a company which does not notify an accounting reference date, will have a first accounting period of not more than 13 months. For example, a company incorporated on 2 July 1991, and failing to notify the Registrar of an accounting reference date within the required nine month period, will be obliged to prepare its first accounts for the period ending 31 July 1992. If, however, the same company gives notice to the Registrar that its chosen accounting reference date is 31 December in each year, it will prepare its first accounts for the period ending 31 December 1992. Accounts for the shortened period to 31 December 1991 could not be prepared as they would be for a period of less than six months.

Except in the circumstances set out below, a company may only change its accounting reference period during the course of a current accounting period and this change will have effect for that period and for subsequent periods (s 225(1); CA 1989 s 3). Notice must be given of this change to the Registrar on Form G225(1) during the course of the accounting reference period it is wished to change.

The financial year of a subsidiary must coincide with the financial year of its parent undertaking, except where in the opinion of the directors, there are good reasons against it (s 223(5); CA 1989 s 3).

In pursuance of this requirement, a subsidiary or a parent company may change its accounting reference date to make it co-terminus with the accounting reference date of its parent or subsidiary company, as the case may be (s 225(2); CA 1989 s 3). The notice, to be given to the Registrar on Form G225(2) may be given in relation to the company's previous accounting period and all subsequent periods. The notice will only be effective if the period allowed for laying and delivering accounts in relation to the previous accounting period has not already expired. This period is 10 months in the case of a private company and 7 months in the case of a public company.

A company may shorten its accounting reference period as often as it wishes (subject always to a minimum accounting period of six months) but may not extend its accounting period more than once in every five years. This limitation does not apply where a parent or a subsidiary company changes its accounting period in terms of s 225(2).

ANNUAL ACCOUNTS

The directors of every company are obliged to prepare, for each financial year of the company, a balance sheet as at the last day of the year, and a profit and loss account (s 226(1); CA 1989 s 4). A parent company must also prepare group accounts as well as individual accounts in respect of each year (s 227; CA 1989 s 5). A parent company is excused the preparation of such consolidated accounts in the following circumstances:

(1) the company is a subsidiary and its immediate parent undertaking is established under the laws of a member state of the EEC and complies with certain requirements (s 228; CA 1989, s 5);

(2) where the inclusion of the subsidiary is not material for the purpose of giving a true and fair view (s 229(2); CA 1989 s 5); or

(3) severe long term restrictions substantially hinder the exercise of the rights of the parent company over the assets and management of the particular undertaking (s 229(3); CA 1989 s 5); or

(4) the information necessary for the preparation of group accounts cannot be obtained without disproportionate expense or undue delay (s 229(3); CA 1989 s 5); or

(5) the interest of the parent company is held exclusively with a view to subsequent resale and the undertaking has not previously been included in consolidated group accounts prepared by the parent (s 229(3); CA 1989 s 5); or

(6) the activities of one or more undertakings is so different from those of other undertakings to be included in the consolidation that their inclusion would be incompatible with the obligation to give a true and fair view (s 229(4); CA 1989 s 5).

The Companies Act 1989 introduces new concepts of 'parent undertaking' and 'subsidiary undertaking' (s 258; CA 1989 s 21). The definitions do not require the 'undertakings' to be companies, and group accounts may now include the results of not just companies but other forms of business, e.g. partnerships and sole traders. It should be noted that the new definitions of parent undertaking and subsidiary undertaking are only for the purpose of preparing group accounts and do not apply for other purposes of the Acts, where the expressions 'holding company' and 'subsidiary' are retained but redefined (ss 736, 736A, 736B; CA 1989 s 144). The new provisions are designed to curb off-balance sheet financing. Under the old rules, a company could be excluded from consolidation even though it was effectively controlled by another company, by specially constructed

voting rights or capital structure. The new tests include voting control and whether one company is able to exercise 'a dominant influence' over another (s 258(2); CA 1989 s 21).

Reference should be made to Sch 4 (as amended) of the Companies Act 1985 as to the preparation of individual company accounts and to new Sch 4A, introduced into the Companies Act 1985, for the form and content of group accounts.

APPROVAL AND SIGNING OF ACCOUNTS

A company's annual accounts must be approved by the board of directors and signed, on the balance sheet, by a director of the company on behalf of the board (s 233; CA 1989 s 7). The copy of the company's balance sheet which is delivered to the Registrar of Companies must also be signed by a director of the company.

Every copy of the balance sheet which is laid before the company in general meeting or which is otherwise circulated, published or issued must state the name of the person who has signed the balance sheet on behalf of the board.

DIRECTORS' REPORT

A Directors' report must be prepared for each financial year. (s 234; CA 1989 s 8). It must be approved by the board of directors and signed on behalf of the board by a director or the secretary (s 234 A; CA 1989 s 8). The copy of the report delivered to the Registrar must be signed on behalf of the board by a director or the secretary of the company. Every copy of the directors' report which is laid before the company in general meeting or which is otherwise circulated, published or issued must state the name of the person who signed it on behalf of the board.

The directors' report must contain the following information required by s 234 and Sch 7. The information to be given for an individual company is as follows:

(1) A fair review of the development of the business of the company and its subsidiary undertakings (if any) during the financial year and of their position at the end of it.

(2) The amount (if any) which the directors recommend should be paid as dividend and the amount (if any) which they propose to carry to reserves.

(3) The names of the persons who at any time during the financial year were directors of the company.

(4) The principal activities of the company and its subsidiary undertakings in the course of the year and any significant changes in those activities during the year.

(5) Details of any significant changes in fixed assets of the company or any of its subsidiary undertakings during the year.

(6) Any difference in the market value of interests in land over the value disclosed in the balance sheet, if the difference is, in the directors

opinion, of such significance as to require that the attention of members or debenture holders should be drawn to it.

(7) Interests of directors in shares or debentures of the company or any other body corporate in the same group at the beginning and end of the financial year. The information to be given must be extracted from the register of directors' interests maintained by the company. Details of directors' interests may be included in the notes to the accounts rather than the directors' report.

(8) Particulars of contributions made for political or charitable purposes if the total exceeds £200.

(9) Particulars of any important events affecting the company or any of its subsidiary undertakings which have occurred since the end of the financial year.

(10) An indication of likely future developments in the business of the company and its subsidiary undertakings.

(11) An indication of the activities (if any) of the company and its subsidiary undertakings in the field of research and development.

(12) Details of any acquisition of its own shares during the year.

(13) Where the average numbers of employees of the company exceeds 250,

   (a) a statement describing the company's policy towards disabled persons;

   (b) a statement concerning employee involvement; and

   (c) a statement of the company's policy for securing the health and safety and welfare at work of employees of the company and its subsidiary undertakings and for protecting other persons against risks to health or safety arising out of or in connection with the activities at work of those employees.

It should be remembered that a directors' report is not required for inclusion in modified accounts prepared by a small company, or the accounts of dormant companies (see later in this chapter).

AUDITORS' REPORT

The auditors' report to annual accounts must state whether, in the auditors' opinion, the annual accounts have been properly prepared in accordance with the Act and in particular whether a true and fair view is given (s 235; CA 1989 s 9). The report must state the names of the auditors and be signed by them and every copy which is laid before the company in general meeting or which is otherwise circulated, published or issued shall state the names of the auditors (s 236; CA 1989 s 9). The copy of the auditor's report delivered to the Registrar of Companies shall state the names of the auditors and be signed by them.

PUBLICATION OF ACCOUNTS AND REPORTS

A copy of the company's annual accounts, together with copies of the directors' report and the auditors' report must be sent to:

(1) every member of the company,

(2) every holder of the company's debentures, and
(3) every person who is entitled to receive notice of general meetings. This would include directors who are not members and the auditors (s 238; CA 1989 s 10).

These copies must be sent not less than 21 days before the date of the meeting at which copies of the accounts are to be laid before the shareholders.

Copies need not be sent to:

(1) a person who is not entitled to receive notices of general meetings and of whose address the company is unaware;
(2) more than one of the joint holders of shares or debentures, none of whom is entitled to receive notices; and
(3) in the case of joint holders of shares or debentures, some of whom are, and some not, entitled to receive such notices, to those who are not so entitled.

Where copies are not sent within 21 days of the date of the meeting to those entitled to receive them, the copies may be deemed to have been duly sent if by all members entitled to attend and vote at the meeting agree (s 238(4); CA 1989 s 10).

Any member or any debenture holder may request to be sent, without charge, a copy of the last annual accounts in addition to the copy which must be sent in accordance with s 238.

Every copy of published statutory accounts must be accompanied by the relevant auditors' report. If the company publishes non-statutory accounts, they must include a statement indicating, amongst other things, that they are not statutory accounts (s 240; CA 1989 s 10).

LAYING AND DELIVERING OF ACCOUNTS AND REPORTS

In each financial year, the directors of a company must lay before the company in general meeting copies of the company's annual accounts and the directors' report and auditors' report thereon and deliver a copy of such accounts and reports to the Registrar of Companies (ss 241 and 242; CA 1989 s 11). A private company may, however, elect to dispense with the laying of accounts and reports before a general meeting (s 252; CA 1989 s 16 and hereafter).

A private company must lay accounts before a general meeting and deliver a copy of such accounts to the Registrar within 10 months of the end of the appropriate accounting reference period. This period is 7 months in the case of a public company (s 244(1); CA 1989 s 11). However, in the case of the first accounting period of the company which is for a period of more than 12 months, the period allowed is 10 months or seven months, as the case may be, from the first anniversary of the incorporation of the company or three months from the end of the accounting reference period, whichever last expires (s 244(2); CA 1989 s 11).

Where a company carries on business or has interests outside the United Kingdom, the Channel Islands, or the Isle of Man, the directors may give notice to the Registrar before the end of an accounting reference period, claiming a three month extension of the period allowed for laying and delivering accounts and reports (s 244(3); CA 1989 s 11). The extension has effect only for the particular period.

The Companies Act 1989 has greatly increased the penalties that can be levied on the company and its directors for failure to lay and deliver accounts. The penalties are as follows:

(1) Every director found guilty of an offence will be liable to a fine and, for continued contravention, to a daily default fine.

(2) The company will be liable to a civil penalty calculated by reference to the length of the period between the end of the period allowed for laying and delivering accounts and the day on which the requirements are complied with (s 242A(2); CA 1989 s 11). The penalty shall be determined as follows:

Length of period	Public company	Private company
Not more than 3 months	£500	£100
More than 3 months but not more than 6 months	£1000	£250
More than 6 months but not more than 12 months	£2000	£500
More than 12 months	£5000	£1000

ELECTION TO DISPENSE WITH THE LAYING OF ACCOUNTS AND REPORTS

A private company may approve an elective resolution to dispense with the laying of accounts or reports before the company in general meeting (s 252; CA 1989 s 16). Such an election will have effect both for the financial year for which the election is made and for subsequent financial years.

An election does not relieve a company from the obligation to send copies of the accounts to every member and to those other persons entitled to receive copies in terms of s 238. Where an election has been made, copies of accounts must be sent to those entitled to receive them not less than 28 days before the end of the period allowed for laying and delivering accounts and reports (s 253; CA 1989 s 16). Therefore, where an election is in place, the directors will normally be obliged to send copies of the accounts and reports to members and others within nine months of the year end.

A notice must accompany every copy of the accounts sent to members, informing them of their right to require the laying of accounts and reports before a general meeting. Before the end of 28 days beginning with the day on which the accounts and reports are sent out to members and others, any member or auditor may, by notice in writing, deposited at the registered office of the company, require that a general meeting be held for the purpose of laying the accounts and reports before the company (s 253(2); CA 1989 s 16).

Within 21 days of receiving the notice, the directors must proceed to convene a general meeting to be held not more than three months from the date of receipt of the notice from the member or the auditor, as the case may be. If the directors fail to convene such a meeting, the person who deposited the notice may do so and all reasonable expenses shall be made good to him by the company and shall be recouped by the company out of any fees or other remuneration paid to the directors in default.

A specimen elective resolution is set out at Precedent 5.8.

REVISION OF DEFECTIVE ACCOUNTS AND REPORTS

If it appears to the directors of a company that any accounts or reports do not comply with requirements of the Act, they may prepare and file revised accounts with the Registrar of Companies (s 245; CA 1989 s 12). The Secretary of State is also empowered to serve a notice on a company stating that the accounts do not, in his opinion, comply with the provisions of the Acts. Having served such notice, the Secretary of State may make application to the Court for an Order, requiring, amongst other things, the preparation of revised accounts (ss 245A, 245B; CA 1989 s 12).

SMALL AND MEDIUM SIZED COMPANIES AND GROUPS

A company which qualifies as a small or medium sized company is entitled to prepare and file with the Registrar modified accounts in accordance with Sch 8 of the Act (s 246(1); CA 1989 s 13). This does not release a company from the obligation to prepare and submit full audited accounts to each member.

The modified accounts for a small company consist of an abbreviated balance sheet for a particular financial year together with abbreviated notes. Copies of the profit and loss account and directors' report for the year are not required.

A medium sized company is exempted from supplying certain information set out in its profit and loss account. In all other respects, full accounts must be prepared and submitted to the Registrar for a medium sized company.

A public company, a banking or insurance company, or an authorised person under the Financial Services Act 1986 are not entitled to the exemptions, nor is any company which is in a group containing such a company. A parent company is also unable to enjoy the exemptions unless the group, as a whole, qualifies as a small or medium sized group, as the case may be.

To qualify as small or medium sized, a company must satisfy at least two of the following qualifying conditions, either in its first financial year, or in the case of any subsequent financial year, in that year and the preceding year:

Small company

Turnover	Not more than £2 million
Balance sheet total	Not more than £975,000
Number of employees	Not more than 50

Medium sized company

Turnover	Not more than £8 million
Balance sheet total	Not more than £3.9 million
Number of employees	Not more than 250.

Turnover must be adjusted proportionately where the period is less than one year. (s 247; CA 1989 s 13).

SMALL AND MEDIUM SIZED GROUPS

The Companies Act 1989 has introduced a concession for small and medium sized groups of companies relieving them of the obligation to prepare group accounts. A group is ineligible if it contains a public company, a banking or insurance company, or an authorised person under the Financial Services Act 1986 (s 248; CA 1989 s 13). A group qualifies as small and medium sized, as the case may be, if two of the following qualifying conditions are met, either in the first financial year of the parent company or in the case of any subsequent financial year, in that year and the preceding year:

Small group

Aggregate turnover	Not more than £2 million net (or £2.4 million gross)
Aggregate balance sheet total	Not more than £1 million net (or £1.2 million gross)
Aggregate number of employees	Not more than 50

Medium sized group

Aggregate turnover	Not more than £8 million net (or £9.6 million gross)
Aggregate balance sheet total	Not more than £3,900,000 net (or £4.7 million gross)
Aggregate number of employees	Not more than 250

The 'net' figures referred to in the tables are to be calculated after the set-offs and other adjustments required by Sch 4A to the Companies Act 1985 (Form and Content of Group Accounts) and 'gross' figures are without the benefit of such set-offs and adjustments.

DORMANT COMPANIES

Any company which qualifies as a dormant company, may by special resolution, resolve not to appoint auditors (s 250; CA 1989 s 14). A public company, banking or insurance company or an authorised person under the Financial Services Act 1986 may not qualify as a dormant company.

To qualify a company must either:

(1) be dormant from the time of its formation and exempt itself from the

    obligation to appoint auditors by a special resolution passed before the first general meeting of the company at which annual accounts are laid, or

(2) have been dormant since the end of the previous financial year, qualify as a small company or would so qualify if it were not a member of an ineligible group, and is not required to prepare group accounts for that year. Such a company may resolve not to appoint auditors by a special resolution passed at a general meeting of the company at which annual accounts to that year are laid (s 250(1); CA 1989 s 14).

A company is dormant if, during the particular period, no significant accounting transactions occur (s 250(3); CA 1989 s 14). 'Significant accounting transactions' are defined as those transactions requiring entry in the company's accounting records pursuant to s 221.

Dormant accounts must be prepared and sent to members and other persons entitled to receive copies and must be laid before the members in general meeting, unless the company has elected otherwise. The copy of the balance sheet delivered to the Registrar of Companies must contain a statement by the directors that the company was dormant throughout the financial year.

A special resolution exempting a company from the requirement to appoint auditors and an example of dormant accounts are set out at Precedents 9.1 and 9.2.

SUMMARY FINANCIAL STATEMENT TO SHAREHOLDERS

The Secretary of State is empowered to make regulations permitting listed public companies to send summary financial statements to shareholders rather than the full annual accounts and report. Any member will have the right to ask for a set of the full accounts and report to be sent to him. The information to be given in the summary financial statement shall be prescribed by the Secretary of State (s 251; CA 1989 s 15).

10 Company Auditors

Sections 24 to 54 of the Companies Act 1989 replace the provisions of the Companies Act 1985 relating to the appointment, resignation and removal of company auditors.

The main purposes of the Act are 'to secure that only persons who are properly supervised and appropriately qualified are appointed company auditors, and that audits by persons so appointed are carried out 'properly and with integrity and with a proper degree of independence' (CA 1989 s 24(1)). Such persons may now include a body corporate, as well as an individual or partnership (CA 1989; s 25(2)).

ELIGIBILITY FOR APPOINTMENT

A person is eligible for appointment as a company auditor only if he is a member of a recognised supervisory body and is eligible for the appointment under the rules of that body (CA 1989 s 25(1)).

Section 26 makes it clear that where a partnership is appointed as a company auditor, the appointment is an appointment of the partnership as such and not of the individual partners.

An officer or an employee of the company or a partner or employee of such a person, or a partnership of which such a person is a partner, may not be auditor of a company (CA 1989 s 27).

An auditor who becomes ineligible during his term of office shall thereupon vacate office and give notice in writing to the company concerned that he has vacated it by reason of ineligibility (CA 1989 s 28).

Where a person has audited accounts whilst ineligible, the Secretary of State has the power to require the company to appoint another auditor to either audit the relevant accounts again or to review the first audit and to report whether a second audit is needed (CA 1989 s 29).

Those persons who may hold office as auditor include members of the relevant accountancy bodies or a person who holds an approved overseas qualification. An auditor who is qualified by virtue of the Board of Trade authorisation granted under the Companies Act 1967, may only audit an unquoted company.

The Secretary of State is empowered to make regulations requiring the keeping of a register of the individuals and firms eligible for appointment as company auditors (s 35).

The Secretary of State is also empowered to make regulations requiring recognised supervisory bodies to keep and make available to the public, information with respect to the firms eligible under their rules for appointment as a company auditor. In the case of a body corporate the information must include the names and addresses of each person who is a director of the body corporate or who holds any shares in it and in relation to a partnership, the name and address of each partner (s 36).

APPOINTMENT AND REMOVAL OF AUDITORS

The Companies Act 1989 amends the law relating to the appointment and removal of auditors.

Appointment of Auditors

Every company (except a company which is dormant in terms of s 250) must appoint an auditor or auditors (s 384; CA 1989 s 119).

The first auditors of the company may be appointed by the directors at any time before the first general meeting of the company at which accounts are laid, in which case the auditors so appointed shall hold office until the conclusion of that meeting (s 385; CA 1989 s 119). If the directors fail to appoint an auditor or auditors prior to the first general meeting, the power of appointment may be exercised by the company in general meeting. A resolution of the directors to appoint an auditor is set out at Precedent 10.1.

Every public company, and every private company which has *not* elected to dispense with the laying of accounts, shall, at each general meeting at which accounts are laid, appoint an auditor or auditors to hold office from the conclusion of that meeting until the conclusion of the next general meeting at which accounts are laid (s 385(2); CA 1989 s 119).

Different provisions apply to the appointment of an auditor or auditors, where a private company has elected in accordance with s 252 to dispense with the laying of accounts before the company in general meeting. In such cases, the first auditors may be appointed by the directors at any time before the end of 28 days from the day on which copies of the company's first annual accounts are sent to members in accordance with the Acts (s 385A; CA 1989 s 119).

If however, notice is given by a member under s 253(2) requiring the laying of accounts before the company in general meeting, the first auditors may be appointed by the directors at any time before the beginning of that meeting. Such first auditors shall hold office until the end of that period or, as the case may be, the conclusion of that meeting.

Subsequent appointments may be made by the company in general meeting within 28 days of the day on which copies of the company's annual accounts for the previous financial year are sent to members under s 238 or, if notice is given by a member under s 253(2), requiring the laying of the accounts before the company in general meeting, the conclusion of the meeting. Auditors appointed in such cases shall hold office from the end of that period or, as the case may be, the conclusion of that meeting until the end of the time for appointing auditors for the next financial year.

Auditors holding office when an election is made shall, unless the company in general meeting determines otherwise, continue to hold office until the end of the time for appointing auditors for the next financial year. The auditors holding office when an election ceases to have effect, shall continue to hold office until the conclusion of the next general meeting of the company at which accounts are laid.

Normally, a company which has elected to dispense with the laying of accounts, will also have elected to dispense with the annual re-appointment of auditors (see following section).

Election not to Reappoint Auditors Annually (Private Company)

Section 386 permits a private company to approve an elective resolution to dispense with the obligation to appoint auditors annually. Where such an election is made, the company's auditors shall automatically be deemed to be reappointed for each succeeding financial year, unless a special resolution is approved pursuant to s 250 exempting a dormant company from the obligation to appoint auditors or, a resolution is passed pursuant to s 393 (see hereafter) resolving that the auditors' appointment be brought to an end (s 386(1)(2); CA 1989 s 119).

When an election ceases to be in force, the auditors then holding office continue in office until the conclusion of the next general meeting of the company at which accounts are laid, or if a company has elected not to lay accounts before a general meeting, the auditors shall continue in office until the end of the time for appointing auditors for the next financial year under s 385A.

An elective resolution to dispense with the reappointment of auditors is set out at Precedent 5.8.

An election may be brought to an end by a notice deposited by any member at the registered office. Upon receiving such a notice, the directors must convene a general meeting of the company for a date not more than 28 days after the date on which the notice is given. The notice convening the general meeting must propose a resolution in a form enabling the company to decide whether the appointment of the company's auditors should be brought to an end (s 393; CA 1989 s 122). (See Precedent 10.2.)

If it is the decision of the company in general meeting to terminate the appointment of the auditors, the appointment ceases from the date upon which they would next otherwise be reappointed. If however the notice calling for the appointment to be brought to an end is deposited within the period beginning with the day on which copies of the company's annual accounts are sent to members of the company under s 238 and ending 14 days after that day, any deemed reappointment for the following financial year shall cease to have effect.

If within 14 days of the date of deposit of a notice by a member, the directors do not proceed to convene a general meeting, the member who deposited the notice may himself convene the meeting for a date no later than three months from that date. Any reasonable expenses incurred by the member in convening the meeting shall be made good by the company and the company may itself look to the directors for reimbursement.

The statement to be given by an auditor in terms of s 394 must be given whenever an auditor ceases for any reason to hold office. (See later in this chapter.)

Casual Vacancy

The directors, or the company in general meeting, may fill a casual vacancy in the office of auditor. While such a vacancy continues, any surviving or continuing auditor or auditors may continue to act (s 388; CA 1989 s 119).

Special notice is required of a resolution to be proposed at a general meeting of the company filling a casual vacancy in the office of auditor or reappointing as auditor a retiring auditor who was appointed by the directors to fill a casual vacancy. On receipt of special notice the company shall forthwith send a copy of it to the person proposed to be appointed and, if the casual vacancy was caused by the resignation of an auditor, to the auditor who resigned (s 388; CA 1989 s 119 and see Chapter 5 page 62).

RIGHTS OF AUDITORS

Every auditor has the right to receive all notices of and other communications relating to any general meeting which a member of a company is entitled to receive. They may also attend any general meeting of the company and be heard on any part of the business of the meeting which concerns them as auditors (s 390(1); CA 1989 s 120).

A copy of any written resolution proposed to be agreed by a private company in accordance with s 381A, must be sent to a company's auditors. If the resolution concerns the auditors as auditors, they may within seven days of receiving a copy give notice to the company stating that in their opinion the resolution should be considered by the company in general meeting or, if appropriate, by a meeting of the relevant class of members (s 390; CA 1989 s 119).

An auditor's right to attend or be heard at a meeting is exercised, in the case of the body corporate or partnership which are auditors, by an individual authorised by it in writing to act as its representative at the meeting (s 390(3); CA 1989 s 120).

REMUNERATION OF AUDITORS

The remuneration of auditors appointed by the company in general meeting shall be fixed by the company in general meeting or in such manner as the company in general meeting may determine (s 390A; CA 1989 s 121). Normally a general meeting would authorise the directors to fix the remuneration of the auditors.

The remuneration of the auditors must be set out in a company's accounts. It should be noted that 'remuneration' includes any sums paid in respect of expenses and also includes the estimated money value of any benefits in kind received. The nature of any benefit must be disclosed in a company's annual accounts.

The Secretary of State is now empowered to make regulations requiring the disclosure of the amount of any remuneration received or receivable by a company's auditors or their associates in respect of services other than as auditors (s 390B; CA 1989 s 121).

REMOVAL OF AUDITORS

A company may remove an auditor from office by ordinary resolution (s 391; CA 1989 s 122). Special notice of the intention to propose such a resolution must be given to the company (s 391A; CA 1989 s 122 and see Chapter 5 page 62). **An example of a special notice proposing the removal of an auditor** is set out at Precedent 5.17.

An auditor who has been removed may nevertheless receive notice of and attend, and be heard at any general meeting at which his term of office would otherwise have expired, or at which it is proposed to fill the vacancy caused by his removal.

Special notice is also required of an ordinary resolution proposing to appoint as auditor a person other than a retiring auditor.

Upon receipt of special notice, the company must immediately send a copy of the notice to the person proposed to be removed or, as the case may be, to the person proposed to be appointed and to the retiring auditor.

The auditor to be removed or retiring, may make representations in writing to the company, not exceeding a reasonable length, and request the notification of the representations to members of the company.

Unless the representations are received too late (in which case the auditor may require the representations to be read out at the meeting), the notice of the resolution given to members must state the fact that representations have been made and a copy of the representations must be sent to every member of the company to whom notice of the meeting is or has been sent.

RESIGNATION OF AUDITORS

An auditor of a company may resign by depositing a notice in writing to that effect at the company's registered office (s 392; CA 1989 s 122). The notice must be accompanied by a statement of any circumstances connected with his resignation which he considers should be brought to the attention of the members or creditors of the company or, if he considers that there are no such circumstances, a statement that there are none (s 394; CA 1989 s 123). A specimen letter of resignation is set out at Precedent 10.3.

A copy of the notice of resignation must be sent by the company to the Registrar within 14 days of the deposit of the notice (s 392; CA 1989 s 123).

If the statement accompanying the auditors' notice of resignation, sets out circumstances which the auditors consider should be brought to the attention of the members or creditors to the company, the company shall within 14 days of the deposit of the statement send a copy of it to every person who is entitled to receive copies of the accounts.

Unless the auditor receives notice of an application to court within 21 days of the date on which he deposited the statement, he must, within a further seven days, send a copy of the statement to the Registrar.

Where an auditor makes a statement setting out circumstances which he considers should be brought to the attention of members or creditors of the company, he may also deposit with his notice of resignation a signed requisition calling on the directors of the company to forthwith convene an extraordinary general meeting for the purpose of receiving and considering such explanation of the circumstances connected with his resignation as he may wish to place before the meeting.

He may also request the company to circulate a statement in writing of the circumstances connected with his resignation. Unless the statement is received too late, the company shall, in the notice of the requisitioned general meeting, state the fact of the statement having been made and send a copy of the statement to every member to whom notice is or has been sent. If the statement is received too late or, in the event of default by the company, the auditor may require that the statement be read out at the meeting. This is in addition to the auditor's right to be heard orally.

Notwithstanding his resignation, an auditor has the right to receive notice of any general meeting and to attend and to be heard on any part of the business which concerns him as former auditors.

11 Miscellaneous

THE SECRETARY

Every company must have a secretary (s 283(1)).

The Act does not define the duties of the secretary but he is an officer of the company and is assumed by the Acts to be responsible to the directors for ensuring compliance by the company with the provisions of the Companies Acts, the Articles, and commercial law in general. It is modern practice for the secretary of larger private companies and public companies also to have managerial responsibilities.

There are certain restrictions on the appointment of a secretary:-

(1) A sole director cannot also be secretary.

(2) Whilst a corporation can be secretary, no company may have as secretary a corporation, the sole director of which is a sole director of the company; nor may a company have as its sole director a corporation whose sole director is secretary to the company.

(3) By virtue of s 286, the directors of a public company must take all reasonable steps to ensure that the secretary is 'a person who appears to them to have the requisite knowledge and experience to discharge the functions of secretary of the company'. To this end, the secretary of a public company must be a person falling within one of the five following categories:-

(a) a person holding the office of secretary or assistant or deputy secretary on 22 December 1980;

(b) a person who for at least three of the five years immediately preceding his appointment as secretary has held the office of secretary of a company other than a private company;

(c) a member of the Institute of Chartered Accountants in England and Wales, or of Scotland or Ireland, or of the Institute of Chartered Secretaries and Administrators or the Chartered Association of Certified Accountants or the Institute of Cost and Management Accountants or the Chartered Institute of Public Finance and Accountancy;

(d) a person who is a barrister, advocate or solicitor called or admitted in the United Kingdom; or

(e) a person who appears to the directors to be capable of discharging the function of secretary, by virtue of holding or having held any other position, or of being a member of any other body (s 286).

Both the Act and normally the company's articles contemplate the possibility of joint or deputy secretaries being appointed. Section 283(3) states that if the office of secretary is vacant or if for any other reason there is no secretary capable of acting, an assistant or deputy secretary or any officer of the company authorised in that behalf by the directors, may perform any act required of the secretary. Article 1 of Table A defines a secretary as 'the secretary of the company or any other person appointed to perform the duties of the secretary, including a joint, assistant or deputy secretary'.

Appointment of Secretary

A secretary is appointed as follows:

(1) Upon incorporation of the company, the person named as the secretary in Form G10 delivered with the Memorandum and Articles of Association for registration is deemed to be appointed as secretary of the company as from the date of incorporation.
(2) Subsequent appointments of the secretary are made by the directors who have the power to appoint and to remove a secretary at any time (see Precedent 11.1).
(3) The new secretary should complete Form G288 for delivery to the Registrar of Companies within 14 days of the date of appointment. Notification of removal or resignation must also be given to the Registrar on Form G288 within 14 days of the event.
(4) Enter details of the appointment in the register of directors and secretary.
(5) Notification must be given to the company's bankers if the secretary is to be an authorised signatory to the bank account.

ANNUAL RETURN

The Companies Act 1989 has broken the linkage between a company's annual return and its annual general meeting. In addition the contents of an annual return have been simplified, particularly the information relating to the numbers and classes of shares issued and the amounts called up thereon.

Every company is obliged to deliver to the Registrar, on Form A363, a return made up in every year to a date not later than the company's 'return date' (s 363; CA 1989 s 139). The return date is a date not later than:

(1) the anniversary of the company's incorporation for any company whose first return is made after the commencement of s 139 of the Companies Act 1989, or
(2) where a company has submitted a return prior to the commencement of s 139, the anniversary of the date of that last return. Accordingly, any company incorporated before the commencement of s 139 which has already submitted a return to the Registrar before the commencement date, will submit further returns made up to a date not later than the anniversary of the date of the last return submitted.

A return must be delivered to the Registrar within 28 days of the date to which it is made up.

The contents of an annual return are as follows:

(1) The date to which it is made up.
(2) The address of the company's registered office.
(3) The company's principal business activities.

(4) The name and address of the company secretary.

(5) The name and address of every director of the company.

(6) The nationality, date of birth, and business occupation of every director. In addition, the particulars required to be contained in the company's Register of Directors in respect of other directorships and former names must also be shown.

(7) Any other directorships of any corporate director.

(8) The address of the situation of the register of members, if it is not kept at the company's registered office.

(9) The address of the situation of the register of debenture holders if it is not kept at the company's registered office.

(10) The fact of any election to dispense with the laying of accounts before the company in general meeting or to dispense with the holding of annual general meetings.

(11) The company's principal business activities.

(12) Where a company has a share capital, certain information regarding its share capital and members, including the number and nominal value of the shares in issue and details of members as at the date of the return and changes in membership since the last return.

The Secretary of State is empowered by regulations to amend or augment, the information to be given in an annual return.

COMMON SEAL

The Companies Act 1989 removes the need for any company to have a common seal in England and Wales. Whether or not a company has a seal, any document signed by a director and the secretary of the company and expressed to be executed by the company has the same effect as if it were executed under the company's seal (s 36A; CA 1989 s 130). If a document executed by a company makes clear on its face that it is intended to be a deed, it will have effect as a deed.

This change in contractual procedure has resulted in consequential amendments to various sections of the Companies Act 1985. These amendments provide that certain documents, previously required to be executed under the seal may, in future, only require sealing where the company has a seal. It is recommended that reference be made to a company's Articles as to whether any documents or deeds specifically require execution under the common seal. In this event it may be necessary to amend the Articles, if a company decides not to employ a seal.

In small private companies it is normal for each use of the seal to be specifically approved by the directors. Where, however, frequent use is made of a company seal, it is convenient to establish a seal book into which details of all sealings are entered. The seal book is then produced at meetings of the directors and the entries approved.

A public company will normally have an official seal which is a copy of the common seal of the company with the addition of the word 'securities'. This may be employed by a committee of the Board or sealing share certificates. If permitted by its articles, a company may also have one or more official seals for use abroad.

Authentification of Documents

Section 41 (as amended), provides that any document or proceeding which requires authentification by a company will be sufficiently authenticated for the purposes of the law of England and Wales by the signature of the director, secretary or other authorised officer of the company (s 41; CA 1989 Para 4 Sch 17). A document may be authenticated in the following form:

Certified True Copy

_____

Secretary

Dated in   this   day of   199   .

DISCLOSURE OF INTEREST IN SHARES

A person who acquires a substantial interest in the voting shares of a public company is obliged to disclose such interest to the company (ss 198 and 199). The notifiable interest is any holding equal to or more than 3% of the nominal value of the voting shares of the company (s 199(2); CA 1989 s 134(2)).

The obligation to notify the company must be performed within the period of two days next following the day upon which the obligation arises (s 202(1); CA 1989 s 134(3)). Such obligation arises both upon the acquisition of a notifiable interest and upon the disposal of such interest.

The definition of a 'notifiable interest' is set out in great detail in ss 198 to 210. Such interests includes so-called 'concert parties' whereby persons acting in concert together hold 3% or more of the relevant share capital.

Every public company is obliged to maintain a register for the purposes of recording such interests as are notified to it (s 211). Entries must be made in the register within three days of the receipt of notification.

A public company is also empowered to make enquiries as to the interest of any person in the shares of the company (s 212). If a public company knows or has reasonable cause to believe a person to be interested or to have been interested at any time during the preceding three years in the voting share capital of the company, it may serve a notice upon that person requiring him to make a disclosure of such interest.

REGISTRATION OF CHARGES

The law relating to the registration of charges has been amended by the Companies Act 1989. This has involved the repeal of ss 395 to 408 and 410 to 423 of the Companies Act 1985 and the enactment of new provisions with corresponding section numbers.

The new provisions seek to simplify and alleviate the responsibilities of the Registrar. In particular, a company is no longer obliged to forward a copy of the instrument creating or evidencing a charge and it is merely sufficient to supply the registrar with details in the prescribed form. In addition, rectification of details previously delivered, may be corrected by agreement of the company and the chargee without the need for a court order.

Charges requiring registration differ for those companies incorporated in England and Wales, and those incorporated in Scotland (see s 396(1); CA 1989 s 93).

Charges requiring registration with the Registrar of Companies include:-

(1) a charge on land or any interest in land,
(2) a charge on goods or any interest in goods,
(3) a charge on intangible moveable property consisting of either goodwill, intellectual property, book debts or uncalled share capital or calls made but not paid,
(4) a charge for securing an issue of debentures, or
(5) a floating charge on the whole or part of the company's property.

Charges Register Maintained by the Registrar of Companies

The Registrar of Companies, either in England and Wales or in Scotland, is obliged to maintain a register of charges for every company (s 397; CA 1989 s 94). The register must include, amongst other things, details of all particulars of charges delivered to him, any memoranda of satisfaction or release received, details of the issue of debentures of a series, the appointment of receivers or managers and the crystallisation or attachment of a floating charge and other matters (s 397(2); CA 1989 s 94).

Any person may require the Registrar to provide a certificate stating the date on which any specified particulars of a charge, or other information relating thereto, were delivered to him. The certificate is conclusive evidence that the particulars or other information were duly delivered to the Registrar. The Registrar is no longer obliged to issue a certificate and will now do so only on request.

Delivery of Particulars to the Registrar for Registration

It is the duty of a company which creates a charge or acquires property subject to an existing charge, to notify the Registrar in prescribed form (s 398; CA 1989 s 95). Such notification must be made within 21 days of the date of the creation of the charge, or, the date on which property was acquired subject to an existing charge, as the case may be. The duty of the company does not prevent any other person interested in the charge from delivering particulars to the Registrar. This is usual in practice as banks and other secured lenders are anxious to ensure that details of a charge are properly lodged with the Registrar.

Upon receipt of the prescribed form, details are noted on the company's register by the Registrar who will send a copy of the particulars filed by him and a note of the date on which they were delivered, to the company, the chargee and, if the particulars were delivered by another person interested in the charge, to that person (s 398(5); CA 1989 s 95).

The Registrar is no longer required to check the particulars delivered against the charge.

Failure to deliver particulars

Failure to deliver particulars in the prescribed form to the Registrar shall render the charge void against an administrator or liquidator of the company and any person who for value acquires an interest in or right over property subject to the charge (s 399; CA 1989 s 95). A charge may also be rendered void if the registered particulars are inaccurate or contain an omission.

Late Delivery of Particulars

It is no longer necessary for a court order to be obtained to register particulars delivered after the end of the 21 day period.

Where particulars of a charge in the prescribed form are delivered to the registrar after the 21 day period, the following provisions apply:-

(1) If a 'relevant event' occurs after the particulars are delivered, the charge will *not* be void (s 400(1); CA 1989 s 95). A relevant event includes the presentation of an administration or winding up order, a resolution for voluntary winding up or the acquisition of an interest in or right over property subject to a charge (s 399(2); CA 1989 s 95).

(2) If the company is, at the date of delivery of the particulars, unable to pay its debts in terms of the Insolvency Act 1986 or, subsequently becomes unable to pay its debts in consequence of the transaction under which the charge is created, the charge may be void as against the administrator or liquidator if insolvency proceedings begin before the end of:-.

(a) two years in the case of a floating charge created in favour of a 'connected person' of the company. (For this purpose a connected person is defined by s 249 of the Insolvency Act 1986), or

(b) one year in the case of the floating charge created in favour of the person not so connected, and

(c) six months in any other case, (s 400(3); CA 1989 s 95).

Delivery of Further Particulars

It is open to the company and the chargee to file further particulars of a charge with the Registrar, where the particulars previously delivered, omitted or mistated information or the particulars given are no longer accurate. (s 401(1); CA 1989 s 96). For example, such further particulars may be filed where, the terms of a charge are varied or where property subject to the charge is substituted or released or following a change in identity of the chargee.

The further particulars must be given on the prescribed form and be signed by or on behalf of *both* the company and the chargee.

On noting further particulars in the register, the Registrar will send to the company, the chargee or where a person other than the company delivered the particulars, that other person, a copy of the particulars so filed and a note of the date on which they were delivered.

Memorandum of Satisfaction or Release

A memorandum of satisfaction or release, given on the prescribed form, may be delivered to the Registrar when a particular charge no longer affects the company's property or the debt for which a charge was given is paid or otherwise satisfied (s 403; CA 1989 s 98).

The memorandum must be signed by or on behalf of *both* the company and the chargee. Upon receipt of the memorandum the registrar will file the memorandum in the register, note the date upon which it was delivered to him and send to the company, the chargee, and if the memorandum was delivered by a person other than the company, that person, a copy of the memorandum filed by him and a note made by him as to the date upon which it was delivered.

Issue of Debentures of a Series

In addition to the delivery for registration of particulars of a charge securing a series of debentures, a company must also deliver particulars in the prescribed form, giving the date and amount of *each* issue of debentures of the series within the period of 21 days after the date of each issue (s 408; CA 1989 s 100).

Notice of Appointment of Receiver or Manager

Any person obtaining an order for the appointment of a receiver or a manager of a company's property, or any person who appoints such receiver or manager under powers contained in an instrument must, within seven days of the order or of the appointment, give notice of that fact to the Registrar. Thereupon the Registrar will file notice in the register of the company (s 409; CA 1989 s 100). Notice must also be given to the Registrar of any person ceasing to act as receiver or manager.

Register of Charges

Every company must keep at its registered office a copy of every instrument creating or evidencing a charge. This applies whether or not the charge is one requiring registration with the Registrar of Companies (s 411; CA 1989 s 101).

Every company must maintain at its registered office a register of charges, containing entries for each charge and giving a short description of the property so charged, the amount of the charge and the names of the persons entitled thereto. It should be noted that all charges must be entered in the register, whether or not a charge is registerable with the Registrar of Companies (s 412(2); CA 1989 s 101).

Copies of the instruments and the register must be open to inspection by any person, who may request the company to provide copies of any instrument or copies of any entry in the register. The company must send such copies within 10 days of the date of the request.

Overseas Companies

A foreign company (a company incorporated outside Great Britain) which establishes a place of business in Great Britain must, within 1 month of establishing such place of business, register as an overseas company with the Registrar of Companies (s 691). 'An established place of business' would normally consist of an office and merely an occasional presence in Great Britain, or the carrying on of business through an agent, would not usually be sufficient to require registration.

An overseas company applying for registration must submit to the Registrar of Companies a certified copy of its Memorandum and Articles of Association or other charter. If this is written in a foreign language, a certified translation in English is required. In addition a return must be made on Form G691 listing the Company's directors and secretary, a list of the names and addresses of the person or persons resident in Great Britain authorised to accept service of process and notices on behalf of the Company, and a statutory declaration made by a director or the secretary or the authorised person resident in Great Britain, stating the date on which the Company's place of business in Great Britain was established. In addition, notice must be given of the Company's Accounting Reference Date.

Thereafter, an overseas company must notify the Registrar, from time to time, of any changes in directors, secretary, accounting reference date and other particulars filed. Copies of the audited accounts of the overseas company must also be filed for each accounting reference period, together with a filing fee which is at present £20 (s 700; CA 1989 Para 13 Part 1 Sch 10). An overseas company is also obliged to give particulars, in the prescribed form, to the Registrar of any charge created or, any property acquired subject to charge, in Great Britain (s 703A; CA 1989 Sch 15).

DISSOLUTION

The directors of a company which has no assets or liabilities and is not trading may make application to the Registrar of Companies to strike the company from the Register (s 652). This is a useful procedure obviating the need for a formal liquidation. The following procedures should be followed:

(1) Make such investigations and carry out such action as is necessary to ensure that the company has no assets or liabilities. This may involve the settlement of any inter-group balances and a waiver by directors of any loans made to the company.

(2) Make application to the Registrar of Companies for the dissolution to be commenced.

(3) If the Registrar considers that the company is capable of dissolution, he will forward a certificate, for signature by a director, formally requesting the company to be struck from the register.

(4) Upon receipt of the certificate the Registrar will cause a notice to be published in the London Gazette or Edinburgh Gazette (as appropriate) stating that unless cause is shown to the contrary, the company will be struck from the register within three months of the date of

publication and the company will be dissolved. The Registrar informs the company of this action.

(5) At the expiration of the three month period, the company will be struck off the register and a notice will be published in the London Gazette or Edinburgh Gazette (as appropriate), that the company has been dissolved.

A company which has been dissolved may be restored to the register by application to the court within 2 years of dissolution (s 651). It has become increasingly common in the last few years for companies to be struck off by the Registrar whilst still active, in cases where audited accounts and annual returns have not been submitted and it appears to the Registrar that the company is no longer trading. Any assets of the company at the date of dissolution become vested in the crown as bona vacantia and to reclaim such assets and to enter into transactions in the name of the company, it will be necessary for the company to be restored.

Before the Registrar can agree to restoration, all outstanding audited accounts, annual returns and other unfiled documents must be submitted to the Registrar. It will be necessary to consult and retain a solicitor for the purpose of making the appropriate application to court.

Materials and Precedents

Precedent 1.1

TABLE C

A COMPANY LIMITED BY GURANTEE AND NOT HAVING A SHARE CAPITAL

Memorandum of Association

1. The company's name is 'The Dundee School Association Limited'.

2. The company's registered office is to be situated in Scotland.

3. The company's objects are the carrying on of a school for boys and girls in Dundee and the doing of all such other things as are incidental or conducive to the attainment of that object.

4. The liability of the members is limited.

5. Every member of the company undertakes to contribute such amount as may be required (not exceeding £100) to the company's assets if it should be wound up while he is a member or within one year after he ceases to be a member, for payment of the company's debts and liabilities contracted before he ceases to be a member, and of the costs, charges and expenses of winding up, and for the adjustment of the rights of the contributories among themselves.

We, the subscribers to this memorandum of association, wish to be formed into a company pursuant to this memorandum.

Names and Addresses of Subscribers.

(1) Kenneth Brodie, 14 Bute Street, Dundee.

(2) Ian Davis, 2 Burns Avenue, Dundee.

Dated   19 .

Witness to the above signatures,
Anne Brown, 149 Princes Street, Edinburgh.

Articles of association

Preliminary

1. Regulations 2 to 35 inclusive, 54, 55, 57, 59, 102 to 108 inclusive, 110, 114, 116, and 117 inclusive of Table A, shall not apply to the company but the articles hereinafter contained and, subject to the modifications hereinafter expressed, the remaining regulations of Table A shall constitute the articles of association of the company.

Interpretation

2. In regulation 1 of Table A, the definition of 'the holder' shall be omitted.

Members

3. The subscribers to the memorandum of association of the company and such other persons as are admitted to membership in accordance with the articles shall be members of the company. No person shall be admitted a member of the company

unless he is approved by the directors. Every person who wishes to become a member shall deliver to the company an application for membership in such form as the directors require executed by him.

4. A member may at any time withdraw from the company by giving at least seven clear days' notice to the company. Membership shall not be transferable and shall cease on death.

Notice of General Meetings

5. In regulation 38 of Table A:

 (1) in paragraph (b) the words 'or the total voting rights at the meeting of all the members' shall be substituted for 'in nominal value of the shares giving that right' and
 (2) the words 'The notice shall be given to all the members and to the directors and auditors' shall be substituted for the last sentence.

Proceedings at General Meetings

6. The words 'and at any separate meeting of the holders of any class of shares in the company' shall be omitted from regulation 44 of Table A.

7. Paragraph (d) of Regulation 46 of Table A shall be omitted.

Votes of Members

8. On a show of hands every member present in person shall have one vote. On a poll every member present in person or by proxy shall have one vote.

Directors' Expenses

9. The words 'of any class of shares or' shall be omitted from regulation 83 of Table A.

Proceedings of Directors

10. In Paragraph (c) of Regulation 94 of Table A the word 'debentures' shall be substituted for the words 'shares, debentures or other securities' where they twice occur.

Minutes

11. The words 'of the holders of any class of shares in the company' shall be omitted from regulation 100 of Table A.

Notices

12. The second sentence of Regulation 111 of Table A shall be omitted.

13. The words 'or of the holders of any class of shares in the company' shall be omitted from Regulation 113 of Table A.

Precedent 1.2

TABLE E

AN UNLIMITED COMPANY HAVING A SHARE CAPITAL

Memorandum of Association

1. The company's name is 'The Woodford Engineering Company'.

2. The company's registered office is to be situated in England and Wales.

3. The company's objects are the working of certain patented inventions relating to the application of microchip technology to the improvement of food processing, and the doing of all such other things as are incidental or conducive to the attainment of that object.

We, the subscribers to this memorandum of association, wish to be formed into a company pursuant to this memorandum; and we agree to take the number of shares shown opposite our respective names.

Names and Addresses of Subscribers	Numbers of shares taken by each Subscriber
1. Brian Smith, 24 Nibley Road, Wotton-under-Edge, Gloucestershire.	3
2. William Green, 278 High Street, Chipping Sodbury, Avon.	5
Total shares taken	8

Witness to the above signatures,
Anne Brown, 108 Park Way, Bristol 8.

Articles of Association

1. Regulations 3, 32, 34 and 35 of Table A shall not apply to the company, but the articles hereinafter contained and, subject to the modifications hereinafter expressed, the remaining regulations of Table A shall constitute the articles of association of the company.

2. The words 'at least seven clear days' notice' shall be substituted for the words 'at least 14 clear days' notice' in Regulation 38 of Table A.

3. The share capital of the company is £20,000 divided into 20,000 shares of £1 each.

4. The company may by special resolution:

(1) increase the share capital by such sum to be divided into shares of such amount as the resolution may prescribe;

(2) consolidate and divide all or any of its share capital into shares of a larger amount than its existing shares;

(3) subdivide its shares, or any of them, into shares of a smaller amount than its existing shares;

(4) cancel any shares which at the date of the passing of the resolution have not been taken or agreed to be taken by any person;

(5) reduce its share capital and any share premium account in any way.

Precedent 1.3

APPENDIX A

The following words and expressions will require the consent of the Secretary of State for Trade & Industry before their use will be allowed in a company name. The words fall into the following categories:

(1) Words which imply national or international pre-eminence:

International	Scotland
National	Scottish
European	Wales
United Kingdom	Welsh
Great Britain	Ireland
British	Irish
England	
English	

(2) Words which imply governmental patronage or sponsorship:

Authority
Board
Council

(3) Words which imply business pre-eminence or representative status:

Association
Federation
Society
Institute
Institution

(4) Words which imply specific objects or functions:

Assurance	Patent	Group	Friendly Society
Insurance	Patentee	Holdings	Industrial & Provident Society
Reinsurance	Chamber of Commerce	Post Office	
Reassurance	Chamber of Trade	Giro	Building Society
Insurer	Chamber of Industry	Trust	Trade Union
Assurer	Co-operative		Foundation
Re-assurer	Chemist	Stock Exchange	Fund
Reinsurer	Chemistry	Register Registered	Charter Chartered Sheffield Benevolent

APPENDIX B

The following words and expressions also require the Secretary of State's consent and normally a company would be registered by a name containing any of the following words or expressions only if the applicant had obtained a letter of non-objection from the relevant Department or Body. Any correspondence should be submitted with the appropriate registration documents.

WORD OR EXPRESSION	RELEVANT BODY FOR COMPANIES INTENDING TO HAVE REGISTERED OFFICE IN ENGLAND OR WALES	RELEVANT BODY FOR COMPANIES INTENDING TO HAVE REGISTERED OFFICE IN SCOTLAND
Royal, Royale Royalty, King Queen, Prince Princess, Windsor Duke, His/Her Majesty	E2 Division (Room 829) Home Office Queen Anne's Gate London SW1H 9AT	Scottish Home and Health Department Old St Andrews House Edinburgh EH1 3DE
Police	F1 Division Police Department Home Office Queen Anne's Gate London SW1H 9AT	Police Division Scottish Home and Health Department Old St Andrews House Edinburgh EH1 3DE
Special School	School RN 11 Branch Department of Education and Science Elizabeth House York Road London SE1 7PH	As for England and Wales
Contact Lens	The Registrar General Optical Council 41 Harley Street London W1N 2DJ	As for England and Wales
Dental Dentistry	The Registrar General Dental Council 37 Wimpole Street London W1M 8DQ	As for England and Wales
District Nurse, Health Visitor, Midwife, Midwifery, Nurse	Principal Administrative Officer English National Board for Nursing, Midwifery and Health Visiting Victory House 170 Tottenham Court Rd London W1P 0HA	The Registrar National Board for Nursing, Midwifery and Health Visiting 22 Queen Street Edinburgh EH2 1JX

WORD OR EXPRESSION	RELEVANT BODY FOR COMPANIES INTENDING TO HAVE REGISTERED OFFICE IN ENGLAND OR WALES	RELEVANT BODY FOR COMPANIES INTENDING TO HAVE REGISTERED OFFICE IN SCOTLAND
Health Centre	Division PMC1 (c) Room B1205 Department of Health and Social Security Alexander Fleming House Elephant and Castle London SE1 6TE	As for England and Wales
Health Service	HS2D Division (Room 1115) Department of Health and Social Security Hannibal House Elephant and Castle London SE1 6TE	As for England and Wales
Nursing Home	H43A Division Room 1221 Department of Health and Social Security Hannibal House Elephant and Castle London SE1 6TE	As for England and Wales
Pregnancy Termination Abortion	PMC2A Division Room B1210 Department of Health and Social Security Alexander Fleming House Elephant and Castle London SE1 6TE	As for England and Wales
Breed, Breeder Breeding	Animal Health III Division Ministry of Agriculture Fisheries and Food Tolworth Tower Surbiton Surrey KT6 7DX	As for England and Wales
Charity, Charitable	Registration Division Charity Commission St Alban's House 57/60 Haymarket London SW1Y 4QX	Civil Law and Charities Division Scottish Home and Health Department St Andrews House Edinburgh EH1 3DE

WORD OR EXPRESSION	RELEVANT BODY FOR COMPANIES INTENDING TO HAVE REGISTERED OFFICE IN ENGLAND OR WALES	RELEVANT BODY FOR COMPANIES INTENDING TO HAVE REGISTERED OFFICE IN SCOTLAND
Apothecary	The Worshipful Society of Apothecaries of London Apothecaries Hall Blackfriars Lane London EC4	The Pharmaceutical Society of Great Britain 1 Lambeth High Street London SE1 7JN
University, Polytechnic	FHE3 Department of Education and Science Elizabeth House York Road London SE1 7PH	As for England and Wales

APPENDIX C

The use of certain words in company names is covered by other legislation and their use may constitute a criminal offence (see s 26(1)(d) of the Companies Act 1985). Some of these words are listed below but the list is not exhaustive. Applicants wishing to use any of these words may therefore be asked to seek confirmation from the relevant body listed that the use of the word does not contravene the relevant legislation. The Department of Trade & Industry also reserve the right to seek advice in each case direct from the relevant body if necessary.

WORD OR EXPRESSION	RELEVANT LEGISLATION	RELEVANT BODY
Architect, Architectural	Section 1 Architects Registration Act 1938	The Registrar Architects Registration Council of the United Kingdom 73 Hallam Street London W1N 6EE
Credit Union	Credit Union Act 1979	The Registrar of Friendly Societies 15/17 Great Marlborough Street London W1V 2AX
Veterinary Surgeon	Sections 19/20 Veterinary Surgeons Act 1966	The Registrar Royal College of Veterinary Surgeons 32 Belgrave Square London SW1X 8QP

WORD OR EXPRESSION	RELEVANT LEGISLATION	RELEVANT BODY
Dentist, Dental Surgeon, Dental Practitioner	Dentist Act 1984	The Registrar General Dental Council 37 Wimpole Street London W1M 8DQ
Drug Druggist Pharmaceutical Pharmaceutist Pharmacist Pharmacy	Section 78 Medicines Act 1968	The Head of the Law Dept The Pharmaceutical Society of Great Britain 1 Lambeth High Street London SE1 7JN
Optician, Ophthalmic Optician Dispensing Optician, Enrolled Optician Registered Optician, Optometrist	Sections 4 & 22 Opticians Act 1958 and Health and Social Security Act 1984	The Registrar General Optical Council 41 Harley Street London W1N 2DJ
Bank, Banker, Banking Deposit	Banking Act 1979	Bank of England Threadneedle Street London EC2R 8AH
Red Cross	Geneva Convention Act 1957	Seek Advice of CRO
Anzac	Section 1 Anzac Act 1916	Seek Advice of CRO
Insurance Broker Assurance Broker Re-Insurance Broker Re-Assurance Broker	Sections 2 & 3 Insurance Brokers (Registration) Act 1977	Seek Advice of CRO
Chiropodist, Dietician, Medical Laboratory Technician, Occupational Therapist, Orthoptist, Physiotherapist, Radiographer Remedial Gymnast	Professions Supplementary to Medicine Act 1960 if preceded by Registered, State	Room 77 Department of Health and Social Security Hannibal House Elephant & Castle London SE1 6TE

APPENDIX D

'Too Like' Names

In considering whether names are 'too like', the Secretary of State must be prepared to take account of all factors which may be considered to suggest similarity and lead to confusion between the names of two companies. These will include, for example, the nature and location of the businesses concerned.

Subject to this requirement names may be considered to be 'too like' in the opinion of the Secretary of State:

(1) if the names are phonetically identical;

(2) if there is only a slight variation in the spelling of the two names and the variation does not make a significant difference between the names;

(3) if in the case of an overseas company registered under Part XXIII of the Companies Act 1985 the names differ from a name already on the Index only by the substitution of the overseas country equivalent of LIMITED, UNLIMITED or PUBLIC LIMITED COMPANY;

(4) if the names contain a word or words which might be regarded as a distinctive element, unless that element is qualified in such a way as would minimise risk of confusion. A distinctive element will normally be defined as 'made up words', 'non-dictionary words' or 'combinations of two or more letters as a prefix'. In some cases everyday words used in a 'distinctive' way may also be considered as distinctive elements. Place names, or everyday descriptive words in general use will not normally be regarded as distinctive. Similar descriptive elements, eg press/printing, staff agency/employment agency, or the inclusion in one name of only a general or 'weak' qualification such as holding, group, system, services, etc. would not normally be regarded as a sufficient qualification.

Examples

(1) Names which are the same—*MAYFAIR ENGINEERING LIMITED v MAYFAIR ENGINEERING COMPANY LIMITED.*

(2) Names which are phonetically identical—*LYFESTYLE LIMITED v LIFESTYLE LIMITED and AB-CHEM LIMITED v ABKEM LIMITED.*

(3) Names in which the slight variation in spelling does not make a significant difference—*CONSOLAIR LTD v CONSULAIR LTD.*

(4) Names which contain the same distinctive element:

   (a) Where the names are sufficiently qualified—*FACTROMATIC COMPUTERS LIMITED v FACTROMATIC PLANT HIRE LIMITED.*
   (b) Where the names are not sufficiently qualified—*MECHALA LIMITED v MECHALA HOLDINGS LIMITED or ODDBODS PRESS LIMITED v ODDBODDS PRINTING LIMITED.*

(5) Names which are 'like' where other factors may be relevant—*PLAN TRAVEL LIMITED v PLANNED TRAVEL LIMITED.*

Precedent 1.4

SCHEDULE: TABLE A

REGULATIONS FOR MANAGEMENT OF A COMPANY LIMITED BY SHARES

Interpretation

1. In these regulations:

(1) 'The Act' means the Companies Act 1985 including any statutory modification or re-enactment thereof for the time being in force.

(2) 'The articles' means the articles of the company.

(3) 'Clear days' in relation to the period of a notice means that period excluding the day when the notice is given or deemed to be given and the day for which it is given or on which it is to take effect.

(4) 'Executed' included any mode of execution.

(5) 'Office' means the registered office of the company.

(6) 'The holder' in relation to shares means the member whose name is entered in the register of members as the holder of the shares.

(7) 'The seal' means the common seal of the company.

(8) 'Secretary' means the secretary of the company or any other person appointed to perform the duties of the secretary of the company, including a joint, assistant or deputy secretary.

(9) 'The United Kingdom' means Great Britain and Northern Ireland.

Unless the context otherwise requires, words or expressions contained in these regulations bear the same meaning as in the Act but excluding any statutory modification thereof not in force when these regulations become binding on the company.

Share Capital

2. Subject to the provisions of the Act and without prejudice to any rights attached to any existing shares, any share may be issued with such rights or restrictions as the company may by ordinary resolution determine.

3. Subject to the provisions of the Act, shares may be issued which are to be redeemed or are to be liable to be redeemed at the option of the company of the holder on such terms and in such manner as may be provided by the articles.

4. The company may exercise the powers of paying commissions conferred by the Act. Subject to the provisions of the Act, any such commission may be satisfied by the payment of cash or by the allotment of fully or partly paid shares or partly in one way and partly in the other.

5. Except as required by law, no person shall be recognised by the company as holding any share upon any trust and (except as otherwise provided by the articles or by law) the company shall not be bound by or recognise any interest in any share except an absolute right to the entirety thereof in the holder.

Share Certificates

6. Every member, upon becoming the holder of any share, shall be entitled without payment to one certificate for all the shares of each class held by him (and, upon transferring a part of his holding of shares of any class, to a certificate for the balance of such holding) or several certificates each for one or more of his shares upon payment for every certificate after the first of such reasonable sum as the directors may determine. Every certificate shall be sealed with the seal and shall specify the number, class and distinguishing numbers (if any) of the shares to which it relates and the amount or respective amounts paid up thereon. The company shall not be bound to issue more than one certificate for shares held jointly by several persons and delivery of a certificate to one joint holder shall be sufficient delivery to all of them.

7. If a share certificate is defaced, worn-out, lost or destroyed, it may be renewed on such terms (if any) as to evidence and indemnity and payment of the expenses reasonably incurred by the company in investigating evidence as the directors may determine but otherwise free of charge, and (in the case of defacement or wearing-out) on delivery up of the old certificate.

Lien

8. The company shall have a first and paramount lien on every share (not being a fully paid share) for all monies (whether presently payable or not) payable at a fixed time or called in respect of that share. The directors may at any time declare any share to be wholly or in part exempt from the provisions of this regulation. The company's lien on a share shall extend to any amount payable in respect of it.

9. The company may sell in such manner as the directors determine any shares on which the company has a lien if a sum in respect of which the lien exists is presently payable and is not paid within 14 clear days after notice has been given to the holder of the share or to the person entitled to it in consequence of the death or bankruptcy of the holder, demanding payment and stating that if the notice is not complied with the shares may be sold.

10. To give effect to a sale the directors may authorise some person to execute an instrument of transfer of the shares sold to, or in accordance with the directions of, the purchaser. The title of the transferee to the shares shall not be affected by any irregularity in or invalidity of the proceedings in reference to the sale.

11. The net proceeds of the sale, after payment of the costs, shall be applied in payment of so much of the sum for which the lien exists as is presently payable, and any residue shall (upon surrender to the company for cancellation of the certificate for the shares sold and subject to a like lien for any moneys not presently payable as existed upon the shares before the sale) be paid to the person entitled to the shares at the date of the sale.

Calls on Shares and Forfeiture

12. Subject to the terms of allotment, the directors may make calls upon the members in respect of any monies unpaid on their shares (whether in respect of nominal value or premium) and each member shall (subject to receiving at least 14 clear days' notice specifying when and where payment is to be made) pay to the company as required by the notice the amount called on his shares. A call may be required to be paid by instalments. A call may, before receipt by the company of any sum due thereunder, be revoked in whole or part. A person upon whom a call is made

shall remain liable for calls made upon him notwithstanding the subsequent transfer of the shares in respect whereof the call was made.

13. A call shall be deemed to have been made at the time when the resolution of the directors authorising the call was passed.

14. The joint holders of a share shall be jointly and severally liable to pay all calls in respect thereof.

15. If a call remains unpaid after it has become due and payable the person from whom it is due and payable shall pay interest on the amount unpaid from the day it became due and payable until it is paid at the rate fixed by the terms of allotment of the share or in the notice of the call or, if not rate is fixed, at the appropriate rate (as defined by the Act) but the directors may waive payment of the interest wholly or in part.

16. An amount payable in respect of a share on allotment or at any fixed date, whether in respect of nominal value or premium or as an instalment of a call, shall be deemed to be a call and if it is not paid the provisions of the articles shall apply as if that amount had become due and payable by virtue of a call.

17. Subject to the terms of allotment, the directors may make arrangements on the issue of shares for a difference between the holders in the amounts and times of payment of calls on their shares.

18. If a call remains unpaid after it has become due and payable the directors may give to the person from whom it is due not less than 14 clear days' notice requiring payment of the amount unpaid together with any interest which may have accrued. The notice shall name the place where payment is to be made and shall state that if the notice is not complied with the shares in respect of which the call was made will be liable to be forfeited.

19. If the notice is not complied with any share in respect of which it was given may, before the payment required by the notice has been made, be forfeited by a resolution of the directors and the forfeiture shall include all dividends or other monies payable in respect of the forfeited shares and not paid before the forfeiture.

20. Subject to the provisions of the Act, a forfeited share may be sold, re-allotted or otherwise disposed of on such terms and in such manner as the directors determine either to the person who was before the forfeiture the holder or to any other person and at any time before sale, re-allotment or other disposition, the forfeiture may be cancelled on such terms as the directors think fit. Where for the purposes of its disposal a forfeited share is to be transferred to any person the directors may authorise some person to execute an instrument of transfer to that person.

21. A person any of whose shares have been forfeited shall cease to be a member in respect of them and shall surrender to the company for cancellation the certificate for the shares forfeited but shall remain liable to the company for all monies which at the date of forfeiture were presently payable by him to the company in respect of those shares with interest at the rate at which interest was payable on those monies before the forfeiture or, if no interest was so payable, at the appropriate rate (as defined in the Act) from the date of forfeiture until payment but the directors may waive payment wholly or in part or enforce payment without any allowance for the value of the shares at the time of forfeiture or for any consideration received on their disposal.

22. A statutory declaration by a director or the secretary that a share has been forfeited on a specified date shall be conclusive evidence of the facts stated in it as against all persons claiming to be entitled to the share and the declaration shall (subject to the execution of an instrument of transfer if necessary) constitute a good title to the share and the person to whom the share is disposed of shall not be bound to see to the application of the consideration, if any, nor shall his title to the share be

affected by any irregularity in or invalidity of the proceedings in reference to the forfeiture or disposal of the share.

Transfer of Shares

23. The instrument of transfer of a share may be in any usual form or in any other form which the directors may approve and shall be executed by or on behalf of the transferor and, unless the share is fully paid, by or on behalf of the transferee.

24. The directors may refuse to register the transfer of a share on which the company has a lien. They may also refuse to register a transfer unless:

    (1) it is lodged at the office or at such other place as the directors may appoint and is accompanied by the certificate for the shares to which it relates and such other evidence as the directors may reasonably require to show the right of the transferor to make the transfer;

    (2) it is in respect of only one class of shares; and

    (3) it is in favour of not more than four transferees.

25. If the directors refuse to register a transfer of a share, they shall within two months after the date on which the transfer was lodged with the company send to the transferee notice of the refusal.

26. The registration of transfers of shares or of transfers of any class of shares may be suspended at such times and for such periods (not exceeding 30 days in any year) as the directors may determine.

27. No fee shall be charged for the registration of any instrument of transfer or other document relating to or affecting the title to any share.

28. The company shall be entitled to retain any instrument of transfer which is registered, but any instrument of transfer which the directors refuse to register shall be returned to the person lodging it when the notice of refusal is given.

Transmission of Shares

29. If a member dies the survivor or survivors where he was a joint holder, and his personal representatives where he was a sole holder or the only survivor of joint holders, shall be the only persons recognised by the company as having any title to his interest; but nothing herein contained shall release the estate of a deceased member from any liability in respect of any share which had been jointly held by him.

30. A person becoming entitled to a share in consequence of the death or bankruptcy of a member may, upon such evidence being produced as the directors may properly require, elect either to become the holder of the share or to have some person nominated by him registered as the transferee. If he elects to have another person registered he shall execute an instrument of transfer of the share to that person. All the articles relating to the transfer of share shall apply to the notice or instrument of transfer as if it were an instrument of transfer executed by the member and the death or bankruptcy of the member had not occurred.

31. A person becoming entitled to a share in consequence of the death or bankruptcy of a member shall have the rights to which he would be entitled if he were the holder of the share, except that he shall not, before being registered as the holder of the share, be entitled in respect of it to attend or vote at any meeting of the company or at any separate meeting of the holders of any class of shares in the company.

Alteration of Share Capital

32. The company may by ordinary resolution:

    (1) increase its share capital by new shares of such amount as the resolution prescribes;

    (2) consolidate and divide all or any of its share capital into shares of larger amount than its existing shares;

    (3) subject to the provisions of the Act, sub-divide its shares, or any of them, into shares of smaller amount and the resolution may determine that, as between the shares resulting from the sub-division, any of them may have any preference or advantage as compared with the others; and

    (4) cancel shares which, at the date of the passing of the resolution, have not been taken or agreed to be taken by any person and diminish the amount of its share capital by the amount of the shares so cancelled.

33. Whenever as a result of a consolidation of shares any members would become entitled to fractions of a share, the directors may, on behalf of those members, sell the shares representing the fractions for the best price reasonably obtainable to any person (including, subject to the provisions of the Act, the company) and distribute the net proceeds of sale in due proportion among those members, and the directors may authorise some person to execute an instrument of transfer of the shares to, or in accordance with the directions of, the purchaser. The transferee shall not be bound to see to the application of the purchase money nor shall his title to the shares be affected by any irregularity in or invalidity of the proceedings in reference to the sale.

34. Subject to the provisions of the Act, the company may by special resolution reduce its share capital, any capital redemption reserve and any share premium account in any way.

Purchase of Own Shares

35. Subject to the provisions of the Act, the company may purchase its own shares (including any redeemable shares) and, if it is a private company, make a payment in respect of the redemption or purchase of its own shares otherwise than out of distributable profits of the company or the proceeds of a fresh issue of shares.

General Meetings

36. All general meetings other than annual general meetings shall be called extraordinary general meetings.

37. The directors may call general meetings and, on the requisition of members pursuant to the provisions of the Act, shall forthwith proceed to convene an extraordinary general meeting for a date not later than eight weeks after receipt of the requisition. If there are not within the United Kingdom sufficient directors to call a general meeting, any director or any member of the company may call a general meeting.

Notice of General Meetings

38. An annual general meeting and an extraordinary general meeting called for the passing of a special resolution or a resolution appointing a person as a director shall be called by at least 21 clear days' notice. All other extraordinary general meetings

shall be called by a least fourteen clear days' notice but a general meeting may be called by shorter notice if it is so agreed:

(1) in the case of an annual general meeting, by all the members entitled to attend and vote thereat; and

(2) in the case of any other meeting by a majority in number of the members having a right to attend and vote being a majority together holding not less than 95 per cent in nominal value of the shares giving that right.

The notice shall specify the time and place of the meeting and the general nature of the business to be transacted and, in the case of an annual general meeting, shall specify the meeting as such.

Subject to the provisions of the articles and to any restrictions imposed on any shares, the notice shall be given to all the members, to all persons entitled to a share in consequence of the death or bankruptcy of a member and to the directors and auditors.

39. The accidental omission to give notice of a meeting to, or the non-receipt of notice of a meeting by, any person entitled to receive notice shall not invalidate the proceedings at that meeting.

Proceedings at General Meetings

40. No business shall be transacted at any meeting unless a quorum is present. Two persons entitled to vote upon the business to be transacted, each being a member or a proxy for a member or a duly authorised representative of a corporation, shall be a quorum.

41. If such a quorum is not present within half an hour from the time appointed for the meeting, or if during a meeting such a quorum ceases to be present, the meeting shall stand adjourned to the same day in the next week at the same time and place or such time and place as the directors may determine.

42. The chairman, if any, of the board of directors or in his absence some other director nominated by the directors shall preside as chairman of the meeting, but if neither the chairman nor such other director (if any) be present within 15 minutes after the time appointed for holding the meeting and willing to act, the directors present shall elect one of their number to be chairman and, if there is only one director present and willing to act, he shall be chairman.

43. If no director is willing to act as chairman, or if no director is present within 15 minutes after the time appointed for holding the meeting, the members present and entitled to vote shall choose one of their number to be chairman.

44. A director shall, notwithstanding that he is not a member, be entitled to attend and speak at any general meeting and at any separate meeting of the holders of any class of shares in the company.

45. The chairman may, with the consent of a meeting at which a quorum is present (and shall if so directed by the meeting) adjourn the meeting from time to time and place to place, but no business shall be transacted at an adjourned meeting other than business which might properly have been transacted at the meeting had the adjournment not taken place. When a meeting is adjourned for 14 days or more, at least seven clear days' notice shall be given specifying the time and place of the adjourned meeting and the general nature of the business to be transacted. Otherwise it shall not be necessary to give any such notice.

46. A resolution put to the vote of a meeting shall be decided on a show of hands

unless before, or on the declaration of the result of, the show of hands a poll is duly demanded. Subject to the provisions of the Act, a poll may be demanded:

(1) by the chairman; or

(2) by at least two members having the right to vote at the meeting; or

(3) by a member or members representing not less than one-tenth of the total voting rights of all the members having the right to vote at the meeting; or

(4) by a member or members holding shares conferring a right to vote at the meeting being shares on which an aggregate sum has been paid up equal to not less than one-tenth of the total sum paid up on all shares conferring that right;

and a demand by a person as proxy for a member shall be the same as a demand by the member.

47. Unless a poll is duly demanded a declaration by the chairman that a resolution has been carried or carried unanimously, or by a particular majority, or lost, or not carried by a particular majority and an entry to that effect in the minutes of the meeting shall be conclusive evidence of the fact without proof of the number or proportion of the votes recorded in favour of or against the resolution.

48. The demand for a poll may, before the poll is taken, be withdrawn but only with the consent of the chairman and a demand so withdrawn shall not be taken to have invalidated the result of a show of hands declared before the demand was made.

49. A poll shall be taken as the chairman directs and he may appoint scrutineers (who need not be members) and fix a time and place for declaring the result of the poll. The result of the poll shall be deemed to be the resolution of the meeting at which the poll was demanded.

50. In the case of a quality of votes, whether on a show of hands or on a poll, the chairman shall be entitled to a casting vote in addition to any other vote he may have.

51. A poll demanded on the election of a chairman or on a question of adjournment shall be taken forthwith. A poll demanded on any other question shall be taken either forthwith or at such time and place as the chairman directs not being more than 30 days after the poll is demanded. The demand for a poll shall not prevent the continuance of a meeting for the transaction of any business other than the question on which the poll was demanded. If a poll is demanded before the declaration of the result of a show of hands and the demand is duly withdrawn, the meeting shall continue as if the demand had not been made.

52. No notice need be given of a poll not taken forthwith if the time and place at which it is to be taken are announced at the meeting at which it is demanded. In any other case at least seven clear days' notice shall be given specifying the time and place at which the poll is to be taken.

53. A resolution in writing executed by or on behalf of each member who would have been entitled to vote upon it if it had been proposed at a general meeting at which he was present shall be as effectual as if it had been passed at a general meeting duly convened and held and may consist of several instruments in the like form each executed by or on behalf of one or more members.

Votes of Members

54. Subject to any rights or restrictions attached to any shares, on a show of hands every member who (being an individual) is present in person or (being a corporation) is present by a duly authorised representative, not being himself a member entitled to

vote, shall have one vote and on a poll every member shall have one vote for every share of which he is the holder.

55. In the case of joint holders the vote of the senior who tenders a vote, whether in person or by proxy, shall be accepted to the exclusion of the votes of the other joint holders; and seniority shall be determined by the order in which the names of the holders stand in the register of members.

56. A member in respect of whom an order has been made by any court having jurisdiction (whether in the United Kingdom or elsewhere) in matters concerning mental disorder may vote, whether on a show of hands or on a poll, by his receiver, curator bonis or other person may, on a poll, vote by proxy. Evidence to the satisfaction of the directors of the authority of the person claiming to exercise the right to vote shall be deposited at the office, or at such other place as is specified in accordance with the articles for the deposit of instruments of proxy, not less than 48 hours before the time appointed for holding the meeting or adjourned meeting at which the right to vote is to be exercised and in default the right to vote shall not be exercisable.

57. No member shall vote at any general meeting or at any separate meeting of the holders of any class of shares in the company, either in person or by proxy, in respect of any share held by him unless all moneys presently payable by him in respect of that share have been paid.

58. No objection shall be raised to the qualification of any voter except at the meeting at which the vote objected to is tendered, and every vote not disallowed at the meeting shall be valid. Any objection made in due time shall be referred to the chairman, whose decision shall be final and conclusive.

59. On a poll votes may be given either personally or by proxy. A member may appoint more than one proxy to attend on the same occasion.

60. An instrument appointing a proxy shall be in writing, executed by or on behalf of the appointor and shall be in the following form (or in a form as near thereto as circumstances allow or in any other form which is usual or which the directors may approve):

'PLC/Limited

I/We,   , of
                                                                  , being a
member/members of the above-named company, hereby appoint
          of   , or failing him,
          of   , as my/our proxy to vote in my/
our name(s) and on my/our behalf at the annual/extraordinary general meeting of the company to be held on   19   , and at any adjournment thereof.
Signed on   19   .'

61. Where it is desired to afford members an opportunity of instructing the proxy how he shall act the instrument appointing a proxy shall be in the following form (or in a form as near thereto as circumstances allow or in any other form which is usual or which the directors may approve):

'PLC/Limited

I/We,   , of
                                                                  , being a
member/members of the above-named company, hereby appoint
          of   , or failing him,
          of   , as my/our proxy to vote in my/
our name(s) and on my/our behalf at the annual/extraordinary general meeting of

the company to be held on   19   , and at any adjournment
thereof.
This form is to be used in respect of the resolutions mentioned below as follows:
    Resolution No. 1 *for *against
    Resolution No. 2 *for *against.
*Strike out whichever is not desired.
Unless otherwise instructed, the proxy may vote as he thinks fit or abstain from
voting.
Signed this   day of   19   .'

62. The instrument appointing a proxy and any authority under which it is executed
or a copy of such authority certified notarially or in some other way approved by the
directors may:

(1) be deposited at the office or at such other place within the United Kingdom as
is specified in the notice convening the meeting or in any instrument of proxy
sent out by the company in relation to the meeting not less than 48 hours before
the time for holding the meeting or adjourned meeting at which the person
named in the instrument proposes to vote; or

(2) in the case of a poll taken more than 48 hours after it is demanded, be deposited
as aforesaid after the poll has been demanded and not less than 24 hours before
the time appointed for the taking of the poll; or

(3) where the poll is not taken forthwith but is taken not more than 48 hours after it
was demanded, be delivered at the meeting at which the poll was demanded to
the chairman or to the secretary or to any director;

and an instrument of proxy which is not deposited or delivered in a manner so
permitted shall be invalid.

63. A vote given or poll demanded by proxy or by the duly authorised representative
of a corporation shall be valid notwithstanding the previous determination of the
authority of the person voting or demanding a poll unless notice of the determination
was received by the company at the office or at such other place at which the
instrument of proxy was duly deposited before the commencement of the meeting or
adjourned meeting at which the vote is given or the poll demanded or (in the case of
the poll taken otherwise than on the same day as the meeting or adjourned meeting)
the time appointed for taking the poll.

Number of Directors

64. Unless otherwise determined by ordinary resolution, the number of directors
(other than alternate directors) shall not be subject to any maximum but shall be not
less than two.

Alternate Directors

65. Any director (other than an alternate director) may appoint any other director,
or any other person approved by resolution of the directors and willing to act, to be
an alternate director and may remove from office an alternate director appointed by
him.

66. An alternate director shall be entitled to receive notice of all meetings of
directors and of all meetings of committees of directors of which his appointor is a
member, to attend and vote at any such meeting at which the director appointing him
is not personally present, and generally to perform all the functions of his appointor
as a director in his absence but shall not be entitled to receive any remuneration from

the company for his services as an alternate director who is absent from the United Kingdom.

67. An alternate director shall cease to be an alternate director if his appointor ceases to be a director; but, if a director retires by rotation or otherwise but is reappointed or deemed to have been reappointed at the meeting at which he retires, any appointment of an alternate director made by him which was in force immediately prior to his retirement shall continue after his reappointment.

68. Any appointment or removal of an alternate director shall be by notice to the company signed by the director making or revoking the appointment or in any other manner approved by the directors.

69. Save as otherwise provided in the articles, an alternate director shall be deemed for all purposes to be a director and shall alone be responsible for his own acts and defaults and he shall not be deemed to be the agent of the director appointing him.

Powers of Directors

70. Subject to the provisions of the Act, the memorandum and the articles and to any directions given by special resolution, the business of the company shall be managed by the directors who may exercise all the powers of the company. No alteration of the memorandum or articles and no such direction shall invalidate any prior act of the directors which would have been valid if that alteration had not been made or that direction had not been given. The powers given by this regulation shall not be limited by any special power given to the directors by the articles and a meeting of directors at which a quorum is present may exercise all powers exercisable by the directors.

71. The directors may, by power of attorney or otherwise, appoint any person to be the agent of the company for such purposes and on such conditions as they determine, including authority for the agent to delegate all or any of his powers.

Delegation of Directors' Powers

72. The directors may delegate any of their powers to any committee consisting of one or more directors. They may also delegate to any managing director or any director holding any other executive office such of their powers as they consider desirable to be exercised by him. Any such delegation may be made subject to any conditions the directors may impose, and either collaterally with or to the exclusion of their own powers and may be revoked or altered. Subject to any such conditions, the proceedings of a committee with two or more members shall be governed by the articles regulating the proceedings of directors so far as they are capable of applying.

Appointment and Retirement of Directors

73. At the first annual general meeting all the directors shall retire from office, and at every subsequent annual general meeting the one-third of the directors who are subject to retirement by rotation or, if their number is not three or a multiple of three, the number nearest to one-third shall retire from office; but, if there is only one director who is subject to retirement by rotation, he shall retire.

74. Subject to the provisions of the Act, the directors to retire by rotation shall be those who have been longest in office since their last appointment or reappointment, but as between persons who became or were last reappointed directors on the same day those to retire shall (unless they otherwise agree among themselves) be determined by lot.

75. If the company, at the meeting at which a director retires by rotation, does not fill the vacancy the retiring director shall, if willing to act, be deemed to have been reappointed unless at the meeting it is resolved not to fill the vacancy or unless a resolution for the reappointment of the director is put to the meeting and lost.

76. No person other than a director retiring by rotation shall be appointed or reappointed a director at any general meeting unless:

 (1) he is recommended by the directors; or

 (2) not less than 14 nor more than 35 clear days before the date appointed for the meeting, notice executed by a member qualified to vote at the meeting has been given to the company of the intention to propose that person for appointment or reappointment stating the particulars which would, if he were so appointed or reappointed, be required to be included in the company's register of directors together with notice executed by that person of his willingness to be appointed or reappointed.

77. Not less than 7 nor more than 28 clear days before the date appointed for holding a general meeting notice shall be given to all who are entitled to receive notice of the meeting of any person (other than a director retiring by rotation at the meeting) who is recommended by the directors for appointment or reappointment as a director at the meeting or in respect of whom notice has been duly given to the company of the intention to propose him at the meeting for appointment or reappointment as a director. The notice shall give the particulars of that person which would, if he were so appointed or reappointed, be required to be included in the company's register of directors.

78. Subject as aforesaid, the company may by ordinary resolution appoint a person who is willing to act to be a director either to fill a vacancy or as an additional director and may also determine the rotation in which any additional directors are to retire.

79. The directors may appoint a person who is willing to act to be a director, either to fill a vacancy or as an additional director, provided that the appointment does not cause the number of directors to exceed any number fixed by or in accordance with the articles as the maximum number of directors. A director so appointed shall hold office only until the next following annual general meeting and shall not be taken into account in determining the directors who are to retire by rotation at the meeting. If not reappointed at such annual general meeting, he shall vacate office at the conclusion thereof.

80. Subject as aforesaid, a director who retires at an annual general meeting may, if willing to act, be reappointed. If he is not reappointed, he shall retain office until the meeting appoints someone in his place, or if it does not do so, until the end of the meeting.

Disqualification and Removal of Directors

81. The office of a director shall be vacated if:

 (1) he ceases to be a director by virtue of any provision of the Act or he becomes prohibited by law from being a director; or

 (2) he becomes bankrupt or makes any arrangement or composition with his creditors generally; or

 (3) he is, or may be, suffering from mental disorder and either:

  (a) he is admitted to hospital in pursuance of an application for admission for treatment under the Mental Health Act 1983, or in Scotland, an application for admission under the Mental Health (Scotland) Act 1960, or

(b) an order is made by a court having jurisdiction (whether in the United Kingdom or elsewhere) in matters concerning mental disorder for his detention or for the appointment of a receiver, curator bonis or other person to exercise powers with respect to his property or affairs; or

(4) he resigns his office by notice to the company; or

(5) he shall for more than six consecutive months have been absent without permission of the directors from meetings of directors held during that period and the directors resolve that his office be vacated.

Remuneration of Directors

82. The directors shall be entitled to such remuneration as the company may by ordinary resolution determine and, unless the resolution provides otherwise, the remuneration shall be deemed to accrue from day to day.

Directors' Expenses

83. The directors may be paid all travelling, hotel, and other expenses properly incurred by them in connection with their attendance at meetings of directors or committees of directors or general meetings or separate meetings of the holders of any class of shares or of debentures of the company or otherwise in connection with the discharge of their duties.

Directors' Appointments and Interests

84. Subject to the provisions of the Act, the directors may appoint one or more of their number to the office of managing director or to any other executive office under the company and may enter into an agreement or arrangement with any director for his employment by the company or for the provision by him of any services outside the scope of the ordinary duties of a director. Any such appointment, agreement or arrangement may be made upon such terms as the directors determine and they may remunerate any such director for his services as they think fit. Any appointment of a director to an executive office shall terminate if he ceases to be a director but without prejudice to any claim to damages for breach of the contract of service between the director and the company. A managing director and a director holding any other executive office shall not be subject to retirement by rotation.

85. Subject to the provisions of the Act, and provided that he has disclosed to the directors the nature and extent of any material interest of his, a director notwithstanding his office:

(1) may be a party to, or otherwise interested in, any transaction or arrangement with the company or in which the company is otherwise interested;

(2) may be a director or other officer or employed by, or a party to any transaction or arrangement with, or otherwise interested in, any body corporate promoted by the company or in which the company is otherwise interested; and

(3) shall not, by reason of his office, be accountable to the company for any benefit which he derives from any such office or employment or from any such transaction or arrangement or from any interest in any such body corporate and no such transaction or arrangement shall be liable to be avoided on the ground of any such interest or benefit.

86. For the purposes of regulation 85:

(1) a general notice given to the directors that a director is to be regarded as having an interest of the nature and extent specified in the notice in any transaction or arrangement in which a specified person or class of person is interested shall be deemed to be a disclosure that the director has an interest in any such transaction of the nature and extent so specified; and

(2) an interest of which a director has no knowledge and of which it is unreasonable to expect him to have knowledge shall not be treated as an interest of his.

Directors' Gratuities and Pensions

87. The directors may provide benefits, whether by the payment of gratuities or pensions or by insurance or otherwise, for any director who has held but no longer holds any executive office or employment with the company or with any body corporate which is or has been a subsidiary of the company or a predecessor in business of the company or of any such subsidiary, and for any member of his family (including a spouse and a former spouse) or any person who is or was dependent on him, and may (as well before as after he ceases to hold such office or employment) contribute to any fund and pay premiums for the purchase or provision of any such benefit.

Proceedings of Directors

88. Subject to the provisions of the articles, the directors may regulate their proceedings as they think fit. A director may, and the secretary at the request of a director shall, call a meeting of the directors. It shall not be necessary to give notice of a meeting to a director who is absent from the United Kingdom. Questions arising at a meeting shall be decided by a majority of votes. In the case of a quality of votes, the chairman shall have a second or casting vote. A director who is also an alternate director shall be entitled in the absence of his appointor to a separate vote on behalf of his appointor in addition to his own vote.

89. The quorum for the transaction of the business of the directors may be fixed by the directors and unless so fixed at any other number shall be two. A person who holds office only as an alternate director shall, if his appointor is not present, be counted in the quorum.

90. The continuing directors or a sole continuing director may act notwithstanding any vacancies in their number, but, if the number of directors is less than the number fixed as the quorum, the continuing directors or director may act only for the purpose or filling vacancies or of calling a general meeting.

91. The directors may appoint one of their number to be the chairman of the board of directors and may at any time remove him from that office. Unless he is unwilling to do so, the director so appointed shall preside at every meeting of directors at which he is present. But if there is no director holding that office, or if the director holding it is unwilling to preside or is not present within five minutes after the time appointed for the meeting, the directors present may appoint one of their number to be chairman of the meeting.

92. All acts done by a meeting of directors, or of a committee of directors, or by a person acting as a director shall, notwithstanding that it be afterwards discovered that there was a defect in the appointment of any director or that any of them were disqualified from holding office, or had vacated office, or were not entitled to vote, be as valid as if every such person had been duly appointed and was qualified and had continued to be a director and had been entitled to vote.

93. A resolution in writing signed by all the directors entitled to receive notice of a meeting of directors or of a committee of directors shall be as valid and effectual as if it had been passed at a meeting of directors or (as the case may be) a committee of directors duly convened and held and may consist of several documents in the like form each signed by one or more directors; but a resolution signed by an alternate director need not also be signed by his appointor and if it is signed by a director who has appointed an alternate director, it need not be signed by the alternate director in that capacity.

94. Save as otherwise provided by the articles, a director shall not vote at a meeting of directors or of a commitee of directors on any resolution concerning a matter in which he has, directly or indirectly, an interest or duty which is material and which conflicts or may conflict with the interests of the company unless his interest or duty arises only because the case falls within one or more of the following paragraphs:

(a) the resolution relates to the giving to him of a guarantee, security, or indemnity in respect of money lent to, or an obligation incurred by him for the benefit of, the company or any of its subsidiaries;

(b) the resolution relates to the giving to a third party of a guarantee, security, or indemnity in respect of an obligation of the company or any of its subsidiaries for which the director has assumed responsibility in whole or part and whether alone or jointly with others under a guarantee or indemnity or by the giving of security;

(c) his interest arises by virtue of his subscribing or agreeing to subscribe for any shares, debentures or other securities of the company or any of its subsidiaries, or by virtue of his being, or intending to become, a participant in the underwriting or sub-underwriting of an offer of any such shares, debentures, or other securities by the company or any of its subsidiaries for subscription, purchase or exchange;

(d) the resolution relates in any way to a retirement benefits scheme which has been approved, or is conditional upon approval, by the Board of Inland Revenue for taxation purposes.

For the purposes of this regulation, an interest of a person who is, for any purpose of the Act (excluding any statutory modification thereof not in force when this regulation becomes binding on the company), connected with a director shall be treated as an interest of the director and, in relation to an alternate director without prejudice to any interest which the alternate director has otherwise.

95. A director shall not be counted in the quorum present at a meeting in relation to a resolution on which he is not entitled to vote.

96. The company may by ordinary resolution suspend or relax to any extent, either generally or in respect of any particular matter, any provision of the articles prohibiting a director from voting at a meeting of directors or of a committee of directors.

97. Where proposals are under consideration concerning the appointment of two or more directors to offices or employments with the company or any body corporate in which the company is interested the proposals may be divided and considered in relation to each director separately and (provided he is not for another reason precluded from voting) each of the directors concerned shall be entitled to vote and be counted in the quorum in respect of each resolution except that concerning his own appointment.

98. If a question arises at a meeting of directors or of a committee of directors as to the the right of a director to vote, the question may, before the conclusion of the meeting, be referred to the chairman of the meeting and his ruling in relation to any director other than himself shall be final and conclusive.

Secretary

99. Subject to the provisions of the Act, the secretary shall be appointed by the directors for such term, at such remuneration and upon such conditions as they may think fit; and any secretary so appointed may be removed by them.

Minutes

100. The directors shall cause minutes to be made in books kept for the purpose:

(1) of all appointments of officers made by the directors; and

(2) of all proceedings at meetings of the company, of the holders of any class of shares in the company, and of the directors, and of committees of directors, including the names of the directors present at each such meeting.

The Seal

101. The seal shall only be used by the authority of the directors or of a committee of directors authorised by the directors. The directors may determine who shall sign any instrument to which the seal is affixed and unless otherwise so determined it shall be signed by a director and by the secretary or by a second director.

Dividends

102. Subject to the provisions of the Act, the company may by ordinary resolution declare dividends in accordance with the respective rights of the members, but no dividend shall exceed the amount recommended by the directors.

103. Subject to the provisions of the Act, the directors may pay interim dividends if it appears to them that they are justified by the profits of the company available for distribution. If the share capital is divided into different classes, the directors may pay interim dividends on shares which confer deferred or non-preferred rights with regard to dividend as well as on shares which confer preferential rights with regard to dividend, but no interim dividend shall be paid on shares carrying deferred or non-preferred rights if, at the time of payment, any preferential dividend is in arrear. The directors may also pay at intervals settled by them any dividend payable at a fixed rate if it appears to them that the profits available for distribution justify the payment. Provided the directors act in good faith they shall not incur any liability to the holders of shares conferring preferred rights for any loss they may suffer by the lawful payment of an interim dividend on any shares having deferred or non-preferred rights.

104. Except as otherwise provided by the rights attached to shares, all dividends shall be declared and paid according to the amounts paid up on the shares on which the dividend is paid. All dividends shall be apportioned and paid proportionately to the amounts paid up on the shares during any portion or portions of the period in respect of which the dividend is paid; but, if any share is issued on terms providing that it shall rank for dividend as from a particular date, that shall rank for dividend accordingly.

105. A general meeting declaring a dividend may, upon the recommendation of the directors, direct that it shall be satisfied wholly or partly by the distribution of assets and, where any difficulty arises in regard to the distribution, the directors may settle the same and in particular may issue fractional certificates and fix the value for distribution of any assets and may determine that cash shall be paid to any member

upon the footing of the value so fixed in order to adjust the rights of members and may vest any assets in trustees.

106. Any dividend or other moneys payable in respect of a share may be paid by cheque sent by post to the registered address of the person entitled or, if two or more persons are the holders of the share or are jointly entitled to it by reason of the death or bankruptcy of the holder, to the registered address of that one of those persons who is first named in the register of members or to such person and to such address as the person or persons entitled may in writing direct. Every cheque shall be made payable to the order of the person or persons entitled or to such other person as the person or persons entitled may in writing direct and payment of the cheque shall be good discharge to the company. Any joint holder or other person jointly entitled to a share as aforesaid may give receipts for any dividend or other moneys payable in respect of the share.

107. No dividend or other moneys payable in respect of a share shall bear interest against the company unless otherwise provided by the rights attached to the share.

108. Any dividend which has remained unclaimed for twelve years from the date when it became due for payment shall, if the directors so resolve, be forfeited and cease to remain owing by the company.

Accounts

109. No member shall (as such) have any right of inspecting any accounting records or other book or document of the company except as conferred by statute or authorised by the directors or by ordinary resolution of the company.

Capitalisation of Profits

110. The directors may with the authority of an ordinary resolution of the company:

(a) subject as hereinafter provided, resolve to capitalise any undivided profits of the company not required for paying any preferential dividend (whether or not they are available for distribution) or any sum standing to the credit of the company's share premium account or capital redemption reserve;

(b) appropriate the sum resolved to be capitalised to the members who would have been entitled to it if it were distributed by way of dividend and in the same proportions and apply such sum on their behalf either in or towards paying up the amounts, if any, for the time being unpaid on any shares held by them respectively, or in paying up in full unissued shares or debentures of the company of a nominal amount equal to that sum, and allot the shares or debentures credited as fully paid to those members, or as they may direct, in those proportions, or partly in one way and partly in the other: but the share premium account, the capital redemption reserve, and any profits which are not available for distribution may, for the purposes of this regulation, only be applied in paying up unissued shares to be allotted to members credited as fully paid;

(c) make such provision by the issue of fractional certificates or by payment in cash or otherwise as they determine in the case of shares or debentures becoming distributable under this regulation in fractions; and

(d) authorise any person to enter on behalf of all the members concerned into an agreement with the company providing for the allotment to them respectively, credited as fully paid, of any shares or debentures to which they are entitled upon such capitalisation, any agreement made under such authority being binding on all such matters.

Notices

111. Any notice to be given to or by any person pursuant to the articles shall be in writing except that a notice calling a meeting of the directors need not be in writing.

112. The company may give any notice to a member either personally or by sending it by post in a prepaid envelope addressed to the member at his registered address or by leaving it at that address. In the case of joint holders of a share, all notices shall be given to the joint holder whose name stands first in the register of members in respect of the joint holding and notice so given shall be sufficient notice to all the joint holders. A member whose registered address is not within the United Kingdom and who gives to the company an address within the United Kingdom at which notices may be given to him shall be entitled to have notices given to him at that address, but otherwise no such member shall be entitled to receive any notice from the company.

113. A member present, either in person or by proxy, at any meeting of the company or of the holders of any class of shares in the company shall be deemed to have received notice of the meeting and, where requisite, of the purposes for which it was called.

114. Every person who becomes entitled to a share shall be bound by any notice in respect of that share which, before his name is entered in the register of members, has been duly given to a person from whom he derives his title.

115. Proof that an envelope containing a notice was properly addressed, prepaid and posted shall be conclusive evidence that the notice was given. A notice shall be deemed to be given at the expiration of 48 hours after the envelope containing it was posted.

116. A notice may be given by the company to the persons entitled to a share in consequence of the death or bankruptcy of a member by sending or delivering it, in any manner authorised by the articles for the giving of notice to a member, addressed to them by name, or by the title of representatives of the deceased, or trustee of the bankrupt or by any like description at the address, if any, within the United Kingdom supplied for that purpose by the persons claiming to be so entitled. Until such an address has been supplied, a notice may be given in any manner in which it might have been given if the death or bankruptcy had not occurred.

Winding up

117. If the company is wound up, the liquidator may, with the sanction of an extraordinary resolution of the company and any other sanction required by the Act, divide among the members in specie the whole or any part of the assets of the company and may, for that purpose, value any assets and determine how the division shall be carried out as between the members or different classes of members. The liquidator may, with the like sanction, vest the whole or any part of the assets in trustees upon such trusts for the benefit of the members as he with the like sanction determines, but no member shall be compelled to accept any assets upon which there is a liability.

Indemnity

118. Subject to the provisions of the Act but without prejudice to any indemnity to which a director may otherwise be entitled, every director or other officer or auditor of the company shall be indemnified out of the assets of the company against any liability incurred by him in defending any proceedings, whether civil or criminal, in which judgment is given in his favour or in which he is acquitted or in connection with any application in which relief is granted to him by the court from liability for negligence, default, breach of duty or breach of trust in relation to the affairs of the company.

Precedent 1.5

ARTICLES OF ASSOCIATION—PUBLIC COMPANY (SHORT FORM)

THE COMPANIES ACTS 1985 AND 1989
PUBLIC COMPANY LIMITED BY SHARES
ARTICLES OF ASSOCIATION
OF

Preliminary

1. Subject as hereinafter provided the Regulations contained in Table A set out in the Schedule to The Companies (Tables A to F) Regulations 1985 shall apply to the Company.

2. Regulations 3, 23 and 35 of Table A shall not apply to the Company, but the Regulations hereinafter contained together with the remaining Regulations of Table A shall, subject to the modifications hereinafter expressed, constitute the regulations of the Company.

3. Any reference in these Regulations to an enactment shall be construed as a reference to that enactment as amended or extended by or under any other enactment.

Interpretation

4. In Regulation 1 of Table A there shall be inserted before the words 'office' and 'secretary' the word 'the' and between the words 'regulations' and 'the Act' the words 'and in any regulations adopting the whole or in part the same'.

Shares

5. Subject to the provisions of the next following Regulation the Directors are authorised for the purposes of Section 80 of the Act to exercise the power of the Company to allot shares to the amount of the authorised but unissued share capital of the Company at the date hereof and the Directors may allot, grant options over or otherwise dispose of such shares, to such persons, on such terms and in such manner as they think fit provided always that:

(i) save as provided in sub-paragraph (ii) of this Regulation the authority given in this Regulation to the Directors to exercise the power of the Company to allot shares shall expire five years after the date of incorporation of the Company.

(ii) the Members in General Meeting may by Ordinary Resolution:

(a) renew the said authority (whether or not it has been previously renewed) for a period not exceeding five years, but such Resolution must state (or restate) the amount of shares which may be allotted under such authority or renewed authority or, as the case may be, the amount remaining to be allotted thereunder, and must specify the date on which the authority or renewed authority will expire:

(b) revoke or vary any such authority (or renewed authority); and

(iii) notwithstanding the provisions of sub-paragraphs (i) and (ii) of this Regulation the Company may make an offer or agreement which would or might require shares to be allotted after such authority has expired and in pursuance of such an offer or agreement the Directors may allot shares notwithstanding that such authority or renewed authority has expired.

In this regulation any reference to the allotment of shares shall include a reference to the grant of any right to subscribe for, or to convert any security into shares, but shall not include any reference to the allotment of shares pursuant to such a right.

6. Subject to Chapter VII of the Act, the Company may purchase its own shares (including redeemable shares) out of distributable profits or the proceeds of a fresh issue of shares.

7. Subject to Chapter VII of the Act, any shares may, with the sanction of an Ordinary Resolution, be issued on the terms that they are, or, at the option of the Company or the shareholder are liable, to be redeemed on such terms and in such manner as the Company before the issue of the shares may by Special Resolution determine, and whether out of distributable profits or the proceeds of a fresh issue of shares.

Transfers

8. The instrument of transfer of a fully paid share shall be executed by or on behalf of the transferor and in the case of a share which is not fully paid, the instrument of transfer shall in addition be executed by or on behalf of the transferee. The transferor shall be deemed to remain a holder of the share until the name of the transferee is entered in the Register of Members in respect thereof.

Proceedings at General Meetings

9. In every notice convening a General Meeting of the Company there shall appear with reasonable prominence a statement that a Member entitled to attend and vote is entitled to appoint a proxy to attend and on a poll vote instead of him and that such proxy need not also be a Member. Regulation 38 of Table A shall be modified accordingly.

10. Proxies may be deposited at the Registered Office of the Company at any time before the time of the Meeting for which they are to be used unless otherwise specified in the notice convening such Meeting. Regulation 62 of Table A shall be modified accordingly.

Directors

11. The Directors may exercise all the powers of the Company to borrow money, whether in excess of the nominal amount of the share capital of the Company for the time being issued or not, and to mortgage or charge its undertaking, property and uncalled capital or any part thereof, and to issue debentures, debenture stock or any other securities whether outright or as security for any debt, liability or obligation of the Company or of any third party.

12. In Regulation 87 there shall be inserted between the words 'the directors' and 'may' the words 'on behalf of the Company'.

13. Any Director or member of a committee of the Directors may participate in a meeting of the Directors or such committee by means of conference telephone or similar communications equipment whereby all persons participating in the meeting can hear each other and participation in a meeting in this manner shall be deemed to constitute presence in person at such meeting.

14. Any appointment or removal of an alternate director may be made by letter, cable, telex, telegram, fascimile or radiogram or in any other manner approved by the Directors. Any cable, telex, telegram, facsimile or radiogram shall be confirmed in writing as soon as possible by letter but is a valid appointment in the meantime. Accordingly Regulation 68 in Table A shall not apply to the Company.

Dividends

15. No dividend or interim dividend shall be paid otherwise than in accordance with the provisions of Part VIII of the Act which apply to the Company.

Precedent 1.6

ARTICLES OF ASSOCIATION—PRIVATE COMPANY (TABLE A WITH AMENDMENTS)

THE COMPANIES ACTS 1985 TO 1989
COMPANY LIMITED BY SHARES
ARTICLES OF ASSOCIATION
OF

Preliminary

1. The Regulations contained or incorporated in Table A in the Schedule to The Companies (Tables A to F) Regulations 1985 (such Table being hereinafter called 'Table A') shall apply to the Company save in so far as they are excluded or varied hereby and such Regulations (save as so excluded or varied) and the Articles hereinafter contained shall be the Regulations of the Company.

Private Company

2. The Company is a private limited company within the meaning of The Companies Act 1985 and accordingly no shares or debentures of the Company shall be offered to the public.

Shares

3. (a) Shares which are comprised in the authorised share capital with which the Company is incorporated shall be under the control of the Directors who may (subject to paragraph (d) below) allot, grant options over or otherwise dispose of the same, to such persons, on such terms and in such manner as they think fit.

(b) After the first allotment of shares by the Directors any further shares proposed to be issued shall first be offered to the Members in proportion as nearly as may be to the number of the existing shares held by them respectively unless the Company shall by Special Resolution otherwise direct. The offer shall be made by notice specifying the number of shares offered, and limiting a period (not being less than fourteen days) within which the offer, if not accepted, will be deemed to be declined. After the expiration of that period, those shares so deemed to be declined shall be offered in the proportion aforesaid to the persons who have, within the said period, accepted all the shares offered to them; such further offer shall be made in like terms in the same manner and limited by a like period as the original offer. Any shares not accepted pursuant to such offer or further offer as aforesaid or not capable of being offered as aforesaid except by way of fractions and any shares released from the provisions of this Article by such Special Resolution as aforesaid shall be under the control of the Directors, who may (subject to paragraph (d) below) allot, grant options over or otherwise dispose of the same to such persons, on such terms, and in such manner as they think fit, provided that, in the case of shares not accepted as aforesaid , such shares shall not be disposed of on terms which are more favourable to the subscribers therefor than the terms on which they were offered to the Members.

(c) In accordance with Section 91 of the Companies Act 1985 Sections 89(1) and 90 of the said Act shall not apply to the Company.

(d) The Directors are generally and unconditionally authorised for the purposes of Section 80 of the Companies Act 1985 to exercise any power of the Company to allot and grant rights to subscribe for or convert securities into shares of the Company up to the amount of the authorised share capital with which the Company is incorporated at any time or times during the period of five years from the date of incorporation and the Directors may after that period, allot any shares or grant any such rights under this authority in pursuance of an offer or agreement so to do made by the Company within that period. The authority hereby given may at any time (subject to the said Section 80) be renewed, revoked or varied by Ordinary Resolution.

4. The lien conferred by Regulation 8 in Table A shall attach also to fully paid up shares. Regulation 8 in Table A shall be modified accordingly.

5. The liability of any Member in default in respect of a call shall be increased by the addition at the end of the first sentence of Regulation 18 in Table A of the words 'and all expenses that may have been incurred by the Company by reason of such non-payment'.

Transfer of Shares

6. The Directors may, in their absolute discretion and without assigning any reason therefor, decline to register any transfer which would otherwise be permitted under the succeeding provisions of this Article if it is a transfer:

    (i) of a share on which the Company has a lien;

    (ii) of a share (not being a fully paid share) to a person of whom they shall not approve.

    Regulation 24 in Table A shall not apply to the Company.

Redemption of Shares

7. Subject to the provisions of the Companies Acts shares may be issued which are to be redeemed or are to be liable to be redeemed at the option of the Company or the holder, provided that the terms on which and the manner in which any such redeemable shares shall or may be redeemed shall be specified by Special Resolution before the issue thereof.

General Meetings and Resolutions

8. Every notice convening a General Meeting shall comply with the provisions of Section 372(3) of the Companies Act 1985 as to giving information to Members

in regard to their right to appoint proxies; and notices of and other communications relating to any General Meeting which any Member is entitled to receive shall be sent to the Directors and to the Auditor for the time being of the Company.

9. In Regulation 41 of Table A there shall be inserted at the end the words 'and if at the adjourned meeting a quorum is not present within half an hour from the time appointed for the meeting, the members present shall be a quorum.'

Appointment of Directors

10. (a) The number of the Directors may be determined by Ordinary Resolution of the Company but unless and until so fixed there shall be no maximum number of Directors and the minimum number of Directors shall be one. In the event of the minimum number of Directors fixed by or pursuant to these Articles or Table A being one, a sole Director shall have authority to exercise all the powers and discretions by Table A or these Articles expressed to be vested in the Directors generally and the quorum for the transaction of the business of the Directors shall be one. Regulation 64 in Table A shall not apply to the Company.

(b) The Directors shall not be required to retire by rotation and accordingly Regulations 73, 74 and 75 in Table A shall not apply to the Company and Regulations 76, 77, 78 and 79 in Table A shall be modified accordingly.

11. Any appointment or removal of an alternate Director may be made by letter, cable, telex, telegram, facsimile or radiogram or in any other manner approved by the Directors. Any cable, telex, telegram, facsimile or radiogram shall be confirmed as soon as possible by letter but is a valid appointment in the meantime. Accordingly Regulation 68 in Table A shall not apply to the Company.

Powers of Directors

12. In addition to and without prejudice to the generality of the powers conferred by Regulation 70 of Table A the Directors may mortgage or charge all the undertaking and property of the Company including the uncalled capital or any part thereof, and to issue debentures, debenture stock and other securities whether outright or as security for any debt, liability or obligation of the Company or of any third party.

13. A Director may vote as a Director in regard to any contract or arrangement in which he is interested or upon any matter arising thereout, and if he shall so vote his vote shall be counted and he shall be reckoned in estimating a quorum when any such contract or arrangement is under consideration and Regulations 94 to 97 in Table A shall be modified accordingly.

14. Any Director or member of a committee of the Directors may participate in a meeting of the Directors or such committee by means of conference telephone or similar communications equipment whereby all persons meeting in this manner shall be deemed to constitute presence in person at such meeting.

Precedent 1.7

ARTICLES OF ASSOCIATION—SUBSIDIARY COMPANY

THE COMPANIES ACTS 1985 AND 1989
COMPANY LIMITED BY SHARES
ARTICLES OF ASSOCIATION
OF

Preliminary

1. The Regulations contained or incorporated in Table A in the Schedule to the Companies (Tables A to F) Regulations 1985 (such Table being hereinafter called 'Table A') shall apply to the Company save in so far as they are excluded or varied hereby and such Regulations (save as so excluded or varied) and the Articles hereinafter contained shall be the Regulations of the Company.

2. The following provisions of Table A shall not apply to the Company; in Regulation 62 the words 'not less than 48 hours' and 'not less than 24 hours', Regulations 65 to 69 (inclusive) and 94 to 98 (inclusive).

Private Company

3. The Company is a private limited company within the meaning of the Companies Act 1985 and accordingly no shares or debentures of the Company shall be offered to the public.

Shares

4. The lien conferred by Regulation 8 in Table A shall attach also to fully paid up shares. Regulation 8 in Table A shall be modified accordingly.

5. The liability of any Member in default in respect of a call shall be increased by the addition at the end of the first sentence of Regulation 18 in Table A of the words 'and all expenses that may have been incurred by the Company by reason of such non-payment'.

Transfer of Shares

6. (a) The immediate holding company (if any) for the time being of the Company may at any time transfer all or any shares to any person and the provisions of Regulation 24 of Table A shall not apply to such transfer.

(b) Except in the case of a transfer of shares expressly authorised by the last preceding Article the right to transfer shares in the Company shall be subject to the following restrictions for as long as the Company has an immediate holding company:

(i)   Any person (hereinafter called 'the proposing transferor') proposing to transfer any shares shall give notice in writing (hereinafter called 'the transfer notice') to the Company and to the immediate holding company that he desires to transfer the same and specifying the price per share which in his opinion constitutes the fair value thereof. The transfer notice shall constitute the Company the agents of the proposing transferor for the sale of all (but not some of) the shares comprised in the transfer notice to the immediate holding company at the price specified therein or at the fair value certified in accordance with paragraph (iii) below (whichever shall be the lower). A transfer notice shall not be revocable except with the sanction of the Directors.

(ii) The shares comprised in any transfer notice shall be offered to the immediate holding company by notice in writing (hereinafter called 'the offer notice') within seven days after the receipt by the Company of the transfer notice. The offer notice shall state the price per share specified in the transfer notice and shall limit the time in which the offer may be accepted, being not more than forty-two days after the date of the offer notice, provided that if a certificate of fair value is requested under paragraph (iii) below the offer shall remain open for acceptance for a period of fourteen days after the date on which notice of the fair value certified in accordance with that paragraph shall have been given by the Company to the immediate holding company or until the expiry of the period specified in the offer notice whichever is the later. For the purpose of this Article an offer shall be deemed to be accepted on the day on which the acceptance is received by the Company.

(iii) The immediate holding company may, not later than eight days after the date of the offer notice, serve on the Company a notice in writing requesting that the Auditor for the time being of the Company (or at the discretion of the Auditor, a person nominated by the President for the time being of the Institute of Chartered Accountants in the Country of the situation of its Registered Office) certify in writing the sum which in his opinion represents the fair value of the shares comprised in the transfer notice as at the date of the transfer notice and for the purpose of this Article reference to the Auditor shall include any person so nominated. Upon receipt of such notice the Company shall instruct the Auditor to certify as aforesaid and the costs of such valuation shall be borne by the Company. In certifying the fair value as aforesaid the Auditor shall be considered to be acting as an expert and not as an arbitrator or arbiter and accordingly any provisions of law or statute relating to arbitration shall not apply. Upon receipt of the certificate of the Auditor, the Company shall by notice in writing inform the immediate holding company of the fair value of each share and of the price per share (being the lower of the price specified in the transfer notice and the fair value of each share) at which the shares comprised in the transfer notice are offered for sale. For the purpose of this Article the fair value of each share comprised in the transfer notice shall be the sum certified as aforesaid divided by the number of shares comprised in the transfer notice.

(iv) If the immediate holding company shall signify its willingness to purchase all or any of the shares comprised in the transfer notice within the appropriate period specified in paragraph (iii) above, the Company shall not later than seven days after the expiry of such appropriate period give notice in writing (hereinafter called 'the sale notice') to the proposing transferor and the proposing transferor shall be bound upon payment of the price due in respect of all the shares comprised in the transfer notice to transfer the shares to the immediate company.

(v) If in any case the proposing transferor after having become bound as aforesaid makes default in transferring any shares the Company may receive the purchase money on his behalf, and may authorise some person to execute a transfer of such shares in favour of the immediate holding company. The receipt of the Company for the purchase money shall be a good discharge to the immediate holding company. The Company shall pay the purchase money into a separate bank account.

(vi) If the Company shall not give a sale notice to the proposing transferor within the time specified in paragraph (iv) above, he shall, during the period of thirty days next following the expiry of the time so specified, be at liberty to transfer all or any of the shares comprised in the transfer notice to any person or persons.

(vii) Upon the liquidation of any Member (being a corporation other than the immediate holding company) or upon any director or employee who is a Member or whose nominee or spouse, child, parent, brother, sister or other relation is a Member ceasing for any reason to be a director or an employee of the Company or its holding company or its subsidiary company or its fellow subsidiary company such Member shall be deemed to have given immediately prior to such liquidation or ceasing to be a director or an employee (as the case may be) a transfer notice in respect of all shares registered in the name of such Member and the provisions of this Article shall apply as to the transfer of his shares.

(viii) Regulations 29 to 31 of Table A shall apply subject to the following provisions:

(a) Any person becoming entitled to a share in consequence of the death or bankruptcy of a Member shall give a transfer notice;

(b) If a person so becoming entitled shall not have given a transfer notice in respect of any share within six months of the death or bankruptcy, the Directors may at any time thereafter upon resolution passed by them give notice requiring such person within thirty days of such notice to give a transfer notice in respect of all the shares to which he has so become entitled and for which he has not previously given a transfer notice and if he does not do so he shall at the end of such thirty days be deemed to have given a transfer notice pursuant to paragraph 6(b) of this Article relating to those shares in respect of which he has still not done so;

(c) Where a transfer notice is given or deemed to be given under these paragraphs (vii) and (viii) and no price per share is specified therein the transfer notice shall be deemed to specify the sum which shall, on the application of the Directors, be certified in writing by the Auditors in accordance with paragraph (iii) of this article as the fair value thereof.   ·

Directors

7. A Director shall not be required to vacate his office and no person shall be ineligible for appointment or re-appointment as a Director by reason of his attaining the age of seventy or any other age.

Alternate Director

8. (a) Each Director shall have the power at any time to appoint as an alternate Director either another Director or any other person approved for that purpose by a resolution of the Directors, and, at any time, to terminate such appointment. Every appointment and removal of an alternate Director shall be in writing signed by the appointor and (subject to any approval required) shall (unless the Directors agree otherwise) only take effect upon receipt of such written

appointment or removal at the Registered Office of the Company. The appointment of an alternate Director shall automatically determine on the happening of any event which if he were a Director would cause him to vacate such office or if his appointor shall cease for any reason to be a Director otherwise than by retiring and being re-appointed at the same meeting.

(b) An alternate Director shall not be entitled as such to receive any remuneration from the Company except only such part (if any) of the remuneration otherwise payable to his appointor as such appointor may by notice in writing to the Company from time to time direct, but shall otherwise be subject to the provisions of these Articles with respect to Directors. An alternate Director shall during his appointment be an officer of the Company and shall not be deemed to be an agent of his appointor.

(c) An alternate Director shall be entitled to receive notices of all meetings of the Directors and of any committee of the Directors of which his appointor is a Member and to attend and to vote as a Director at any such meeting at which his appointor is not personally present and generally in the absence of his appointor to perform and exercise all functions, rights, powers and duties as a Director of his appointor and to receive notice of all general meetings. A Director or any other person may act as alternate Director to represent more than one Director and an alternate Director shall be entitled at meetings of the Directors or any committee of the Directors to one vote for every Director whom he represents in addition of his own vote (if any) as a Director, but he shall count as only one for the purpose of determining whether a quorum is present.

Interest of Directors

9. A Director may, notwithstanding his interest, vote in respect of any contract or arrangement with the Company in which he is interested, directly or indirectly, and be taken into account for the purpose of a quorum and may retain for his own absolute use and benefit all profits and advantages accruing to him.

Powers of Directors

10. In addition to and without prejudice to the generality of the powers conferred by Regulation 70 of Table A the Directors may mortgage or charge all the undertaking and property of the Company including the uncalled capital or any part thereof, and to issue debentures, debenture stock and other securities whether outright or as security for any debt, liability or obligation of the Company or of any third party.

Appointment and Removal of Directors

11. (a) The immediate holding company (if any) for the time being of the Company may appoint any person to be a Director or remove any Director from office. Every such appointment or removal shall be in writing and signed by or on behalf of the said holding company and shall take effect upon receipt at the Registered Office of the Company or by the Secretary.

(b) While the Company is a subsidiary, the Directors shall have power to appoint any person to be a Director either to fill a casual vacancy or as an addition to the existing Directors, subject to any maximum for the time being in force, and any Director so appointed shall (subject to Regulation 81 of Table A) hold office until he is removed pursuant to Article 11(a).

(c) While the Company is a subsidiary, regulations 73 to 80 (inclusive) of Table A shall not apply and all references elsewhere in Table A to retirement by rotation shall be modified accordingly.

Proceedings of Directors

12. (a) A resolution agreed upon by Directors (not being less than the number of Directors required to form a quorum of the Directors) shall be valid and effectual whether or not it shall be passed at a meeting of the Directors duly convened and held and if in writing, may consist of several documents in the like form each signed by one or more Directors.

(b) For the purposes of determining whether there exists the quorum fixed by or in accordance with Regulation 89 of Table A as that necessary for the transaction of the business of the Directors, there shall be counted in the quorum (a) in the case of a resolution agreed by Directors in telephonic communication, all such directors and (b) in the case of a meeting of Directors, in addition to the Directors present at the meeting, any Director in telephonic communication with such meeting.

13. Any Director or member of a committee of the Directors may participate in a meeting of the Directors or such committee by means of conference telephone or similar communications equipment whereby all persons meeting in this manner shall be deemed to constitute presence in person at such meeting.

Precedent 1.8

Transfer of Shares-A

1. (a) The Directors may, in their absolute discretion and without assigning any reason therefor, decline to register any transfer which would otherwise be permitted under the succeeding provisions of this Article if it is a transfer:

   (i) of a share on which the Company has a lien;

   (ii) of a share (not being a fully paid share) to a person of whom they shall not approve;

   (iii) of a share (whether or not it is fully paid) made pursuant to paragraph (g) below.

   Regulation 24 in Table A shall not apply to the Company.

   (b) Any person (hereinafter called 'the proposing transferor') proposing to transfer any shares shall give notice in writing (hereinafter called 'the transfer notice') to the Company that he desires to transfer the same and specifying the price per share which in his opinion constitutes the fair value thereof. The transfer notice shall constitute the Company the agents of the proposing transferor for the sale of all (but not some of) the shares comprised in the transfer notice to any Member or Members willing to purchase the same (hereinafter called 'the purchasing Member') at the price specified therein or at the fair value certified in accordance with paragraph (d) below (whichever shall be the lower). A transfer notice shall not be revocable except with the sanction of the Directors.

   (c) The shares comprised in any transfer notice shall be offered to the Members (other than the proposing transferor) as nearly as may be in proportion to the number of shares held by them respectively. Such offer shall be made by notice in writing (hereinafter called 'the offer notice') within seven days after the receipt by the Company of the transfer notice. The offer notice shall state the price per share specified in the transfer notice and shall limit the time in which the offer may be accepted, not being less than twenty-one days nor more than forty-two days after the date of the offer notice, provided that if a certificate of fair value is requested under paragraph (d) below the offer shall remain open for acceptance for a period of fourteen days after the date on which notice of the fair value certified in accordance with that paragraph shall have been given by the Company to the Members or until the expiry of the period specified in the offer notice whichever is the later. For the purpose of this Article an offer shall be deemed to be accepted on the day on which the acceptance is received by the Company. The offer notice shall further invite each Member to state in his reply the number of additional shares (if any) in excess of his proportion which he desires to purchase and if all the Members do not accept the offer in respect of their respective proportions in full the shares not so accepted shall be used to satisfy the claims for additional shares as nearly as may be in proportion to the number of shares already held by them respectively, provided that no Member shall be obliged to take more shares than he shall have applied for. If any shares shall not be capable without fractions of being offered to the Members in proportion to their existing holdings, the same shall be offered to the Members, or some of them, in such proportions or in such manner as may be determined by lots drawn in regard thereto, and the lots shall be drawn in such manner as the Directors may think fit.

(d) Any Member may, not later than eight days after the date of the offer notice, serve on the Company a notice in writing requesting that the Auditor for the time being of the Company (or at the discretion of the Auditor, a person nominated by the President for the time being of the Institute of Chartered Accountants in England and Wales) certify in writing the sum which in his opinion represents the fair value of the shares comprised in the transfer notice as at the date of the transfer notice and for the purpose of this Article reference to the Auditor shall include any person so nominated. Upon receipt of such notice the Company shall instruct the Auditor to certify as aforesaid and the costs of such valuation shall be apportioned among the proposing transferor and the purchasing Members or borne by any one or more of them as the Auditor in his absolute discretion shall decide. In certifying the fair value as aforesaid the Auditor shall be considered to be acting as an expert and not as an arbitrator or arbiter and accordingly any provisions of law or statute relating to arbitration shall not apply. Upon receipt of the certificate of the Auditor, the Company shall by notice in writing inform all Members of the fair value of each share and of the price per share (being the lower of the price specified in the transfer notice and the fair value of each share) at which the shares comprised in the transfer notice are offered for sale. For the purpose of this Article the fair value of each share comprised in the transfer notice shall be the sum certified as aforesaid divided by the number of shares comprised in the transfer notice.

(e) If purchasing Members shall be found for all the shares comprised in the transfer notice within the appropriate period specified in paragraph (c) above, the Company shall not later than seven days after the expiry of such appropriate period give notice in writing (hereinafter called 'the sale notice') to the proposing transferor specifying the purchasing Members and the proposing transferor shall be bound upon payment of the price due in respect of all the shares comprised in the transfer notice to transfer the shares to the purchasing Members.

(f) If in any case the proposing transferor after having become bound as aforesaid makes default in transferring any shares the Company may receive the purchase money on his behalf, and may authorise some person to execute a transfer of such shares in favour of the purchasing Member. The receipt of the Company for the purchase money shall be a good discharge to the purchasing Member. The Company shall pay the purchase money into a separate bank account.

(g) If the Company shall not give a sale notice to the proposing transferor within the time specified in paragraph (e) above, he shall, during the period of thirty days next following the expiry of the time so specified, be at liberty subject to paragraph (a) above to transfer all or any of the shares comprised in the transfer notice to any person or persons.

(h) Regulations 29 to 31 of Table A shall apply subject to the following provisions:

(i) Any person becoming entitled to a share in consequence of the death or bankruptcy of a Member shall give a transfer notice before he elects in respect of any share to be registered himself or to execute a transfer;

(ii) If a person so becoming entitled shall not have given a transfer notice in respect of any share within six months of the death or bankruptcy, the Directors may at any time thereafter upon resolution passed by them give notice requiring such person within thirty days of such notice to give a transfer notice in respect of all the shares to which he has so become entitled and for which he has not previously given a transfer notice and if he does not do so he shall at the end of such thirty days be deemed to have given a transfer notice pursuant to paragraph (b) of this Article relating to those shares in respect of which he has still not done so;

(iii) Where a transfer notice is given or deemed to be given under this paragraph (h) and no price per share is specified therein the transfer notice shall be deemed to specify the sum which shall, on the application of the Directors, be certified in writing by the Auditor in accordance with paragraph (d) of this article as the fair value thereof.

Precedent 1.9

Transfer of Shares-B

6. (a) A Member (or other person entitled to transfer the shares registered in the name of a Member) may at any time transfer all or any shares

    (i)   to a privileged relation (as hereinafter defined) of such Member; or

    (ii) to trustees to be held upon family trusts (as hereinafter defined); or

    (iii) in the case of a corporate member to any other body corporate which is the holding company of the Member or a subsidiary of the Member or of its holding company, provided that in the event that any company to whom such shares are transferred ceases to be a holding company or subsidiary as aforesaid such shares shall be transferred back to the company which transferred them or to any other company falling within the required relationship.

    (iv) in the case of a corporate member which holds shares as a nominee or on trust, to any other nominee for the same scheme or schemes, provided that in the event that a nominee or trustee to whom such shares are transferred ceases to be a nominee or trustee such shares shall be transferred back to the Member which transferred them or to any other person falling within the required relationship.

(v) to a nominee of the Member or, where the Member is a nominee for any other person, to that person or to another nominee for him provided that in any such case the transferor certifies to the Company that no beneficial interest in the shares passes by reason of the transfer.

(b) No transfer such as is referred to in paragraph (a) above may be made if the intended Transferee or any of the intended Transferees shall be a minor or a bankrupt.

(c) For the purposes of the foregoing paragraph (a) the expression 'Member' shall not include a trustee holding shares upon family trusts as hereinafter defined but where shares are held by such trustees

(i) such shares may on any change of trustee be transferred to the trustees for the time being;

(ii) such shares may at any time be transferred to any person whom under paragraph (a) hereof the same could have been transferred by the settlor if he had been the holder thereof;

(iii) if and whenever any such shares cease to be held upon family trusts (otherwise than in consequence of a transfer authorised under sub-paragraph (ii) of this paragraph) the trustees shall be bound forthwith to give a transfer notice (as hereinafter defined) in respect of the shares in question.

(d) For the purpose of this Article

(i) the words 'privileged relation' shall mean the father or mother of the Member any lineal descendant of such father and mother or any person who is or has been married to such member such father or mother or to any such lineal descendant or any stepchild or adopted child of the member or of such father or mother or of any such lineal descendant;

(ii) the expression 'family trusts' shall, in relation to any Member, mean trusts (whether arising under a settlement inter vivos or a testamentary disposition by whomsoever made or on an intestacy) for the benefit of the Member or any such privileged relation or privileged relations under which no powers of control over the voting powers conferred by such shares is for the time being exercisable by or subject to the consent of any person other than the trustees as trustees of the Member concerned or a privileged relation of such Member.

Precedent 1.10

MINUTES OF A BOARD MEETING DEALING WITH INITIAL COMPANY SECRETARIAL MATTERS

Minutes of a Meeting of the Board of Directors
of the Company held at
on   at

Present:

In attendance:

Incorporation: There was produced to the Meeting the Certificate of Incorporation of the Company dated (No.   ) together with a copy of the Memorandum and Articles of Association as registered.

Directors: It was noted that   had been appointed first Director(s) of the Company pursuant to Section 10(2) of the Companies Act 1985 and that at a meeting of the first Director(s), held on   ,   had been appointed as (an) additional director(s) of the Company. At the conclusion of the meeting   had resigned as Director(s).

Secretary: It was noted that   had been appointed as the first Secretary to the Company pursuant to Section 10(2) of the Companies Act 1985, and that at a meeting of the first Director(s) held on   had resigned as Secretary and   had been appointed Secretary in his place.

Registered Office: It was noted that the Registered Office of the Company was situated at

Chairman: IT WAS RESOLVED THAT be and is hereby appointed Chairman of the Board of Directors.

Auditors: IT WAS RESOLVED THAT Messrs be and are hereby appointed Auditors of the Company to hold office until the conclusion of the first General Meeting at which accounts are laid before the shareholders.

Common Seal: IT WAS RESOLVED THAT the seal, an impression of which appears in the margin of these Minutes, be and is hereby adopted as the Common Seal of the Company.

Transfer of Shares: There were produced to the Meeting stock transfer forms whereby the subscribers to the Memorandum of Association of the Company transferred the shares which they had agreed to take up upon incorporation of the Company in favour of the following persons:

(a) 1 Ordinary Share of £1.00 from
to

(b) 1 Ordinary Share of £1.00 from
to

IT WAS RESOLVED THAT the said share transfers be and are hereby approved and (subject to stamping by the Inland Revenue) registered in the books of the Company and that the sum of £1.00 on each share be immediately called up and paid by the transferees and that any two directors or one director and the secretary be and are hereby authorised to issue appropriate share certificates to the transferees executed under the seal of the Company.

Allotment of Shares:

It was noted that application had been made for the allotment of the following shares in the capital of the Company:

(a) 499 Ordinary Shares of £1.00 each to

(b) 499 Ordinary Shares of £1.00 each to

The meeting considered the matter and IT WAS RESOLVED THAT pursuant to the authority conferred upon the director(s) by the Articles of Association, the said application(s) be and is (are) hereby approved and that the said shares be allotted to the applicant(s) fully paid at par value for cash and that any two directors or one director and the secretary be and are hereby authorised to issue (an) appropriate share certificate(s) to the allottee(s) executed under the seal of the Company and that the secretary be and is hereby instructed to file Form G88(2) with the Registrar of Companies.

Distinguishing Numbers:

IT WAS RESOLVED THAT all the issued and fully paid shares in the capital of the Company shall not bear distinguishing numbers.

Accounting Reference Date:

IT WAS RESOLVED THAT the Accounting Reference Date of the Company be   of each year and that the secretary be and is hereby instructed to file a Form G224 with the Registrar of Companies.

Bank Account:

IT WAS RESOLVED THAT a Bank Account in the name of the Company be opened with   of   and that the Bank be and is hereby instructed to operate the said Account according to the instructions set down in the Bank's standard form of mandate, a copy of which is attached to and forms part of these Minutes.

There being no further business the meeting closed.

CHAIRMAN

Precedent 1.11

SPECIAL RESOLUTIONS—EXAMPLES OF RESOLUTIONS TO ALTER OBJECTS

1. THAT the Memorandum of Association of the Company be amended in the manner following, that is to say by the deletion of the present clause C(1) and the adoption of a new Clause C(1) namely:

'To carry on business as a general commercial company.'

2. THAT the Memorandum of Association of the Company be amended:

   (a) By deleting in the present Clause C(6) the words 'within the United Kingdom' and substituting therefor the words 'within or without the United Kingdom'.

   (b) By redesignating the present Clauses C(8) to C(22) (inclusive) as clauses C(9) to C(23) inclusive and by adopting a new Clause C(8) namely:

   'To prove the Company to be registered or recognised in any part of the world'

Precedent 1.12

SPECIAL RESOLUTIONS—EXAMPLES OF RESOLUTIONS AMENDING ARTICLES OF ASSOCIATION

1. THAT the draft Regulations produced to the meeting and initialled by the Chairman for the purposes of identification be adopted as the Articles of Association of the Company in substitution for and the exclusion of all the existing Articles of Association.

2. THAT the Articles of Association the Company be amended in the manner following that is to say:

   (a) By deleting in the present Article 18, the words 'by any two directors' and by substituting therefor the words 'by any one director'.

   (b) By deleting the present Article 25 and by adopting a new Article 25 namely:

   (c) By renumbering the present Articles 46 to 153 (inclusive) as Articles 47 to 154 (inclusive) and by adopting a new Article 46 namely:

Precedent 2.1

'A' & 'B' SHARES—SPECIMEN ARTICLES

4. The share capital of the Company at the date of incorporation of the Company is £   divided into   'A Shares of £1.00 each (hereinafter called 'the 'A' Shares') and   'B' Shares of £1.00 each (hereinafter called 'the 'B' Shares'). Save as is hereinafter expressly provided the 'A' Shares and the 'B'

Shares shall rank pari passu in all respects. The respective rights attaching to the 'A' Shares and to the 'B' Shares are as follows:

(a) Unless otherwise provided by Special Resolution of the Company any unissued shares in the capital of the Company for the time being which it shall be desired to issue shall consist of such numbers of 'A' Shares or 'B' Shares, as appropriate, as shall be proportionate to the numbers of 'A' Shares and 'B' Shares in issue immediately prior to such further issue and shall be offered in the first instance (on uniform terms of payment) to the Members for the time being in proportion (as nearly as circumstances shall admit) to the number of shares held by them respectively and so that unissued 'A' Shares shall be offered to the holders of the 'A' Shares for the time being and unissued 'B' Shares shall be offered to the holders of the 'B' Shares for the time being. Upon such offers being made as aforesaid the holders of each class who shall accept their entitlements in full shall be invited to apply for any shares of that class which they are willing to accept in excess of their said entitlements. In the event that a holder or holders of any shares of that class does or do not accept all of any of his or their entitlement the shares representing the same (hereinafter called 'excess shares') shall be offered on the same terms of payment as aforesaid to the shareholders of that class who have applied for excess shares when the following provisions shall apply:

    (i) insofar as the number of excess shares is the same as the aggregate of the numbers so applied for they shall be issued in accordance with applications; or

    (ii) insofar as the number of excess shares is less than the aggregate of the numbers so applied for they shall be issued in proportion as nearly as may be to the aggregate of the numbers of that class of shares already held by the respective holders thereof and of their entitlements as aforesaid; or

    (iii) insofar as the number of excess shares is greater than the aggregate of the numbers so applied for they shall be issued in accordance with applications provided that (a) the balance thereafter remaining unissued shall then be offered to the holders of the same class of shares who shall have made applications for excess shares and in the same proportion as aforesaid (including in the respective entitlements for the purpose only of this sub-paragraph the respective numbers of excess shares issued in accordance with applications) and (b) insofar as the offer of any such balance shall remain wholly or partially unaccepted the shares constituting the same shall be offered (on the same terms of payment as aforesaid) to the holders of the other class in proportion as nearly as may be to the aggregate of the numbers of the other class of shares already held by them and of those numbers of shares of that class forming part of their respective entitlements (including their entitlements to excess shares of that class issued in accordance with applications).

(b) On a show of hands or on a poll every holder of 'A' Shares present in person or by proxy shall have one vote for each 'A' Share of which he is the holder. On a show of hands or on a poll every holder of 'B' Shares present in person or by proxy shall have three votes for each 'B' Share of which he is the holder.

Precedent 2.2

FOUNDER SHARES—SPECIMEN ARTICLES

Subject as hereinafter provided the Founder Shares and the Ordinary Shares shall rank pari passu as if the same constituted one class of Shares.

Voting—Generally

Subject to any special terms as to voting upon which any Shares may from time to time be held and subject to disenfranchisement in the event of non-compliance with a notice under Section 212 of the Act, on a show of hands every member present in person or (being a corporation) being a duly authorised representative shall have one vote and on a poll every member present in person or by proxy shall have one vote for every Share held by him.

Voting—Founder Shares

The holders of the Founder Shares shall as a class (between them pro rata to their respective holdings of Founder Shares) be entitled on any resolution proposed prior to the 1997 AGM to wind up the Company to exercise 25.1 per cent of the total number of votes and the holders of the Ordinary Shares as a class (between them pro rata to their respective holdings of Ordinary Shares) shall be entitled to exercise the balance of such voting rights.

Dividends

The holders of the Founder Shares shall not be entitled to any dividends.

Distribution of Surplus Assets on a Winding Up

The surplus assets of the Company (after payment of its liabilities) shall be divided as follows:

(1) firstly, in paying to the holders of the Ordinary Shares an amount equal to the sums subscribed for the Ordinary Shares (including any premium paid thereon);

(2) secondly, in paying to the holders of the Founder Shares the amount paid up or credited as paid up on the nominal amount of the Founder Shares;

(3) thirdly, the balance shall belong to and be distributed to holders of the Ordinary Shares as a class (between them pro rata to their respective holdings of the Ordinary Shares).

Founder Shares—Ordinary Share Equivalents

(1) Immediately following the conclusion of the 1997 AGM all the Founder Shares shall have automatically attached to them such number of Ordinary Share Equivalents representing the aggregate value of 30% of any increase in excess of $7\frac{1}{2}\%$ per annum on a compound basis of each Ordinary Share in issue at 31st March 1997 above its nominal value calculated from the 5th April 1992 (or from the date of allotment in the case of an Ordinary Share allotted after 6th April 1992) as determined by the Valuation at 31st March 1997.

(2) If prior to 31st March 1997 there shall be any Dealing or a Share Offer the Founder Shares shall have automatically attached to them such number of Ordinary Share Equivalents immediately prior to such event representing the aggregate value equal to 20% of any increase in value of each Ordinary Share in issue at such time above its nominal value as determined by the Dealing Price or the Offer Price (as the case may be).

(3) If there shall be any sub-division or consolidation of the Ordinary Shares or any capitalisation issue or reduction of capital which may or would affect the

rights of the Founder Shares, there shall be made such adjustments to such rights as may be necessary to ensure that the rights of the holder of the Founder Shares are less (and no greater) than those prevailing on the date of adoption of these Articles. Any such adjustment shall be determined by the auditors of the Company acting as experts and not arbitrators and shall be final and binding on the Company.

Precedent 2.3

CUMULATIVE PREFERENCE SHARES—SPECIMEN ARTICLES

The Share Capital of the Company at the date of adoption of these Articles is £   divided into   Ordinary Shares of £1.00 each and   Cumulative Preference Shares of £1.00 each. The Ordinary Shares and the Cumulative Preference Shares shall have the same rights and privileges and shall rank pari passu in all respects save that:

(i) The holders of the Cumulative Preference Shares shall not be entitled to receive notice of, or attend, or vote at any General Meeting of the Company.

(ii) The holders of the Cumulative Preference Shares shall be entitled in priority to any payment of dividend on any other class of shares to a fixed cumulative preferential dividend of   per centum per annum (exclusive of inputed tax credit). Any dividend to be paid on the said shares shall be payable by equal half-yearly instalments on   and   in respect of each year for the half-yearly periods ending on those respective dates. Subject to the above the profits of the Company available for dividend and resolved to be distributed shall be distributed by way of dividend among the holders of the Ordinary Shares.

(iii) The Cumulative Preference Shares shall entitle the holders thereof on a winding up or on a reduction of capital involving a return of capital, pari passu with any further Cumulative Preference Shares created to rank pari passu therewith as regard priority in respect of capital, and in priority to any return of capital on any other class of shares, to repayment of the capital paid up or credited as paid up thereon together with a sum equal to any arrears or accruals of the fixed cumulative preferential dividend thereon calculated down to the date of repayment whether or not such dividend shall have been declared or earned and the balance of the assets of the Company, subject to any special rights which may be attached to any class of shares shall be applied in repaying to the holders of the Ordinary Shares the amounts paid upon such shares and subject thereto shall belong to and be distributed among such holders rateably according to the amounts paid upon such shares and the holders of the Cumulative Preference Shares shall not be entitled to any further or other participation in the profits or assets of the Company.

Precedent 2.4

NON-CUMULATIVE PREFERENCE SHARES—SPECIMEN ARTICLES

The Share Capital of the Company at the date of adoption of these Articles is £   divided into   Ordinary Shares of £1.00 each and   Non-Cumulative Preference Shares of £1.00 each. The Ordinary Shares and the Non-Cumulative Preference Shares shall have the same rights and privileges and shall rank pari passu in all respects save that:

(i) The holders of the Non-Cumulative Preference Shares shall not be entitled to receive notice of, or attend, or vote at any General Meeting of the Company.

(ii) The holders of the Non-Cumulative Preference Shares shall be entitled in priority to any payment of dividend on any other class of shares to a fixed preferential dividend of　　　　　per centum per annum (exclusive of imputed tax credit). Any dividend to be paid on the said shares shall be payable by equal half-yearly instalments on　　　　　and　　　　　in respect of each year for the half-yearly periods ending on those respective dates. Subject to the above the profits of the Company available for dividend and resolved to be distributed shall be distributed by way of dividend among the holders of the Ordinary Shares.

(iii) The Non-Cumulative Preference Shares shall entitle the holders thereof on a winding up or on a reduction of capital involving a return of capital, pari passu with any further Non-Cumulative Preference Shares created to rank pari passu therewith as regards priority in respect of capital, and in priority to any return of capital on any other class of shares, to repayment of the capital paid up or credited as paid up thereon and the balance of the assets of the Company, subject to any special rights which may be attached to any class of shares shall be applied in repaying to the holders of the Ordinary Shares the amounts paid upon such shares and subject thereto shall belong to and be distributed among such holders rateably according to the amounts paid upon such shares and the holders of the Non-Cumulative Preference Shares shall not be entitled to any further or other participation in the profits or assets of the Company.

Precedent 2.5

REDEEMABLE PREFERENCE SHARES—SPECIMEN ARTICLES

The Share Capital of the Company at the date of adoption of these Articles is £　　　　　divided into　　　　　Ordinary Shares of £1.00 each and Redeemable Preference Shares of £1.00 each (hereinafter referred to as 'Preference Shares'). The Ordinary Shares and the Preference Shares shall have the same rights and privileges and shall rank pari passu in all respects save that:

As Regards Voting:

(i) The holders of the Preference Shares shall not be entitled to receive notice of, or attend, or vote at any General Meeting of the Company.

As Regards Income:

(ii) The holders of the Preference Shares shall be entitled in priority to any payment of dividend on any other class of share to a non cumulative preferential dividend of　　　　　per centum per annum (exclusive of imputed tax credit). Subject to the above the profits of the Company available for dividend and resolved to be distributed shall be distributed by way of dividend among the holders of the Ordinary Shares.

As Regards Capital:

(iii) The Preference Shares shall entitle the holders thereof on a winding up or on a reduction of capital involving a return of capital, together with any further Preference Shares created to rank pari passu therewith as regards priority in respect of capital, and in priority to any return of capital on any other class of shares, to repayment of the capital paid up or credited as paid up thereon and the balance of the assets of the Company, subject to any special rights which may be attached to any class of shares shall be applied in repaying to the holders of the Ordinary Shares the amounts paid upon such shares and subject thereto shall belong to and be distributed among such holders rateably according to the amounts paid upon such shares and the holders of the Preference Shares shall not be entitled to any further or other participation in the profits or assets of the Company.

(iv) The following provisions shall apply in regard to the redemption of the Preference Shares:

(a) Subject to the provisions of the Companies Act 1985 the Company shall have the right pursuant to Section 160 of the Companies Act 1985 to redeem at par the whole or any part of the Preference Shares at any time or times after the date of issue of the said Shares upon giving to the holders of the particular Shares to be redeemed not less than three months' previous notice in writing.

(b) In the case of any partial redemption under Paragraph (a) of this Article, the Company shall for the purpose of ascertaining the particular shares to be redeemed cause a drawing to be made at the Registered Office or at such other place as the Directors may decide in the presence of a representative of the Auditors for the time being of the Company.

(c) Any Notice of Redemption shall specify the particular shares to be redeemed, the date fixed for redemption and the time and the place at which the certificates for such shares are to be presented for redemption and upon such date each of the holders of the shares concerned shall be bound to deliver to the Company at such place the certificates for such of the shares concerned as ae held by him in order that the same may be cancelled. Upon such delivery the Company shall pay to such holder the amount due to him in respect of such redemption. If any certificates so delivered to the Company includes any shares not redeemable on that occasion, a fresh certificate for such shares shall be issued to the holder delivering such certificate to the Company.

(d) There shall be paid on each Preference Share redeemed the amount paid up thereon together with a sum equal to any arrears of the dividend thereon to be calculated down to the date fixed for redemptions.

(e) The Company shall not be entitled to reissue as Preference Shares any shares redeemed under the foregoing provisions.

Precedent 2.6

REDEEMABLE CUMULATIVE CONVERTIBLE PREFERENCE SHARE PROVISIONS

A. For the purpose of this Article the following expressions shall have the following meanings:

(1) 'Allotment Date' means in respect of each of the Preference Shares the date on which the same is allotted;

(2) 'Conversion Period' means the period commencing in respect of each Preference Share at 5.00 a.m. on the day after the Allotment Date and expiring in respect of all Preference Shares at 5.00 p.m. on that date years from the date of allotment of each Preference Share;

(3) 'Conversion Price' means in respect of each Preference Share the amount of par value and premium determined by the Directors on allotment of the Preference Share to be payable upon conversion of the Preference Shares into Ordinary Shares as hereinafter provided;

(4) 'Preference Shares' means such of the Redeemable Cumulative Convertible Preference Shares of £1.00 each in the capital of the Company as may be issued or, if the context so requires, some of them and each preference share;

   (a) has attached to it the rights, privileges, restrictions and conditions set out in or determined in accordance with the following provisions of this Article;

   (b) has such term, and carries the right to a fixed cumulative preferential dividend at such rate as is determined by the Directors in their absolute discretion from time to time (the Determined Rate) and

   (c) shall be issued at a premium of £   ;

(5) 'Redemption Amount' means with respect to each Preference Share redeemed the aggregate of the following amounts as at the date of payment thereof:

   (a) the paid up par value of the Preference Shares;

   (b) an amount equal to the premium paid up on the Preference Share; and

   (c) any arrears of dividend and interest accruing thereon calculated up to the Redemption Date;

(6) 'Redemption Date' means that date (being   years) from the date of allotment of the Preference Shares.

B. (i) Each holder of Preference Shares shall be entitled at any time during the Conversion Period to convert any Preference Share held by him into ordinary shares upon payment of the Conversion price as herein provided;

  (ii) Any Preference Share may be converted at the option of the holder thereof by the holder duly completing and delivering to the Company a 'Notice of Conversion' substantially in the form set out below or in any other form that the Directors may approve in respect of each of the Preference Shares sought to be converted ('the Converting Preference Shares').

NOTICE OF CONVERSION

To: The Directors,   Limited

I HEREBY CONVERT   Preference Shares held by me and hand you herewith (a) certificate(s) representing those Preference Shares and I request that you forward to me certificates representing the Ordinary Shares into which those Preference Shares have been converted.

If the certificates herewith represent more than the number of Converting Preference Shares I authorise you to cancel the certificates and issue a new certificate representing the balance of the Preference Shares held by me not converted.

Dated the   day of   199

Signed...

Address for forwarding of certificates

....

(iii) Upon conversion of all or any Preference Shares and receipt of all relevant documents, the Ordinary Shares resulting from conversion shall rank pari passu in all respects with all other Ordinary Shares then issued.

(iv) Notwithstanding the foregoing the Directors may at any time prior to the Redemption Date be entitled upon giving no less than 7 days notice to a holder of Preference Shares to require all or any holder of Preference Shares to convert all or any of the Preference Shares held by him into Ordinary Shares as provided by this Article.

C. Preference Shares pending conversion into Ordinary Shares:

(1) shall carry the right to preferential and cumulative dividends at the Determined Rate expressed as a percentage per annum on the capital for the time being paid up on such Preference Shares;

(2) shall not carry the right to any Ordinary, Non Cumulative or other dividends;

(3) shall rank for payment of the Redemption Amount equally with the holders of other Preference Shares and in priority to all holders of other classes of Preference Shares unless the issue and the terms thereof are previously approved in writing by the holders of not less than three quarters in number of each class of the issued Preference Shares;

(4) shall not entitle their holders to participate in the profits or assets of the Company otherwise than as provided in this Article;

(5) shall if the Company makes an issue of Ordinary Shares by way of capitalisation of profits, reserves, or its share premium account ('a bonus issue') to the holders of the then issued Ordinary Shares, carry the right to participate pari passu with the Ordinary Shares in the bonus issue as if the Preference Shares were Ordinary Shares;

(6) shall if an offer or invitation is made by the Company for subscription for cash with respect to shares, options or other securities of the Company, or any other company, to the holders of the then issued Ordinary Shares in the Company, carry the right to participate pari passu with the Ordinary Shares as if the Preference Shares were Ordinary Shares; and

(7) shall entitle their holders to receive not less than 10 days written notice from the Company prior to the proposed events described in sub-paragraphs (5) and (6) above.

D. The Preferential and Cumulative dividend on the Preference Shares shall be paid in arrears on such date and at such times as shall be determined by the Directors from time to time, provided always that if the dividend on the Preference Shares is in arrears by more than   interest calculated daily at the prime U.K. Clearing Bank's Base Rate shall become immediately due and payable by the Company.

E. (1) The Preference Shares shall confer upon the holders thereof the same rights as the holders of Ordinary Shares have with regard to receiving notices including without limitation notices of general meetings of the Company, reports, accounts and balance sheets and attending general meetings but pending conversion shall not confer on such holders the right to vote or to move or second any resolution, or speak at general meetings except as follows:

(a) upon a proposal to reduce the share capital of the Company;
(b) upon a proposal that affects rights attached to the Preference Shares;
(c) upon a proposal to wind up the Company,

(d) upon a proposal for the disposal of the whole of the property, business and undertaking of the Company;

(e) when the dividend on the Preference Shares is in arrears,

(f) during the winding up of the Company.

(2) In any of the events mentioned in sub-paragraphs (1) (a) to (f) inclusive above each holder of a Preference Share shall have one vote on a show of hands, and on a poll, one vote for every Preference Share held;

(3) None of the foregoing shall affect the right of the holders to have a class meeting pursuant to the provisions of the Companies Act.

F.   On the Redemption Date, the Company shall subject to the provisions of the Companies Act:

(a) pay to the holder of each Preference Share which has not been converted the Redemption Amount; and

(b) redeem all the Preference Shares which have not been converted.

G.   Each holder of a Preference Share shall upon redemption thereof be bound to surrender to the Company the certificate for the Preference Shares to be redeemed. Failure by any holder of a Preference Share to surrender a certificate upon redemption shall not prejudice or affect the redemption of that Preference Share but the amount payable to that holder upon redemption shall immediately be paid by the Company into a bank account established for the purpose of holding suich monies and be held by the Company in trust for that holder and be paid to him forthwith after the certificate (or, if it has been lost or misplaced, satisfactory evidence of such fact and an indemnity and release in favour of the Company in respect thereof) is delivered to the Company, payment of such monies into such bank account to constitute redemption.

H.   No shares ranking in priority to or equally with the Preference Shares shall be issued unless the issue and the terms thereof are previously approved in writing by the holders of not less than three quarters in number of the issued Preference Shares.

I.   Subject to these Articles the Directors shall not decline to register a transfer of Preference Shares to any person.

J.   This paragraph shall apply without prejudice to the obligation of the Company to effect redemption of all the Preference Shares which have not been converted ('the Redeeming Preference Shares') by payment in full of the Redemption Amount on the Redemption Date.

The above paragraph shall apply if:

(1) the company fails or is unable to redeem all the Redeeming Preference Shares in full on the Redemption Date; and

(2) the holders of three quarters of the Redeeming Preference Shares elect (by notice in writing to the company) that this paragraph shall apply.

If the aforementioned paragraph applies, then the Company shall (whether or not it is in the course of being wound-up) pay towards redemption of the Redeeming Preference Shares on a pro rata basis such amount as may from time to time lawfully be applied for that purpose, and the Company shall thereafter continue to apply all funds of the Company that may lawfully be applied until the Redemption Amount has been paid in full. Whereupon the Redeeming Preference Shares shall accordingly be redeemed. The Redemption Amount and the Redemption Date shall both be determined when the Redemption Amount in respect of the Redeeming Preference Shares has been paid in full.

Any amounts paid by the Company towards the Redemption amount shall be applied successively in payment of capital and premium due to the others.

K. Subject to Section 80 of the Companies Act 1985, allotment of the Preference Shares shall be determined by the directors who may dispose of the same in such manner as they think most beneficial to the Company.

L. All payments to be made by the Company to the holder of a Preference Share pursuant to this Article shall be made in Pounds Sterling to such account or address as the holder of the Preference Share shall nominate in writing and failing such nomination to the registered address of the holder.

M. In the event of the Company being wound-up each holder shall have the right to be paid the Redemption Amount in cash in respect of each Preference Share which has not been converted in priority to the holders of all other classes of shares in the capital of the Company but no right to any further participation in the profit or assets of the Company.

N. (1) In the event there is less than three holders only of the Preference Shares the quorum for a class meeting of Preference Shareholders shall be the number of such holders present in person or by proxy attorney or representative;

(2) Subject to the above paragraph, the provisions of the Articles relating to proceedings at general meetings shall apply mutatis mutandis.

O. To the extent that the provisions of this Article are inconsistent with any other Articles the provisions of this Article shall prevail.

P. Upon completion of:

(1) the conversion of all the Preference Shares allotted; and

(2) the redemption of all the Preference Shares allotted and not converted,

the Articles shall be amended by deleting this Article and thereupon this Article shall no longer be of any force or effect whatsoever.

Precedent 2.7

A SIMPLE FORM OF APPLICATION FOR SHARES

The Board of Directors
                     Limited

I HEREBY APPLY for the issue of 500 Ordinary Shares of £1.00 each in the capital of the Company to be issued at £1.00 per share fully paid and hereby request you to allot such shares to me. I enclose herewith a cheque in the sum of £500.00 in full payment for the said shares.

I agree to take the said shares subject to the Memorandum of Articles of Association of the Company and authorise you to enter my name in the Register of Members as the holder of the said shares.

Dated this   day of   199

Precedent 2.8

BOARD RESOLUTION—ALLOTMENT OF SHARES FOR CASH

Allotment of Shares

It was noted that application had been made for the allotment of the following shares in the capital of the Company:

  (i) 1000 Ordinary Shares of £1.00 each to
  (ii) 1000 Ordinary Shares of £1.00 each to

The meeting considered the matter and IT WAS RESOLVED THAT pursuant to the authority conferred upon the director(s) by the Articles of Association (or by the shareholders), the said applications be and are hereby approved and that the said shares be allotted to the applicant(s) fully paid at par value for cash and that any two directors or one director and the secretary be and are hereby authorised to issue appropriate share certificates to the allottees executed under the seal of the Company and that the secretary be and is hereby instructed to file a Form G88(2) with the Registrar of Companies.

Precedent 2.9

BOARD RESOLUTION—APPROVING RIGHTS ISSUE

Rights Issue

The Chairman reported the proposal to make a rights issue of
Ordinary Shares on the basis of   new shares for every
shares already held in the capital of the Company. It was noted that the shares would be offered to the existing shareholders at par value, for cash, the subscription price being payable in full upon application.

The secretary informed the meeting that it would be necessary to convene and hold an Extraordinary General Meeting of the shareholders for the purpose of increasing the authorised share capital to create further shares and also to authorise the directors to allot new shares in terms of Section 80(1) of the Companies Act 1985.

There was now produced to the Meeting a Notice convening an Extraordinary General Meeting of the shareholders of the Company to be held immediately upon short notice and IT WAS RESOLVED THAT an Extraordinary General Meeting of the shareholders be immediately convened and held upon short notice and that the Notice produced to the Meeting be and is hereby approved and that the Secretary be and is hereby authorised to sign and issue the Notice to the shareholders. At this point, the Meeting was adjourned to enable the Extraordinary General Meeting of the shareholders to take place.

Upon resumption of the Meeting it was reported that the Resolutions proposed at the Extraordinary Genereal Meeting of the shareholders had been approved unanimously. There were now produced to the Meeting letters addressed to the shareholders of the Company inviting them to subscribe for additional shares of the Company on the basis of   new shares for every   shares presently held. It was noted that acceptance of the offer was required by no later than
                    on   . Any shares not accepted by that

date would be offered for subscription to those Members of the Company accepting the offer. The Meeting considered the matter and IT WAS RESOLVED THAT a rights issue of   Ordinary Shares of £1.00 each on the basis of   new shares for every   share presently held in the Company at a subscription price payable upon application of £1.00 per share be and is hereby approved and that the Secretary be and is hereby authorised to sign and issue letters of application to the Company's shareholders.

(When the letters of application are returned it will be necessary to hold a further Board meeting to approve the allotment of shares (see Precedent 2.8).

Precedent 2.10

RIGHTS ISSUE—LETTER OF INVITATION

Dear

Rights Issue of   Ordinary Shares of £1.00 each on a
**   for   basis at £1.00 per share.**

At a meeting of the Board of Directors of the Company held on
it was resolved to make a Rights Issue of   Ordinary Shares of £1.00 each in the Capital of the Company for every   shares already held at a subscription price of £1.00 per share. In accordance with this Resolution, you have been allocated   Ordinary Shares of £1.00 each.

If you wish to subscribe for all or any of the Ordinary Shares allocated to you, you are requested to return the enclosed Form of Acceptance to the Company's Registered Office by no later than   on   together with payment in full for the shares accepted. To the extent that payment is not made for the shares by the aforesaid date, this allocation will be deemed to have been declined and any shares not taken up will be offered to other members.

BY ORDER OF THE BOARD
Secretary

Precedent 2.11

FORM OF ACCEPTANCE AND APPLICATION FOR ADDITONAL SHARES

To:
The Board of Directors
            Limited

FORM OF ACCEPTANCE

I/We hereby accept the offer for subscription in respect of ....
....
ordinary shares of .... each at a price of .... per share. I/We enclose herewith my/our cheque in the sum of £................ in full payment for such shares.

APPLICATION FOR ADDITIONAL SHARES

In the event that any shareholder does not take up his/her full entitlement to shares under this Rights Issue, I/we hereby apply for ....
additional ordinary shares of .... each at a price of .... per share. I/
We enclose my/our cheque in the sum of £ .... in full payment for such shares.

GENERAL

I/We agree that my/our acceptance and application for additional shares is subject to the Memorandum and Articles of Association of the Company and request that you register the name of the following person(s) in the Register of Members of the Company as the Registered Holder(s) thereof.

Signature(s) ....   Date   ....   19.......
....
Name of Registered Holder(s) ....
Address ....

PLEASE SIGN, DATE AND RETURN THIS FORM TOGETHER WITH YOUR CHEQUE MADE PAYABLE TO '...........................' TO THE ADDRESS ABOVE SO AS TO ARRIVE NOT LATER THAN ....

Precedent 2.12

BOARD RESOLUTION FOR ACQUISITION OF ANOTHER COMPANY BY AN EXCHANGE OF SHARES

Purchase of Company

It was reported that agreement had been reached between the Company and the shareholders of   Limited for the purchase by the Company of the entire issued share capital of that company. It was noted that the issued share capital of the company to be purchased and the respective shareholders were as follows:

50000 Ordinary Shares of £1.00 each fully paid held by:

It was proposed to purchase the shares by the issue of new shares in the capital of the Company to be issued pro-rata to the registered holders in
Limited as follows:

Ordinary Shares of £1.00 each fully paid in the capital of the Company allotted to:

At this point Mr   formally declared an interest in the proposed acquisition by virtue of being a director and shareholder in   Limited.

It was noted however that having formally declared his interest in the proposed acquisition Mr   would be entitled in terms of the Articles of

Association of the Company to vote upon any question put to the meeting concerning the said matter.

Nevertheless, in terms of Section 320(1) of the Companies Act 1985, it would be necessary for the shareholders of the Company to approve the acquisition of the shares in   Limited as the transaction represented the purchase of a non-cash asset from a director of the Company.

There was now produced to the Meeting a Notice convening an Extraordinary General Meeting of the shareholders of the Company for the purpose of approving the purchase of shares in   Limited pursuant to the said Section 320(1).

There were also produced Letters of Offer addressed to the shareholders of   Limited setting out the terms upon which the Company would purchase their shares.

The meeting considered the matter and IT WAS RESOLVED THAT:

(1) Subject to approval by the Company in General Meeting, the purchase of the entire issued share capital of   Limited by an exchange of shares upon the terms outlined to the meeting be and is hereby approved and the Secretary be and is hereby authorised to sign and issue the Letters of Offer addressed to the shareholders of   Limited for and on behalf of the Company.

(2) An Extraordinary General Meeting of the shareholders of the Company be immediately convened and held upon short notice and that the Secretary be and is hereby authorised to sign and issue the Notice to the shareholders for and on behalf of the Company.

At this point, the meeting was adjourned to enable an Extraordinary General Meeting of the shareholders to be held and, subject to approval by the Meeting, to permit the shareholders of   Limited to consider the offer.

Allotment of Shares

Upon the resumption of the meeting, it was reported that the resolutions prepared at the Extraordinary General Meeting of the shareholders had been approved unanimously. In addition, the shareholders of   Limited had approved the offer for purchase of their shares and letters of acceptance were produced to the meeting.

The meeting now considered the allotment of shares in the Company in consideration of the transfer of shares in   Limited and IT WAS RESOLVED THAT:

(1)   Ordinary Shares of £1.00 each in the capital of the Company credited as fully paid be allotted as follows in respect of the purchase of the entire issued share capital of   Limited.

(2) The Secretary be and is hereby instructed to enter the names of the allottees in the Register of Members of the Company and to file Form G88(2) (Return of Allotments) and Form G88(3) with the Registrar of Companies and that any two directors or one director and the secretary be and are hereby authorised to issue share certificates to the allottees executed under the seal of the Company.

Precedent 2.13

SHARE EXCHANGE—LETTER OF OFFER

Dear

At a meeting of the Board of Directors of this Company held on   it
was agreed to make offer to purchase your holding of Ordinary Shares of £1.00 each
in   Limited in consideration of the allotment to you of
Ordinary Shares of £1.00 each credited as fully paid in this Company.

I have been requested on behalf of my Board to place this offer before you. To accept
the offer, kindly execute the attached stock transfer form and make formal
application for the allotment of shares in the Company by signing the form of
acceptance printed below.

Yours faithfully

SECRETARY

I hereby accept the offer to purchase my registered holding of   Ordinary
Shares of £1.00 each in   Limited in consideration of the
allotment to me of   Ordinary Shares of £1.00 each in
Limited credited as fully paid.

I agree to take the said shares subject to the Memorandum and Articles of
Association and authorise you to enter my name in the Register of Members of the
Company.

Precedent 2.14

BOARD RESOLUTION—APPROVAL OF SHARE TRANSFERS ON A SHARE EXCHANGE

Transfer of Shares:

It was noted that agreement had been reached between the shareholders of the
Company and   Limited for the transfer of the entire issued share
capital of the Company to   Limited in consideration of the
allotment of shares in that Company. At this point,   and
                   formally declared interests in the matter before the
meeting by virtue of being Directors of   Limited but it was
noted that having declared such interest they were entitled in terms of the Articles of
Association, to consider and vote upon any question put to the meeting.

There were now produced stock transfer forms transferring the following shares in
the capital of the Company:

   (1)   Ordinary Shares of £1.00 each fully paid from
     to

   (2)   Ordinary Shares of £1.00 each fully paid from
     to

   (3)   Ordinary Shares of £1.00 each fully paid from
     to

The Meeting considered the said share transfers and IT WAS RESOLVED THAT the said share transfers be and are hereby approved and, subject to stamping by the Inland Revenue, registered in the books of the Company and that any two Directors or one Director and the Secretary are hereby authorised to issue Share Certificates to the transferees executed under the seal of the Company.

Precedent 2.15

SHARE EXCHANGE (RELATED PARTY TRANSACTION)

Ordinary Resolution

THAT pursuant to the provisions of Section 320(1) of the Companies Act 1985 the acquisition by the Company of 500,000 Ordinary Shares of £1.00 each in the issued share capital of   Limited from Mr A. Smith in consideration of the allotment to Mr A. Smith of 500,000 Ordinary Shares of £1.00 each credited as fully paid in the capital of the Company be and is hereby approved.

Precedent 2.16

BOARD RESOLUTION—BONUS ISSUE

Capitalisation

The Chairman reported the proposal to make a capitalisation issue to increase the issued share capital from £100,000 to £150,000 divided into 150,000 Ordinary Shares of £1.00 each. It was noted that the increase would be made by capitalising the sum of £50,000 from revenue reserves.

The meeting noted that it would be necessary to convene and hold an Extraordinary General Meeting of the shareholders for the purpose of approving a resolution declaring a capitalisation issue. There was now produced to the meeting a Notice convening an Extraordinary General Meeting of the Shareholders to be held immediately upon short notice and IT WAS RESOLVED THAT:

(1) the directors do recommend to the shareholders that the sum of £50,000 be capitalised and appropriated to the holders of the Ordinary Shares in the capital of the Company pro rata to their existing holdings.

(2) an Extraordinary General Meeting of the shareholders be immediately convened and held upon short notice and that the secretary be and is hereby instructed to sign and issue to the shareholders the Notice convening the meeting.

At this point, the meeting was adjourned to enable the Extraordinary General Meeting of the shareholders to be held.

Upon resumption of the meeting, the Chairman reported that the Extraordinary General Meeting of the shareholders had been duly held and that the resolutions set out in the Notice of the meeting had been approved unanimously. There were now produced to the meeting renounceable letters of allotment and IT WAS RESOLVED THAT:

(1) pursuant to the authority given by and the directions contained in the resolution of the Company passed at the Extraordinary General Meeting held

this day, the sum of £50,000 therein referred to be capitalised and appropriated as therein set out.

(2) 50,000 Ordinary Shares of £1.00 each credited as fully paid up be and are hereby provisionally allotted to the persons and in the numbers set out in the respective renounceable entitlement forms produced to the meeting, such allotments being as follows:

(a) 25,000 Ordinary Shares of £1.00 each to
(b) 25,000 Ordinary Shares of £1.00 each to

(3) the Secretary be and is hereby authorised to issue renounceable letters of allotment to the provisional allottees, renunciations to be made within 14 days of the date hereof.

Precedent 2.17

ORDINARY RESOLUTION—DECLARATION OF BONUS ISSUE

THAT upon the recommendation of the directors, it is desirable to capitalise the sum of £50,000 (being part of the amount standing to the credit of the Company's revenue reserves) and that such sum be capitalised and accordingly the directors be authorised and directed to appropriate the said sum to the holders of the Ordinary Shares in the capital of the Company registered at the close of business on   and to apply such sum in paying up in full at par on behalf of such holders 500,000 Ordinary Shares of £1.00 each (ranking pari passu in all respects with the existing issued Ordinary Shares of the Company) and that such shares be allotted and distributed credited as fully paid to and among the said holders in the proportion of 1 of the said Ordinary Shares for every 2 Ordinary Shares then held and so that the directors shall have full power to do such acts and things required to give effect to the said capitalisation, allotment and distribution.

Precedent 2.18

BONUS ISSUE—RENOUNCEABLE LETTER OF ALLOTMENT (SIMPLE FORM)

LIMITED

To: A.B. Clark Esq.   No. 1

The Directors have allotted to you 20,000 Ordinary Shares of £1.00 each credited as fully paid, subject to the Memorandum and Articles of Association of the Company.

Renunciation of this allotment can be effected by the use of the forms below which, to be effective, must be lodged with the Company not later than the close of business on

Yours faithfully

Secretary

Form of Renunciation

To: **The Directors of**   **Limited**

I hereby renounce my rights to the above-mentioned shares in favour of the person(s) signing the registration application form below.

Dated: _____

                             A. B. Clark

REGISTRATION APPLICATION FORM

To: **The Directors of**   **Limited**

We hereby request you to register the above mentioned shares in my (our) name(s), subject to the Memorandum and Articles of Association of the Company.

                                  _____

                                  _____

Dated: 199

Precedent 2.19

BOARD MEETING—RESOLUTION TO ALLOT BONUS ISSUE FOLLOWING RENUNCIATION PERIOD

Allotment of Shares

There were produced to the Meeting renounceable share entitlement forms relating to the recent capitalisation issue of shares and it was noted that shares were to be registered as follows:

(1)   Ordinary Shares of £1.00 each credited as fully paid to

(2)   Ordinary Shares of £1.00 each credited as fully paid to

IT WAS RESOLVED THAT the said allotments be and are hereby approved and that the Secretary be and is hereby instructed to enter the names of the said persons in the Register of Members of the Company as the holders of the said shares and to file Forms G88(2) and G88(3) with the Registrar of Companies and that any two directors or one director and the secretary be and are hereby authorised to issue appropriate Share Certificates to the allottees executed under the seal of the Company.

_____

Chairman

Precedent 2.20

DECLARATION OF TRUST

To:

I, the undersigned   hereby acknowledge that I am a
nominee and trustee for you in respect of one share of £1.00 fully paid and held by me
in the capital of
(hereinafter called 'the Company').

I hand you herewith the Certificates for the said share together with a transfer duly
executed by me and I hereby irrevocably authorise you to complete such transfer by
filling in the date and the name and address of the transferee and the amount of the
consideration for the transfer and to pass the duly completed document to the
Company for registration.

I will pay all dividends, bonuses and other payments received by me in respect of the
said share to you and I will, so long as I remain as registered proprietor of the said
share, vote in respect thereof as you may from time to time direct and not otherwise.

Dated this   day of

Signed sealed and delivered
by and above named

      (A Declaration of Trust must be stamped with duty of 50p)

Precedent 2.21

NOTICE OF SEPARATE CLASS MEETING

XYZ LIMITED

NOTICE IS HEREBY GIVEN THAT a separate class meeting of the holders of
the 'A' Ordinary Shares in the capital of the Company will be held at
        on   at   for the purpose of
considering and if deemed fit of approving the following Resolution which will be
proposed as an Extraordinary Resolution namely:

EXTRAORDINARY RESOLUTION

THAT Resolution 2 set out in the Notice convening an Extraordinary General
Meeting of the Shareholders of the Company to be held on   199 ,
a copy of which has been laid before this meeting and initialled by the Chairman for
the purposes of identification, be approved.

Dated:

                          BY ORDER OF THE BOARD
Registered Office:
                                Secretary

A holder of 'A' Ordinary Shares entitled to attend and vote at the meeting is entitled
to appoint a proxy to attend and vote in his place. A proxy need not be a member.

Precedent 2.22

SHAREHOLDERS' AGREEMENT

THIS AGREEMENT is made the   day of   19
BETWEEN
of the first part (all of which parties are hereinafter together called 'the particular shareholders') **AND**   Limited whose registered office is at
       (hereinafter called 'the
Company') of the second part.

WHEREAS

1. The Company is incorporated in the United Kingdom and carries on the business of van delivery services specialising in stage props and theatrical removals.

2. The Company has an authorised share capital of £1,000 divided into 1,000 Ordinary Shares of £1.00 each of which 250 are issued and fully paid at the date hereof.

3. At the date hereof   and   are beneficial holders of 80 shares each and   is the beneficial holder of 90 shares, which shares are registered in the joint names of   and   as nominee for

NOW IT IS HEREBY AGREED as follows:

1. **IN** this Agreement the following expressions shall have the following meanings:

   (a) 'Month' means calendar month.
   (b) The singular shall include the plural and vice versa.

2. **THE** provisions of this Agreement shall apply also to any shares of any description of the company the beneficial interest in which may be acquired by any of the particular shareholders after the date hereof.

3. **IF** at any time during this Agreement any of the particular shareholders shall wish to transfer any shares in the capital of the Company or shall cease or shall wish to cease to be an employee of the Company ('employee' means director whether salaried or not) for any reason whatsoever the following provisions shall have effect:

   (a) The relevant particular shareholder (or his personal representative(s) in the case of death) shall immediately deliver (or in the case of cessation of employment shall not later than the proposed date of determination of his employment with the company) deliver to the company at its registered office his share certificate for the total number of shares in the capital of the company beneficially owned by him at such time together with a letter authorising and requesting the company to act as his agent to sell such shares at the price and in the manner hereinafter set out.
   (b) Upon receipt of the said share certificate and letter of authority the Auditors of the company, for the time being, shall acting as experts and not as arbitrators, immediately fix and certify the fair value of the said shares at the company's expense. In the event that the vending shareholder shall not agree the fair value as certified, the said vending shareholder shall have the right to appoint at his expense an independent firm of Chartered Accountants acceptable to all the parties hereto to fix and certify the fair value of the shares. The said firm shall act as experts and not as arbitrators and their decision as to the fair value shall be final and binding on all the parties hereto.

(c) Upon receipt of the said certificate the directors shall forthwith offer in writing the said shares to the other ordinary shareholders of the said company at the fair value assessed.

(d) The shareholders of the company to whom such offer is made shall accept or decline such offer no later than twenty one days after receipt thereof and so that they shall notify their acceptance by sending to the company's registered office a notice in writing to this effect together with a remittance by way of Banker's draft for the whole of the purchase price for all the said shares made payable to the vending shareholder.

(e) In the event that the said shares or some of them remain unsold after implementation of (d) above

  (i) the other particular shareholders and the company shall have the right exercisable within three months of the date of accepting or declining the offer in accordance with (d) above of finding a person or persons wishing to purchase some or all of the shares at the fair value assessed and the provisions of (g) shall mutatis mutandis apply, and/or

  (ii) the company shall have the right exercisable within three months of the date of accepting or declining the offer in accordance with (d) above of re-purchasing some or all of the shares pursuant to Section 162 of the Companies Act 1985 at the fair value assessed.

(f) In the event that the said shares remain unsold after implementation of (e) above the share certificate (or in the case of a part sale the certificate for the balance of shares) shall be sent to the vending particular shareholders who shall be at liberty to deal with such shares as he thinks fit in accordance with the appropriate provisions of the Articles of Association of the company.

(g) Immediately upon receipt from an accepting shareholder of a Banker's draft for the fair value of the said shares the company shall notify the vending particular shareholder thereof and deal with the said draft as the vending particular shareholder shall direct so that in no circumstances whatsoever shall the company hand over the said share certificate (or issue a new certificate in the case of a part sale) to an accepting shareholder until receipt of the said Banker's draft and further in case of a part sale shall also forthwith issue to the vending particular shareholder a new certificate for the balance of his shares following completion of the procedure set out in this Clause.

4. **THE** parties agree to procure that the Directors of the Company shall approve for registration any transfer of shares in relation to which all the foregoing provisions of this Agreement have been complied with.

5. **NO** resolution for the allotment of any additional shares in the capital of the Company shall be approved without the consent of all the particular shareholders.

6. **NO** particular shareholder will without the previous consent in writing of the other particular shareholders either transfer or part with the beneficial ownership of any shares in the capital of the company held by him at any time during this Agreement.

7. **EACH** particular shareholder shall have the right to appoint one director of the Company (and to remove such director). The maximum number of directors of the Company shall be three.

8. **IN** the event of any particular shareholder not exercising his right to appoint any person to be a director of the Company, the particular shareholder shall be kept fully informed as to all financial and business affairs of the Company and shall be consulted on all important policy matters.

9. **THE** Chairman of the Board of Directors and of the Shareholders shall not have a casting vote.

10. **EACH** particular shareholder undertakes to the other particular shareholders not to propose or to exercise his votes at any general meeting of the company in favour of a resolution for the removal of any other particular shareholder or his appointee from their position as a director of the company and at any general meeting of the Company at which a particular shareholder or his appointee retires from office as a director of the Company the other particular shareholders shall cast their votes for the re-election of such director.

11. **EACH** particular shareholder agrees with the other particular shareholder that the provisions of this Agreement shall apply to shares of the company held by them as trustees as well as shares of the company beneficially owned by them.

12. **UPON** completion of the sale of all the shares of the particular shareholder in the circumstances referred to in this Agreement the other particular shareholders shall jointly and severally release and indemnify such particular shareholder as between each other from and against his obligations as a joint and several guarantor of any of the liabilities of the company to which he may be subject for the time being and further make representations to the person firm or company having the benefit of such guarantee with a view to such vending particular shareholder being released by such third party.

13. **No** remuneration shall be payable to the directors of the Company without the consent of the particular shareholders. Any expenses properly incurred by the directors in the performance of their duties shall be payable with the approval of the particular shareholders.

14. **NO** capital expenditure in excess of £   shall be incurred by the Company without the prior approval of the particular shareholders.

15. **NO** cheques shall be signed or drawn upon the Company's bank account or accounts or instructions given to the Company's bank without the prior written approval of   and

16. **IF** there is any conflict between this Agreement and the Articles of Association of the Company the provisions of this Agreement shall prevail.

17. (a) **IT** is hereby agreed that no Resolution shall be proposed (and no party hereto shall vote in favour of any resolution) for the winding up of the Company unless either:

    (i) each of the particular shareholders shall have agreed that the Company shall be wound up and shall have approved the appointment of the proposed liquidator or joint liquidators; or

    (ii) the parties are deadlocked in regard to matters requiring their unanimous consent and the business operation of the Company is thereby impaired.

  (b) The provisions of the following sub-clauses of this Clause shall arise and become immediately effective if any party shall be in material breach of the terms of this Agreement.

  (c) In any such case any party other than the party in breach under (b) above shall be entitled by notice in writing to the other parties to require the parties to procure the Company's Auditors to determine and certify the fair price of any shares of the Company (disregarding whether such shares represent a minority interest or not) as between a willing vendor and a willing purchaser and in so certifying the Auditors shall be deemed to be acting as experts and not as arbitrators and without personal liability.

  (d) Within twenty eight days after the date of such determination any parties not in breach under (b) above shall be entitled to purchase (and if more than one in such proportions as they may agree) the whole of the shares of the Company beneficially held by the party in breach at the fair price or (failing such purchase) to require the party in breach to purchase the whole of the shares of the Company held by it at the fair price.

(e) If any purchase required in accordance with the foregoing provisions of this Clause shall not be completed within fourteen days, the Company shall be placed in voluntary liquidation.

18. **ANY** notice required hereunder to be given to one of the parties hereto shall be in writing and shall be deemed to have been duly given to that party if deposited by hand or cabled or posted postage pre-paid to the address of that party described above or to such other address as may from time to time have been notified in writing by that party to the others.

17. **THIS** Agreement shall be binding on the personal representatives of the particular shareholders.

AS WITNESS the hands and seals of the parties hereto the day and year first above written.

SIGNED and sealed by the said
in the presence of: ....

SIGNED and sealed by the said
in the presence of: ....

SIGNED and sealed by the said
in the presence of: ....

GIVEN under the Common Seal of
                     Limited in
the presence of: ....
                                                                 Director

                                          ....
                                                                 Secretary

Precedent 3.1

INDEMNITY FOR LOST CERTIFICATE

To the Directors of ....

The original certificate(s) of title relating to the undermentioned securities of the above-named Company has/have been lost or destroyed.

Neither the securities nor the certificate(s) of title thereto have been transferred, charged, lent or deposited or dealt with in any manner affecting the absolute title thereto and the person(s) named in the said certificate(s) is/are the person(s) entitled to be on the register in respect of such securities.

I/We request you to issue a duplicate certificate(s) of title for such securities and in consideration of your doing so, undertake (jointly and severally) to indemnify you and the Company against all claims and demands (and any expenses thereof) which may be made against you or the Company in consequence of your complying with this request and of the Company permitting at any time hereafter a transfer of the said securities, or any part thereof, without the production of the said original certificate(s).

I/We undertake to deliver to the Company for cancellation the said original certificate(s) should the same ever be recovered.

PARTICULARS OF CERTIFICATE(S) LOST OR DESTROYED

Particulars of Certificate	Amount and Class of Securities	In favour of

Dates this ....day of................................... 19..........

Signature(s) ....

*We ....
hereby join in the above indemnity and undertaking.

(*delete as appropriate)

Precedent 4.1

PURCHASE OF OWN SHARES

Special Resolution amending the Articles of Association of a Private Company to Provide the Necessary Power

THAT the Articles of Association of the Company be amended by the adoption of a new Article   namely:

'Subject to the provisions of Part V of the Companies Act 1985 (as amended) the Company shall have power:

(1) pursuant to Sections 159, 159A, 160 of that Act to issue shares which are to be redeemed or are liable to be redeemed at the option of the Company or the shareholder on such terms and in such manner as shall be provided by the Articles of the Company.

(2) pursuant to Section 162 of that Act to purchase its own shares (including any redeemable shares).

(3) pursuant to Section 170 of that Act to make a payment out of capital in respect of any such redemption or purchase.

Regulation 10 in Table A shall not apply to the Company.'

NB. This Resolution is not required for companies adopting Articles 3 and 35 of the Companies (Tables A to F) Regulations 1985.

Precedent 4.2

CONTRACT FOR PURCHASE OF OWN SHARES

THIS AGREEMENT is made the   day of between
of   (hereinafter called 'the
Vendor') and   Limited whose registered office is
at   (hereinafter called 'the Company').

WHEREAS

A) The Company was incorporated in England and Wales on
                         with a registered number of   and
has an authorised share capital of £50,000 divided into 50,000 Ordinary Shares
of £1.00 each of which 25,000 have been issued and are fully paid.

B) The Vendor is the beneficial owner of 15,000 Ordinary Shares of £1.00 each
in the capital of the Company.

C) The parties have proposed to enter into this Agreement pursuant to Part V of
the Company Act 1985, Article _____ of the Articles of Association of the
Company, and a Special Resolution of the Shareholders of the Company
approved at an Extraordinary General Meeting held on

NOW IT IS HEREBY AGREED THAT:

1. The Vendor shall sell and the Company shall purchase 15,000 Ordinary Shares of
£1.00 each beneficially held by the Vendor, free of all liens, charges and
encumbrances.

2. The total purchase price for the shares shall be £   payable in full upon completion.

3. Completion of the sale and purchase of shares hereby agreed shall take place at
          on   at   am/pm
   when

   (a) the Vendor shall deliver to the Company the share certificate(s) in respect of the number of shares to be sold by him pursuant to this Agreement.

   (b) the Company shall deliver to the Vendor a draft for the purchase monies due.

4. This Agreement shall be governed by the laws of England.

AS WITNESS etc.

Precedent 4.3

PURCHASE OF OWN SHARES

Special Resolution Approving an 'Off-market' Purchase

'THAT the contract proposed to be made between the Company and
          for the purchase by the Company of
Ordinary Shares of £1.00 each fully paid in the capital of the Company upon the terms of the draft produced to the meeting and initialled by the Chairman for the purposes of identification be and is hereby authorised.'

Precedent 4.4

PURCHASE OF OWN SHARES

Special Resolution Approving Purchase out of Capital

'THAT the payment of £   out of capital of the Company as defined in sections 171 and 172 of the Companies Act 1985 in respect of the purchase of
          Ordinary shares of £1.00 each under Section 162 of the said Act from
          be and is hereby authorised.'

Precedent 4.5

PURCHASE OF OWN SHARES

Specimen notice for insertion in London Gazette (or Edinburgh Gazette) and a national newspaper re: purchase of shares from capital (s 175).

LIMITED

NOTICE IS HEREBY GIVEN THAT—

(a) By a Special Resolution of the Shareholders of the above-named Company approved at an Extraordinary General Meeting of the Shareholders held on
          the payment out of capital of £
   for the purpose of the Company acquiring   Ordinary Shares of
   £1.00 each from   was authorised.

(b) The amount of the permissible capital repayment as defined by Sections 170, 171 and 172 of the Companies Act 1985 was £

(c) The statutory declaration of the directors and the auditors' report required by Section 173 of the said Act are available for inspection at the Registered Office of the Company situated at

(d) Any creditor of the Company may at any time within the period of 5 weeks immediately following   199   (being the date of the above mentioned Special Resolution) apply to the High Court under Section 176 of the said Act for an order prohibiting the payment.

Precedent 4.6

FINANCIAL ASSISTANCE FOR PURCHASE OF OWN SHARES

Auditors' Report pursuant to Section 156(4) CA 1985

The Board of Directors
                                                          Limited

Dear Sirs,

In accordance with Section 156(4) of the Companies Act 1985 we would report that we have enquired into the state of affairs of the company as at   (insert date of statutory declaration) and are not aware of anything to indicate that the opinion expressed by the directors in the declaration made by them pursuant to Section 155(6) of the Companies Act 1985 as to any of the matters mentioned in Section 156(2) of the Companies Act 1985 is unreasonable in all the circumstances.

Yours faithfully

Precedent 4.7

FINANCIAL ASSISTANCE FOR PURCHASE OF OWN SHARES

Special Resolution approving financial assistance

'THAT in accordance with Section 155 of the Companies Act 1985 the provision by the Company of financial assistance to   in the sum of £   for the purpose of acquiring   Ordinary Shares of £1.00 each in the capital of the Company be and is hereby approved.'

Precedent 5.1

MEETINGS

Notice of Board Meetings

LIMITED

To: The Board of Directors

Upon the instructions of a director, Mr   I hereby call a
meeting of the directors of the Company to be held at   on   at

Secretary

Precedent 5.2

MEETINGS

Article to Provide for Directors' Meetings by Telephone

Any director or member of a committee of the Directors may participate in a meeting
of the Directors or such committee by means of conference telephone or similar
communications equipment whereby all persons meeting in this manner shall be
deemed to constitute presence in person at such meeting

Precedent 5.3

MEETINGS

Resolution in Writing of the Board of Directors of a Company

LIMITED

RESOLUTION IN WRITING

Resolution in Writing of the Board of Directors of the Company taken pursuant to
Regulation 93 of the Articles of Association.

IT IS HEREBY RESOLVED THAT the Registered Office of the Company be
changed to 121/123, High Street, Newtown, Surrey EV5 6DB with immediate
effect.

Date:

_____
Director

_____
Director

Precedent 5.4

ANNUAL GENERAL MEETING

Notice of Annual General Meeting (Private Company)

LIMITED

Notice of Annual General Meeting

(1) To receive the Accounts of the Company for the year ended together with the Reports thereon of the Directors and the Auditors of the Company and to consider the recommendation of the Directors that no dividend be declared in respect of the year.

(2) To reappoint Mr   retiring by rotation as a Director in accordance with the provisions of the Articles of Association and, being eligible, offering himself for re-election as a Director of the Company.

(3) To reappoint Messrs.   as Auditors of the Company until the conclusion of the next General Meeting of the Company at which Accounts are laid before the Members and to authorise the Directors to fix their remuneration.

BY ORDER OF THE BOARD

Dated:

Registered Office:

_____

Secretary

A Member entitled to attend and vote at the meeting is entitled to appoint a proxy to attend and vote in his place. Such proxy need not be a Member of the Company.

Precedent 5.5

ANNUAL GENERAL MEETING

Notice of Annual General Meeting (Public Company)

PLC

NOTICE IS HEREBY GIVEN THAT the 199   Annual General Meeting of the company will be held at the offices of
on
at
for the following purposes:

Resolution on
proxy form

1.   To receive the report of the directors and the audited
     accounts for the period ended   Res. No. 1.

2.   To re-elect   a director
     of the Company   Res. No. 2.

3. To re-elect   a director
    of the Company   Res. No. 3.

4. To re-elect   a director
    of the Company   Res. No. 4.

5. To re-elect   a director
    of the Company   Res. No. 5.

6. To reappoint   the
    retiring auditors and to authorise the directors to
    determine their remuneration   Res. No. 6.

7. As special business to consider the following resolution,
    which will be proposed as a special resolution: Res. No. 7.

'That the directors be unconditionally authorised as if s 89(1) of the Companies Act 1985 did not apply thereto for a period ending on the date of the next Annual General Meeting of the Company, to allot   ordinary shares of the Company (being 5% of ordinary shares issued pursuant to the offer for subscription) as they see fit.'

A member entitled to attend and vote at the meeting is entitled to appoint one or more proxies to attend and vote in his place. A proxy need not also be a member of the company.

Dated: BY ORDER OF THE BOARD

Registered office:

SECRETARY

NOTE:

Copies of the director's service contracts with the Company not expiring or determinable without payment of compensation within one year will be available for inspection at the registered office during normal business hours on any weekday from the date of this notice until the date of the Annual General Meeting and at
                        from   on
until the conclusion of the meeting.

Precedent 5.6

ANNUAL GENERAL MEETING

Minutes of an Annual General Meeting for a Private Company

Minutes of the 199 Annual General Meeting of the Company held at
                    on   at
                             Present

Chairman: Mr   took the Chair of the Meet-
                    ing. The Chairman announced that a quorum was
                    present.

Notice: The Notice convening the meeting was taken as read. All
                    members having consented IT WAS RESOLVED to
                    accept shorter notice of the meeting than the period of
                    notice prescribed by the Companies Act 1985.

Auditors Report:	Mr of the Company's Auditors read the Report of the Auditors to the Members.
Annual Report and Accounts:	IT WAS RESOLVED THAT the Report of the Directors and the Audited Accounts for the year ended be and are hereby received and that the recommendation of the directors that no dividend be declared in respect of the year be and is hereby approved.
Rotation of Director:	IT WAS RESOLVED THAT the Director retiring by rotation in accordance with the provisions of the Articles of Association be and is hereby reappointed as a Director of the Company.
Reappointment of:	IT WAS RESOLVED THAT be and are hereby reappointed to act as the company's Auditors until the next General Meeting at which accounts are laid before the members and that the Directors be and are hereby empowered to fix their remuneration.

_____

CHAIRMAN

Precedent 5.7

ANNUAL GENERAL MEETING

Chairman's script for the Annual General Meeting of a Company

LIMITED

Chairman's Script for the 199   Annual General Meeting of the Company, to be held at   on   at
(Mr   in the chair)

1. The Chairman to say:

   'Ladies and Gentlemen, thank you for coming here today to attend our Annual General meeting'

   'The quorum for this Annual General Meeting is two members entitled to vote present in person or by proxy. As there are more than two shareholders present, I declare the meeting open. Before proceeding to the business of the AGM, I would inform you that   proxies have been received.'

2. The Chairman to say:

   'The notice convening the Meeting has been in your hands for the statutory period and further copies are available here. With your permission I will take the Notice as read.'

3. The Chairman to say:

   'The first item on the agenda is to receive the Accounts for the period ended 30 June 1988 and the Reports of the Directors and Auditors thereon. If you will turn to page 1 of the Accounts you will find the Report of the Directors and with your permission I will take that Report as read.'

'I will now call upon Mr   of the Company's auditors, Messrs   to read the Report of the Auditors to the members.' Mr   will then read the Report.

'Before I propose the adoption of the Accounts, I invite any questions.'

(Questions to follow)

The Chairman to say:

'I now propose that the Report of the Directors and the Audited Accounts for the year ended   , now laid before the meeting be received and the recommendation of the Directors that no dividend be declared in respect of the year be approved.'

Mr   to say:

'I have pleasure in seconding that Resolution.'

The Chairman to say:

'May I call upon you by a show of hands to indicate first those in support of the Resolution   thank you. Those against   thank you.'

If there is a majority on the show of hands in favour of the Resolution, the Chairman to say:

'I now declare the Resolution carried.'

4. 'I now propose that Mr   the director retiring by rotation and, being eligible, offering himself for reelection be and is hereby re-elected a director of the Company.'

'I now call upon Mr   to second the Resolution.'

Mr   to say:

'I have pleasure in seconding the Resolution.'

The Chairman to say:

'Any questions?'

'May I call upon you by a show of hands to indicate first those in support of the Resolution   thank you. Those against   thank you.'

If there is a majority on the show of hands in favour of the Resolution the Chairman to say:

'I now declare the Resolution carried.'

5. The Chairman to say:

'I now propose the reappointment of Messrs   as Auditors of the Company from the conclusion of this meeting until the conclusion of the next Annual General Meeting and to authorise the directors to fix their remuneration.'

'I now call upon Mr   to second the Resolution.'

The Chairman to say:

'Any questions?'

'May I call upon you by a show of hands to indicate first those in support of the Resolution   thank you. Those against   thank you.'

If there is a majority on the show of hands in favour of the Resolution the Chairman to say:

'I now declare the Resolution carried.'

6. If there is no other business, the Chairman to say:

'I now declare the meeting closed.'

Precedent 5.8

MEETINGS
Election by a private company to dispense with the laying of accounts, the holding of annual general meetings, and the appointment of auditors

(a) *By Written Resolution*

LIMITED

ELECTIVE RESOLUTIONS

Written Resolution of the members of the Company taken pursuant to Sections 379A, 252, 366A and 386 of the Companies Act 1985 (as amended)

We being all the members of the Company do hereby elect:

1. To dispense with the laying of accounts and reports before the company in general meeting in respect of the year ended 31st March 1992 and subsequent financial years.

2. To dispense with the holding of the annual general meeting for 1992 and subsequent years.

3. To dispense with the obligation to appoint auditors annually.

Dated:

_____
Signature

_____
Signature

_____
Signature

(b) *By Resolution at General Meeting*

LIMITED

NOTICE IS HEREBY GIVEN THAT an Extraordinary General Meeting of the shareholders of the Company will be held at   on   at   to consider and if deemed fit to approve the following resolutions which will be proposed as Elective Resolutions namely:—

ELECTIVE RESOLUTIONS

1. THAT in accordance with the provisions of Section 252 of the Companies Act 1985 (as amended) the Company does hereby dispense with the laying of accounts and reports before the company in general meeting in respect of the year ended 31st March 1992 and subsequent financial years.

2. THAT in accordance with the provisions of Section 366A of the Companies Act 1985 (as amended) the Company does hereby dispense with the holding of the annual general meeting for 1992 and subsequent years.

3. THAT in accordance with the provisions of Section 386 of the Companies Act 1985 (as amended) the company does hereby dispense with the obligation to appoint auditors annually.

Dated: BY ORDER OF THE BOARD

Registered Office
                                           _____
                                           Secretary

A member entitled to attend and vote at the meeting is entitled to appoint a proxy and vote in his place. A proxy need not be a member.

Precedent 5.9

NOTICE OF EXTRAORDINARY GENERAL MEETING

LIMITED

NOTICE IS HEREBY GIVEN THAT an Extraordinary General Meeting of the shareholders of the Company will be held at   on   at   to consider and if deemed fit to approve the following Resolutions namely:

ORDINARY RESOLUTION

1. THAT the 10000 Ordinary Shares of £1.00 each in the capital of the Company be subdivided into 100,000 Ordinary Shares of 10p each.

SPECIAL RESOLUTION

2. THAT the draft Regulations produced to the meeting and initialled by the Chairman for the purposes of identification be and are hereby adopted as the Articles of Association of the Company in substitution for and to the exclusion of all the existing Articles of Association.

Dated: BY ORDER OF THE BOARD

Registered Office
                                           _____
                                           Secretary

A member entitled to attend and vote at the meeting is entitled to appoint a proxy to attend and vote in his place. A proxy need not be a member.

Precedent 5.10

MINUTES OF EXTRAORDINARY GENERAL MEETING

Minutes of an Extraordinary General Meeting
of the Company held at
on   at
Present:

1. Mr   took the Chair of the Meeting.

2. The Chairman announced that consent to short notice had been given by the holders of all the shares giving a right to attend and vote at this meeting to the convening hereof and to the proposing and the passing hereat as Resolutions of the Company of the Resolutions set out in the Notice of the Meeting.

3. The Chairman announced that a quorum was present.

4. It was unanimously agreed that the Notice convening the Meeting should be taken as read.

5. Resolution No. 1 contained in the Notice was duly proposed, seconded, put to the vote, unanimously passed as an Ordinary Resolution and declared so passed by the Chairman.

6. Resolution No. 2 contained in the Notice was duly proposed, seconded, put to the vote, unanimously passed as a Special Resolution and declared so passed by the Chairman.

7. There being no other business the Chairman declared the meeting concuded.

————————————————
CHAIRMAN

Precedent 5.11

REQUISITION FOR EXTRAORDINARY GENERAL MEETING

The Board of Directors
        Limited

WE, being members of the Company holding at the date hereof
Ordinary Shares of £1.00 each in the capital of the Company, such holding being not less than one tenth of the paid up share capital of the Company carrying the right to vote, do hereby require you, pursuant to Section 368 of the Companies Act 1985, to convene an Extraordinary General Meeting of the Company for the purpose of considering and if deemed fit, of approving the following Resolution which will be proposed as an Ordinary Resolution namely:

ORDINARY RESOLUTION

THAT Mr   be appointed a director of the Company

Date: _____ Signature _____ Name

_____ Address

_____

Signature _____ Name

_____ Address

Precedent 5.12

NOTICE OF CLASS MEETING

NOTICE IS HEREBY GIVEN THAT a separate class meeting of the holders of the 'B' Ordinary Shares of £1.00 each in the capital of the Company will be held at
on   at   for the
purpose of considering and if deemed fit of approving the following resolution which will be proposed as an Extraordinary Resolution:

EXTRAORDINARY RESOLUTION

THAT the authorised share capital of the Company be increased to £500,000 by the creation of an additional 100,000 'A' Ordinary Shares of £1.00 each.

BY ORDER OF THE BOARD

Dated:

Registered Office:

_____
Secretary

A member entitled to attend and vote at the meeting is entitled to appoint a proxy to attend and vote in his place. A proxy need not be a member.

Precedent 5.13

ANNUAL GENERAL MEETING

Agreement to Short Notice

We, the undersigned, all the members for the time being of
having a right to attend and vote at the Annual General Meeting of that Company to be held on   19   hereby agree:

(a) to accept shorter notice of the said meeting than the period of notice prescribed by Section 369 (1)(a) of the Companies Act 1985 and

(b) to accept service of the documents specified in Section 238 of the Companies Act 1985, less than twenty-one days before the date of the said meeting.

Dated this   day of   19

Date: _____ Signature

                                    _____ Signature

Precedent 5.14

EXTRAORDINARY GENERAL MEETING

Agreement to Short Notice

We, the undersigned, being a majority in number of the members together holding not less than 95 per cent of the issued share capital of   having a right to attend and vote at the meeting referred to below, hereby agree to an Extraordinary General Meeting of that Company being held on   notwithstanding that shorter notice has been given of the said meeting than the period of notice prescribed by Section 369(1)(b) of the Companies Act 1985.

Dated this   day of   19

_____
                                                          Signature

_____
                                                          Signature

Precedent 5.15

AGREEMENT TO SHORT NOTICE

Meeting to approve a Special Resolution

We, the undersigned, being a majority in number of the members together holding not less than 95 per cent of the share capital of   Limited having a right to attend and vote at the meeting referred to below, hereby agree to an Extraordinary General Meeting of the company being held on   19   , for the purpose of considering the special resolutions set out in the notice of the said meeting notwithstanding that less than twenty-one days' notice of the meeting has been given.

Date:

_____
                                                          Signature

_____
                                                          Signature

Precedent 5.16

FORM OF SPECIAL NOTICE—REMOVAL OF DIRECTOR

The Board of Directors
                    Limited

I hereby give notice, pursuant to Sections 303 and 379 of the Companies Act 1985 of my intention to propose the following Ordinary Resolution at an Extraordinary General Meeting of the shareholders of the Company requisitioned by Notice dated   served upon the Company pursuant to Section 368 of the Companies Act 1985:

ORDINARY RESOLUTION

THAT Mr   be removed from the office of director of the Company

Date: _____

                                                                    (Signature)

Precedent 5.17

FORM OF SPECIAL NOTICE—REMOVAL OF AUDITOR

The Board of Directors
                    Limited

I hereby give notice, purusant to Sections 379 and 391 of the Companies Act 1985 of my intention to move the following Ordinary Resolution at the next Annual General Meeting of the Company:

ORDINARY RESOLUTION

THAT Messrs   be removed from the office of auditors of the Company with immediate effect and Messrs   be appointed as auditors in their place to hold office until the conclusion of the next General Meeting at which accounts are laid before the shareholders.

                              _____ Signature

NB The Notice convening the Annual General Meeting should describe the item of business as follows:

   To consider the following Resolution, special notice having been given to the Company pursuant to Sections 379 and 391 of the Companies Act 1985 of the intention to move the Resolution as an Ordinary Resolution:

ORDINARY RESOLUTION
                    (resolution to be set out as above)

Precedent 5.18

ORDINARY FORM OF PROXY

LIMITED

Form of Proxy

I,   of   being a member of the above-
named Company hereby appoint   of
or failing him   of   as my proxy to vote
for me on my behalf at the   General Meeting of the Company
to be held on   and at any adjournment thereof

Signed this   day of   199

To be valid this form must be completed and deposited at the Registered Office of the
Company not less than 48 hours before the time fixed for holding the meeting or
adjourned meeting.

Precedent 5.19

TWO-WAY PROXY

PLC

Form of Proxy

I,   of   being a member of the above-
named Company hereby appoint the chairman of the meeting or
                              of   as my proxy to vote for me on my
behalf at the   General Meeting of the Company to be held on
                              199   and at any adjournment thereof.

Signed this   day of   199

Please indicate with an 'X' in the space below how you wish your votes to be cast.

                                                                    For/Against

Resolution 1 To receive the report and accounts
                and declare that no dividend be paid

2 To re-elect   as director

3 To re-elect   as director

5 To reappoint   the retiring
                auditors

NOTES:

1. A Member may appoint a proxy of his own choice. If such an appointment is
   made, delete the words 'the chairman of the meeting' and insert the name of the
   person appointed proxy in the space provided.

2. If the appointor is a corporation, this form must be under its common seal or
   under the hand of some officer or attorney duly authorised in that behalf.

3. In the case of joint holders, the signature of any one holder will be sufficient, but
   the names of all the joint holders should be stated.

4. If this form is returned without any indication as to how the person appointed proxy shall vote, he will exercise his discretion as to how he votes or whether he abstains from voting.

5. To be valid, this form must be completed and deposited with the registered office of the Company not less than 48 hours before the time fixed for holding the meeting or adjourned meeting.

Precedent 5.20

APPOINTMENT OF REPRESENTATIVE BY A CORPORATION

The Board of Directors
               Limited

Dear Sirs

Kindly note that pursuant to Section 375 of the Companies Act 1985 has been appointed as this Company's representative to attend and vote on its behalf at the Annual General Meeting of the shareholders of Limited to be held on 199 and any adjournment thereof.

Yours faithfully

(for and on behalf of
               Limited)

Precedent 5.21

MEETINGS

General Board Resolutions

1 Approval of Lease

It was reported that agreement had been reached between the Company and Co. Limited ('Landlord') for the lease by the Company of the property known as situated at .
There was produced to the Meeting a Lease to be entered into between the Company and the Landlord and it was particularly noted that the lease was for a term of 12 years expiring on 31st December 2003 and for an initial annual rental of £ , with rent reviews on 31st December 1995 and 31st December 1999. The meeting considered the matter and IT WAS RESOLVED THAT the lease of premises situated at upon the terms outlined to the Meeting be and is hereby approved and that any two directors or one director and the secretary be and are hereby authorised to execute the said Lease under seal of the Company.

2 Pension Schemes

It was reported that agreement had been reached between the Company and Assurance Co. Limited for the establishment of a Retirement Benefits Scheme, to be known as the Company

Limited Pension Scheme, whereby nominated employees and Directors would be entitled to retirement and other benefits. The secretary produced to the Meeting a paper outlining the salient points of the Scheme and this was fully considered by the Meeting. There was also produced an interim Declaration of Trust to be executed by the Company, setting out the initial terms and conditions upon which the Scheme would be established.

After full consideration, IT WAS RESOLVED THAT the establishment of a Retirement Benefits Scheme with   Assurance Co. Limited upon the terms disclosed to the Meeting be and is hereby approved and that any two directors or one director and secretary be and are hereby authorised to execute the interim Declaration of Trust produced to the Meeting under the seal of the Company.

3 Bank Account

IT WAS RESOLVED THAT a Bank Account in the name of the Company be opened with   of   and that the said Bank be and is hereby instructed to operate the said account according to the instructions set down in the bank's standard form of mandate, a copy of which, initialled by the chairman for the purposes of identification, is attached to and forms part of these minutes.

Precedent 6.1

RE-REGISTRATION OF PRIVATE COMPANY AS A PUBLIC COMPANY

Specimen Board Meeting Minutes

Public Limited Company

The Chairman reported the proposal to re-register the Company as a Public Limited Company. It was noted that it would be necessary to convene and hold an Extraordinary General Meeting of the Shareholders to pass a Special Resolution approving re-registration and effecting appropriate amendments to the Memorandum and Articles of Association. There was produced to the Meeting a Notice convening an Extraordinary General Meeting of the Shareholders of the Company to be held immediately upon short notice and IT WAS RESOLVED THAT:

1. The Directors recommend to the shareholders that the Company be re-registered as a Public Limited Company.

2. The Notice convening the Extraordinary General Meeting of the shareholders be and is hereby approved and that the Secretary be and is hereby authorised to sign and issue the Notice to the Shareholders.

3. Subject to approval of the Special Resolution to be proposed at the Extraordinary General Meeting, the Directors and Secretary both jointly and severally be and are hereby authorised to do all such acts and to sign and file with the Registrar of Companies all such documents as are necessary or appropriate to give effect to the re-registration of the Company as a Public Limited Company.

CHAIRMAN

Precedent 6.2

RE-REGISTRATION OF PRIVATE COMPANY AS A PUBLIC COMPANY

Specimen Notice convening an Extraordinary General Meeting

NOTICE IS HEREBY GIVEN THAT an Extraordinary General Meeting of the Company will be held at   on   at   to consider and if deemed fit to approve the following Resolution which will be proposed as a Special Resolution:

SPECIAL RESOLUTION

1. THAT the Company be re-registered as a public company limited by shares within the meaning of the Companies Act 1985.

2. THAT the name of the Company be changed to   PLC.

3. THAT the Memorandum of Association of the Company be amended:

   (a) By deleting in Clause 1 the word 'LIMITED' and substituting therefore the word 'PLC'.

   (b) By inserting as a new Clause 2 the words 'The Company is to be a Public Company'.

   (c) By deleting in the present Clause 2 the words 'situate in England' and substituting therefor the words 'situated in England and Wales' and renumbering the said clause as Clause 3.

   (d) By renumbering the remaining clauses of the Memorandum of Association.

4. THAT the Regulations contained in the document produced to the meeting and signed by the Chairman for the purposes of identification be and are hereby adopted as the Articles of Association of the Company in substitution for and to the exclusion of all the existing Articles of Association.

A Member entitled to attend and vote at the meeting is entitled to appoint a proxy to attend and vote in his place. A proxy need not be a Member.

Dated: BY ORDER OF THE BOARD

Registered Office:

SECRETARY

Precedent 6.3

RE-REGISTRATION OF PRIVATE COMPANY AS A PUBLIC COMPANY-WRITTEN STATEMENT OF AUDITORS

Auditors' Statement to the Registrar of Companies pursuant to the Companies Act 1985 s 43(3)(b)

We have audited the attached Balance Sheet and Notes of   Limited as at   in accordance with approved Auditing Standards (and qualified our opinion in so much as the Company is owned and managed by its Directors. In our opinion, the subject of our qualification is not material for the purpose of determining whether at the balance sheet date the net assets of the Company were not less than its called-up share capital and undistributable reserves.

Accordingly in our opinion, the relevant balance sheet as at
shows that at that date the amount of the Company's net assets (within the meaning given to that expression by Section 264(2)) was not less than the aggregate of its called-up share capital and undistributable reserves.

Dated

CHARTERED ACCOUNTANTS

Precedent 7.1

DIVIDENDS

Written Statement of Auditors under s 271(4) of the Act

The Board of Directors
XYZ Limited

Dear Sirs

We refer to the proposed final dividend of   pence per Ordinary Share to be paid in respect of the year ended   .

Pursuant to the provisions of Section 271(4) of the Companies Act 1985 we can state that, in our opinion, the matter in respect of which our report to the audited accounts of the Company for the year ended   is qualified is not material for determining, by reference to items mentioned in Section 270(2) of the Companies Act 1985 whether the dividend would contravene Section 270 of the said Act.

A copy of this statement must be laid before the Company in general meeting.

Yours faithfully

Auditors

Precedent 7.2

DIVIDENDS

Board Resolution declaring an interim dividend

THAT an interim dividend of   p per Ordinary Share in respect of the year ended   be paid on   to those shareholders registered at the close of business on   .

Precedent 7.3

DIVIDENDS

Resolution in General Meeting approving a final dividend

THAT upon the recommendation of the directors a final dividend of   p
per Ordinary Share in respect of the year ended   (which
together with the interim dividend of   p per Ordinary Share paid on
                       make a total dividend for the year of   p per
Ordinary Share) be declared payable on   to those shareholders registered at the close of business on   .

Precedent 7.4

DIVIDEND WARRANT—PRIVATE COMPANY

LIMITED

Mr: Registered Office:

Dear Sir,

**Ordinary Dividend of £   .   per share (net)
for the year ending 31 March 1991**

I have pleasure in enclosing a cheque for the dividend due on your holding of shares
made up as follows:

Registered holding of shares   99 shares

Amount of Cheque   £

Tax Credit   £

I hereby certify that Advance Corporation Tax of an amount equal to that shown
above as a tax credit, will be accounted for to the proper officer for the receipt of
taxes. This statement will be accepted by the Inland Revenue as evidence of tax
credit, in respect of which you may be entitled to claim payment or relief.

Yours faithfully,

Company Secretary.

Precedent 7.5

DIVIDENDS

Waiver of Entitlement to Dividend

I,   of   being the registered holder of
            Ordinary Shares of £1.00 each fully paid in the capital of
                              Limited do hereby irrevocably waive for myself, my
successors and assign all right and entitlement to payment of the final dividend of
                  p per Ordinary Share declared by the company in respect of the year
ended.

Signed and sealed this   day of   by the
said   in the presence of:

(Seal)

_____
Signature

_____
Witness

_____
Name

_____

_____
Address

Precedent 8.1

DIRECTORS

Appointment

Resolution of the Board of Directors of the Company

Director: IT WAS RESOLVED THAT Mr   be
                  and is hereby appointed as an additional Director of the Company
                  with immediate effect.

_____
Chairman

Precedent 8.2

ALTERNATE DIRECTORS

Form of Appointment

I,   being a director of   Limited do
hereby appoint   of   as my alternate
director pursuant to Article   of the Articles of Association and subject to
approval of the appointment by the Board of Directors.

Date:

_____
Signature

Address:

Form of Revocation of Appointment

I   , being a director of   Limited do
hereby revoke the appointment of   as my alternate director
with immediate effect

Date:

_____
Signature

Address:

Precedent 8.3

DIRECTORS

Ordinary Resolution Approving Payment of Compensation for Loss of Office

'THAT the payment of £   proposed to be made to Mr
             in compensation for the loss of his office as director of the
company be and is hereby approved.'

Precedent 8.4

DIRECTORS

Letter of Resignation by Director

The Board of Directors
                    Limited   Date:

Dear Sirs,

I hereby resign as Director of the Company with immediate effect. I confirm that I
have no outstanding claims against the Company whatsoever in respect of
remuneration or otherwise.

Yours faithfully,

Precedent 8.5

DIRECTORS

Resolution accepting the resignation of a director

'There was produced to the meeting a letter from Mr
tendering his resignation as director of the Company with immediate effect and IT
WAS RESOLVED the resignation of Mr   as director of the
Company be and is hereby accepted.'

Precedent 8.6

DIRECTORS

Special Notice to Company of Intention to Remove a Director

The Board of Directors
                Limited

I hereby give notice pursuant to Sections 303 and 379 of the Companies Act 1985 of
my intention to propose the following resolution as an ordinary resolution at the next
annual general meeting of the company:

RESOLUTION

THAT   be removed from the office of director of the
Company forthwith.

Date: _____

                                         Signature

Address:

Precedent 8.7

DIRECTORS

Notice to members of a resolution of which special notice has been given

'To consider the following resolution which will be proposed as an ordinary
resolution, special notice having been given to the company pursuant to Sections 303
and 379 of the Companies Act 1985.

RESOLUTION

THAT   be removed from the office of director of the
company forthwith.'

Precedent 8.8

DIRECTORS

General Notice of Interest

The Board of Directors
                      Limited

Dear Sirs,

Pursuant to Section 317 of the Companies Act 1985, I hereby give notice that I am to be regarded as interested in any contract which may, after the date hereof, be made with any of the undermentioned companies and firms.

Name of Company or Firm   Details of Interest

Yours faithfully,

Director

Precedent 8.9

DIRECTORS

Approval of substantial property transaction—draft ordinary resolution

'THAT in accordance with the provisions of Section 320(1) of the Companies Act 1985 the acquisition by the Company from a Director of the Company, Mr
                  , of the freehold property situated at
for a consideration of £   be and is hereby approved.'

Precedent 8.10

DIRECTORS

Directors' Interest in Shares

To: The Directors
                    Limited   Date:

Dear Sirs,

In fulfilment of an obligation imposed by section 324 of the Companies Act 1985, I give notice of the subsistence of an interest in   shares in the Company on
                , being the day on which I was appointed a Director of the Company.

Yours faithfully,

Precedent 8.11

DIRECTORS

Directors' Interest in Shares

To: The Directors
                    Limited   Date:

Dear Sirs,

In fulfilment of an obligation imposed by Section 324 of the Companies Act 1985, I give notice of the occurrence of the following events:

1. Purchased   shares at   per share on   19

2. Sold   shares at   per share on   19

Yours faithfully,

Precedent 8.12

DIRECTORS

Directors' Interest in Shares

To: The Directors
                    Limited   Date:

Dear Sirs,

In fulfilment of an obligation imposed by Section 324 of the Companies Act 1985, I give notice of the following interests in the shares and debentures of the Company and its subsidiaries on   19   being the day on which I was appointed a Director of the Company.

The Company

(1)   Ordinary Shares beneficially owned by me.

Subsidiaries

(1)   Ordinary Shares in   Limited owned by my infant children

(2)   Ordinary Shares in   Limited owned by my wife

(3)   Ordinary Shares owned by a body corporate whose directors are accustomed to act in accordance with my directions or instructions.

(4)   Ordinary Shares owned by a body corporate of which I control more than one third of the voting power.

Yours faithfully,

Precedent 9.1

DORMANT COMPANIES

Special Resolution not to Appoint Auditors

'THAT in accordance with the provisions of Section 250 of the Companies Act 1985 (as amended) the Company, being dormant within the meaning of the said section, be exempt from the obligation to appoint auditors as otherwise required by Section 384 of the said Act.'

Precedent 9.2

DORMANT COMPANIES

Limited

Company no:

DIRECTORS' REPORT

The Directors hereby submit the Annual Report and Accounts of the Company for the period ended

The Directors of the Company during the financial period and their interests in shares of the Company were:

1/1/199   31/12/199

No. of shares

No. of shares

During the above financial period the Company has not traded and there has been no income or expenditure and therefore no change in the Company's position has arisen. Any expenses have been met by the Directors personally.

Signed on behalf of the Board.

Secretary

BALANCE SHEET AS AT

ASSETS:
Cash in Hand   £

Less
LIABILITIES   £   £_____

Represented by

AUTHORISED SHARE CAPITAL £   SHARES OF £1.00 each

SHARE CAPITAL ISSUED AND FULLY PAID
  Ordinary Shares of £1.00 each   £
  Profit (loss) brought forward   £   £_____

The Company was dormant within the meaning of Section 250 of the Companies Act 1985, throughout the financial period ended   .

SIGNED: Director

Precedent 10.1

AUDITORS

Board resolution to appoint first auditors

IT WAS RESOLVED THAT Messrs   be and are hereby appointed as auditors of the company to hold office until the first General Meeting at which accounts are laid before the shareholders.

Precedent 10.2

AUDITORS

Ordinary Resolution Terminating the Appointment of Auditors whilst an Election is in Force Pursuant to s 386

THAT notice having been served on the company pursuant to Section 393 of the Companies Act 1985 (as amended) the appointment of Messrs   as auditors of the Company be brought to an end.

Precedent 10.3

AUDITORS

The Board of Directors

                    Limited

Dear Sirs,

We hereby resign as auditors of the Company with effect from the date hereof.

In accordance with Section 394(1) of the Companies Act 1985, we hereby state that there are no circumstances connected with our resignation which we consider should be brought to the attention of the members or creditors of the company.

Yours faithfully,

Messrs
Auditors

Precedent 11.1

SECRETARY

Resolution of the Board appointing a Secretary

There was produced to the meeting a letter from Mr
tendering his resignation as secretary of the company with immediate effect and IT
WAS RESOLVED THAT the resignation of Mr   as
secretary of the company be and is hereby accepted and Mr
be and is hereby appointed as secretary in his place.

Index